Flights
of the
Vout Bug

A guide to the
recorded music of
Michael "Dodo" Marmarosa

by Dieter Salemann
and Fabian Grob

Flights of the Vout Bug: A Guide to the Recorded Music of Michael "Dodo" Marmarosa
© 2009 Dieter Salemann and Fabian Grob. All Rights Reserved.

Published in the USA by:
BearManor Media
P O Box 71426
Albany, Georgia 31708
www.bearmanormedia.com

ISBN 1-59393-337-1

Printed in the United States of America.

Book and cover design by Darlene Swanson of Van-garde Imagery, Inc.

Contents

FOREWORD

In 1956 producer Lyle Griffin released a two-sided single record by the co-median and monologist Richard "Lord" Buckley under the futuristic title "Flight of The Saucer". Having become a cult record long since, this early predecessor of the later 'rap' style at least partly was a recycled version of a recording, which had already been made by Griffin in late 1946, only that the 'flying object' then had not been the saucer but the *vout bug*. Actually flying on this older record was legendary jazz pianist Michael "Dodo" Mar-marosa, for whom "Flight of The Vout Bug" - suggesting at least verbally some kind of analogy to Rimsky-Korsakov's "Bumble Bee" - had been writ-ten as a miniature concertino for piano and big band. Marmarosa certainly was not unknown then, nor is he today. Yet his many 'flights' on records or transcriptions from the 1940s to the 1960s - including some of Slim Gaillard's humorous excursions into the language of "Vout" - have never been completely documented in a comprehensive and chronological cata-logue, which is the task the authors have set themselves with the present publication. The approach to this task is twofold: on one side is a detailed discographical listing of the pianist's known recorded performances and on the other an interpretative survey, which seeks to guide the listener's ear to some of the intrinsic artistic values of Marmarosa's ever-beautiful and highly personal piano style.

The output of the pianist's recording career in general has occasionally been characterized as being small, with one commentator judging that Marmarosa must have "deliberately gone out of his way to bypass the sound studio." There are indeed hints, that he kept a hesitant attitude towards recording and showed scruples about his abilities, when being offered a session of his own. The appreciation of his exceptional talent by others, however, nonetheless led to a considerable number of recording opportunities in the 1940s, which made him after all one of the more prolific musicians of the period. The list of the many jazz greats, who chose him to be the piano player on their recording sessions, included such big names as Lester Young or Charlie Parker and made some later commentators nominate him "everyone's favourite pianist out on the West Coast". In addition to his small group activities, Marmarosa was a sought-after musician by the leaders of big bands. Even though the AFM ban on the recording of instrumental music from mid-1942 to late-1944 may have prevented or reduced studio sessions for him with orchestras like those of Gene Krupa and Tommy Dorsey, the ever-increasing recording activities of the Armed Forces Radio Service fortunately provided a large number of transcribed live performances from this period. Preserved copies of these transcriptions allow us to appreciate Marmarosa's special talents as a big band piano player even today.

Until now, there have been only two attempts to comprehensively document Marmarosa's recorded music. Since Frank Gibson's laudable Dodo Marmarosa Discography, which appeared in Britain's *Jazz Journal* in 1965/1966, additional information and many more recordings have come to light. An excellent listing of Marmarosa's small group studio recordings, published in two parts by Gerard J. Hoogeveen in the Dutch discographical magazine *Names & Numbers* in 2003/2004, clearly shows evidence of this improved situation. Nevertheless, Hoogeveen's list contains long-standing errors; he also admits to having avoided the laborious task of documenting Dodo Marmarosa's transcribed live recordings and his appearances with big bands.

On the interpretative side, there have been few more efforts to evaluate the aesthetical virtues of Dodo Marmarosa's music in general. Three of them deserve a brief mention here. The first, written by George Hoefer for *Down Beat* magazine, appeared in 1966 under the title "The Recorded

Flights of Dodo," and was remarkably informative on the course of the pianist's recording career, although it remained superficial in its observations on the music itself. A few years later the English jazz critic Owen Peterson followed with an extensive homage entitled, "The Consummate Artistry of Dodo Marmarosa," published in two parts in Britain's *Jazz & Blues* magazine. His detailed and sensitive comments on Marmarosa's studio recordings show Peterson's deep understanding of the pianist's music. Even without the benefit of access to all of Marmarosa's recorded performances (and probably none of the live transcriptions), this thoughtful analysis after 35 years still remains the best that has been written on the subject thus far. The third and final of the noteworthy works on Marmarosa may be lesser known in the American world. It was written by the French lyricist and former editor-in-chief of *la Nouvelle Revue Française*, Jacques Réda, and published along with essays on other jazz pianists in a small book in 1985. Under the title "Un oiseau rare: Dodo Marmarosa," the author gives an excellent review of the pianist's more important studio recordings and points out Marmarosa's personal contribution to the history of jazz piano playing. Being a poet, Réda also seeks to comprehend and elucidate the artist's mind as it speaks out of Marmarosa's musical creations. The author's interpretations may be subjective, but Réda's effort to grasp the very essence of Dodo Marmarosa's music is nevertheless more penetrating than any other article written on the pianist's art.

The present publication combines the musicologist's view on Dodo Marmarosa's recorded legacy with that of the discographer and seeks to offer an up-to-date chronological listing of all of the pianist's known recorded performances, based on the results of extensive and thorough research, as well as a detailed and annotated appreciation of their inherent musical and artistic values.

Documenting all aspects of Marmarosa's recording career would not have been possible without the help of scholars, specialists, archivists and collectors, all of whom generously provided insight into their research or access to their record collections. Thus our special thanks go to archivists Eric Dawson and Chris Ogrodowski of Los Angeles' professional musicians AFM Local 47, who enabled us to view a set of small company recording contracts from the 1940s still preserved in their archives; to Ken Seavor and George Hulme for generously sharing research for their discographies of Tommy Dorsey (not yet published) and Mel Tormé; to Dave Goldin, Jack McKinney, Bob Conrad, Dan Haefele, Dieter Hartmann, Alastair Robertson, and especially Dr. Hans-Werner Nahme (an avid collector and always ready to help expert on anything concerning the Armed Forces Radio Service) for providing us with copies of or information on very rare radio broadcast transcriptions or commercial recordings; and to Paul Smoker, the late Danny Conn, Neil and Gene Norman of GNP Crescendo, Betty Talbert, and Bruce Talbot for sharing photographs and recollections of Marmarosa.

Even with such strong support, our research cannot claim to be exhaustive in every detail. There may still be undiscovered sources on Marmarosa's recording career, whether in the form of recording contracts or related documents, transcriptions of radio broadcasts, originally rejected alternate takes of recording sessions or even privately made recordings of club performances (similar to the ones in the possession of Marmarosa's long-time Pittsburgh friend and companion Danny Conn; these have finally been released by the label Uptown Records in 1997). So additions or corrections to the present state of knowledge are likely to occur and are always welcomed to the authors.

We nevertheless hope that the present work will fulfill its purpose by serving as a reliable guide for those who love the wonderful music of Dodo Marmarosa, one of the major jazz piano talents of the 1940s, if not of all time.

Dieter Salemann
Fabian Grob

INTRODUCTION

At the base of research like that conducted for the present publication are the major jazz discographies as well as name discographies of bands and musicians. As indispensable as they are, comprehensive discographical publications in the jazz field simply cannot provide verified data for every single entry, and the validity of name discographies to a certain degree depends on their date of publication, often rendering them obsolete. To augment the already-published discographical information, the authors have based their evidence on a few original recording contracts still extant, and when available, on the recorded music itself. As one might expect some sixty years after the time of actual recording, this has not been possible in every case. We were unable to verify a few non-reissued industrial recordings and a considerable number of never-commercially released radio broadcast transcriptions; these were mainly taken from performances by the big bands Marmarosa played with in the early- and mid-1940s. For a few of these big bands we were fortunate enough to rely on the exemplary research of our predecessors, including Dan Mather (on Charlie Barnet), Ken Seavor (on Tommy Dorsey), and Vladimir Simosko (on Artie Shaw). Because Marmarosa's remaining Swing orchestra employments (Johnny "Scat" Davis, Gene Krupa, Ted Fio Rito, Boyd Raeburn, Tommy Pederson) are rather scarcely documented, we have included all information we could gather on these bands for the periods of Marmarosa's presence, even if it was not more than the mere hint at a radio broadcast having taken place at some time at an unknown location. There still remains the possibility that transcriptions or air-checks of such broadcasts may surface among Old-Time Radio collectors. Moreover the inclusion of such information, be it ever so scarce, provides a more detailed view of the engagements and itineraries of the respective orchestras and thus of Dodo Marmarosa's career as a sideman.

Although we could not check everything, the music in general was helpful in verifying or eliminating performances usually referred to as uncertain or doubtful as far as Marmarosa's participation is concerned. In all latter cases we have included separate "notes" in their appropriate chronological place, to reveal, that (and why) these performances have been left out from our discographical listing.

The presentation of the discographical data follows the widely used pattern of giving the **name of the recorded musician or ensemble** and the **type of performance** (such as recording session, radio show or broadcast, or live-concert) in a headline for each entry. Following are documentation of the **band personnel** and the **date and location** of the recorded performance. The term "same as before" or "similar as before" in this context refers to sequences of recording dates by band personnel without changes or possible minor changes. These are indicated if known. Furthermore, vocalists included in the personnel listing for a recording session are denoted after the titles on which they appear in the following way:

(BDv) - Bob Davis, vocal
(VMv) - Virginia Maxey, vocal
(TSv) - The Sentimentalists, vocal etc.

The recorded results of a session or transcribed performance then are given in **lists of titles.** Each title is preceded by **matrix and take numbers** as far as known[1] and followed by indication of the **first release** of the title, be it on industrial 78rpm, 45rpm, or 33rpm records, electrical transcriptions for

---

1. It should be noted that "take numbers" may help to identify existing master and alternate takes of a title, but not necessarily their chronological sequence of recording. Some record companies used take indications to distinguish preferred versions for mastering and release from alternate takes retained for safety reasons or possible later reissues. With these companies, the master take was usually assigned the take number "-1", irrespective of its being recorded before or after an alternate version, which then would be stored as take "-2". Rejected additional takes were routinely destroyed.

use on radio stations or transcription records made by the Armed Forces Radio Service during and after World War II for use on their own radio network. The setting of a small stroke (-) in this context denotes release on the same record as the preceding title.

As we have attempted to gain access to most of the music documented in this discography, we have also included references to **piano solos** or **introductions** by Dodo Marmarosa after each title. They are indicated by the following signs:

(p-intro)	-	denotes the occurrence of a piano introduction by Marmarosa
(s)	-	denotes the occurrence of a piano solo by Marmarosa
(/)	-	denotes that *no* piano solo by Marmarosa is on this title
( )	-	denotes that the title could not be verified by the authors.

Additional comments on the recording date and its original release follow most entries in a small "note" printed in italics. In the case of broadcast transcriptions, these notes may include general information on the radio program series within which the transcribed performances were released, or on special transcription or release usages of the Armed Forces Radio Service. Such information is often helpful in understanding the formation of the repertory of a particular transcription record, which may contain music inserted from other performances by the same band or exist in more than one version with different or reversed title orders.

A **listing of reissues** of the recorded titles—mostly on LP or CD—concludes each note. We have, however, made no attempt at including every single reissue of each title. Only first issue, release in comprehensive anthologies or albums dedicated solely to Marmarosa, and by all possible means, the most recent issue of titles are given. In addition to this, all albums containing reissues that have been cited in the discographical listing can be found with full title and indication of the country of release in a separate LP and CD list following the discographical chapter.

Basic discographical facts are complemented by additional chronological information pertaining to routes and engagements of the bands Marmarosa played in, as to non-recorded performances of his own groups or as a soloist, as far as they are known to date. Such information is valuable in forming links between individual recording dates and thus helps to understand recordings as single occasions within the continuity of a performing career.

The documentation closes with a short bibliography of the relevant sources we relied on for our research and of special literature on Dodo Marmarosa's career. Finally, indexes of musicians and music titles will make the search for particular performers or recorded items an easy and convenient one.

ABBREVIATIONS

The presentation of the discographical data includes the following abbreviations:

INSTRUMENTAL ABBREVIATIONS

arr	arranger
as	alto saxophone
b	bass
bs	baritone saxophone
cl	clarinet
comp	composer
dm	drums
englh	English horn
Ens	Ensemble
fl	flute
frh	French horn
g	guitar
p	piano
perc	percussion
ss	soprano saxophone
tb	trombone
tp	trumpet

ts	tenor saxophone
vib	vibraphone
vl	violin
voc	vocal

OTHER ABBREVIATIONS

AFM	American Federation of Musicians
AFRS	Armed Forces Radio Service
BML	Basic Musical Library
MC	Music Cassette
ONS	One-Night Stand
rpm	revolutions per minute

ILLUSTRATION CREDITS

Unless noted otherwise, illustrations have been provided from the collection of the authors.

"TONE PAINTINGS"

THE RECORDING CAREER OF DODO MARMAROSA:
AN ARTISTIC SURVEY

"I forever liked to live those days over again," reminisced Dodo Marmarosa in 1995 on the occasion of one of his rare interviews, talking to producer Robert E. Sunenblick about a set of privately made recordings from the later 1950s. In "those days" jazz pianist Michael "Dodo" Marmarosa was working in his hometown Pittsburgh, merely unnoticed by the general public, although in jazz circles he enjoyed the status of a somewhat legendary figure. His reputation was the result of the outstanding and much-admired abilities he had shown in a short but brilliant career during the 1940s. Subsequently, the few years he spent completely absent from the national jazz scene had sufficed to add a touch of mystery to the name of Marmarosa. This aura was to remain with him until his very last days in the summer of 2002, and except for a brief attempt to return to the spotlight of nationwide attention in the early 1960s Marmarosa did not do much to lift the veil of obscurity surrounding his existence. On the contrary, the reclusiveness of his later years only added to the "Mystery of Dodo Marmarosa," as one writer put it in the headline of a biographical article on the pianist. But as his introductory words suggest, Marmarosa seemed to enjoy his privacy. And listeners, who were interested enough in his playing, at least had the chance to hear him perform publicly in and around the Pittsburgh area until the early 1970s. For collectors of Marmarosa's recordings, however, things look different. Apart from his already-mentioned set of private recordings and his two comeback albums from 1961 and 1962, virtually none of the pianist's later work has been documented on record. Thus, the major part of his recorded legacy stems from the short period of 1943 to 1948. These testimonies are nevertheless sufficient to characterize him as one of the most capable and fascinating players of early modern jazz piano, and it seems that today the artistic and the historic value of Dodo Marmarosa's music are finally receiving the recognition they deserve.

Marmarosa, who was born on December 12, 1925, started his professional career early. He was sixteen when a recommendation to bandleader Johnny "Scat" Davis by trumpeter and neighbourhood friend Jimmy Pupa procured him his first engagement in a name band. In the years before, while developing his skills in classical piano playing, he rather incidentally took a liking to jazz piano. This came about as a result of meeting a young Erroll Garner. "The first time I ever heard any jazz was when Erroll played," Marmarosa recalled in his interview from 1995.[1] "I studied classical piano, and one time I ran into him. I met Erroll and he played for me. It's the beginning of my influence in jazz ... what started me out." According to Dodo, they both admired Earl Hines, Art Tatum, Mary Lou Williams, Duke Ellington, Count Basie, and Teddy Wilson and used to exchange ideas in mutual sessions with a local player named Tootsie Davis: „Tootsie really never worked anywhere and hardly anyone knew who he was, but he played these fine block chord progressions that had a definite line in the left hand", he remembered.[2] Another pianist, whom Marmarosa mentioned as an early influence was Johnny Guarnieri through his recordings with the Benny Goodman Sextet and Septet in 1940/41. Especially Guarnieri's striding left hand found Marmarosa's admiration: "Guarnieri was a great piano player," he said. "He had a wild left hand. He played something I could never do, something I could play with two hands, he could play with his left hand."[3] In February 1942, Marmarosa received his first mention in a national magazine when DOWN BEAT published

---

1.   Robert E. Sunenblick interviewed Dodo Marmarosa in June 1995 for the release of a CD presenting previously unissued recordings of the pianist from the late 1950s and early 1960s.
2.   cited after Bob Dietsche, "Dodo Marmarosa", Jazz Journal International, June 1991, p.10-11
3.   Interview with Robert E. Sunenblick from June 1995.

a note on his impressive jazz piano playing in a Pittsburgh jam session.[4]

It is not without relevance that Marmarosa entered the Davis band with the reputation as a classically trained prodigy. His arrival at the band's hotel is vividly illustrated by Jimmy Pupa: „I remember Dodo showing up at seven in the morning at this lodge we were staying in. The rest of the band was asleep upstairs, so to have a little fun I switched on the band mike. Then I told Dodo to play the piano. So he starts in on this wild classical thing, and before I know it the whole band including the manager is standing around the piano watching this little genius play."[5]

This classical inclination stayed with Marmarosa throughout his career[6], and can be seen as one of the keys to his jazz style. It expressed itself technically in an immaculately clear articulation combined with a light and feathery touch and the use of unusually fine dynamical shades, all resulting in that particular quality of pianistic sound that classical players seek to develop for the delicate textures of, for example, the music of Mozart or Chopin. On the interpretative side, there was a constant bent for perfection and a well-developed sense of formal unity. This can be heard to best advantage in some of Marmarosa's solos on big band recordings, wherein he manages to make solo statements be at the same time characteristically personal as well as functionally integral to the orchestra as a whole.[7] In general his playing is of the same disciplined precision and transparent elegance that can be found in Teddy Wilson's music, infused, however, with his own unmistakable blend of melodic sense and harmonic invention.

In the Davis band Marmarosa met clarinettist Buddy DeFranco, who became one of his closest friends during those times. In the following two years he and DeFranco, together with trumpeter Jimmy Pupa, successively passed

---

4.   "Do-Do, the sensational 16-year-old 88er here, took most of the honors in a local jam recently", DOWN BEAT magazine of February 1, 1942, p.19, Pittsburgh column.
5.   Dietsche, p.10
6.   Years later fellow musician Barney Kessel and Ross Russell, one of Marmarosa's few promoters, made further statements to underline this classical penchant.
Kessel: "Unlike most of the early boppers, Dodo brought a classical discipline to his music. In fact, the first thing he ever played for me was the Revolutionary Etude."
Russell: "I thought that he was a musician who brought a lot of the technique of the classical piano to jazz and yet had become almost entirely part of the jazz scene - he wasn't a hybrid pianist; he was a real jazz pianist. ... I used to go over to his house, and he would whiz through Bach two-part inventions, playing them at perilous speeds, never faltering on a note."
7.   Listen, for instance, to *S'Wonderful* and the two takes of *Summertime* with the orchestra of Artie Shaw (1945) or the several versions of *Boyd Meets Stravinsky* with Boyd Raeburn's band (1946).

through the bands of Gene Krupa (probably January to June 1943), Ted Fio Rito (at least one month in the summer of 1943), Charlie Barnet (October 1943 to March 1944), and Tommy Dorsey (April to October 1944, without Pupa). As DeFranco later recalled, it was at that time that Marmarosa and he became increasingly aware of the new progressive ideas in jazz. For DeFranco it had been first of all Marmarosa's anxiety to learn, which also led him to discover new directions and musicians like Dizzy Gillespie and Charlie Parker: "Dodo had a concept for grasping new ideas - playing new ideas. ... He was always searching, always into new things. A lot of things escaped me. But I was smart enough to hang on to Dodo. Because he knew. And I knew he knew." [8]

One of the musicians DeFranco mentioned as an influence on Marmarosa is pianist Jimmy Jones, whom both had the opportunity to hear as a member of the Stuff Smith trio in Chicago in the fall of 1943: "They played downstairs in a Chicago club. On our day off [from Barnet] we'd go in and listen to them. We spent three weeks in a row listening to them because it was great music. Jimmy Jones was harmonically very advanced, and Dodo loved his playing. They even let us sit in one time when things were slow." [9]

In January 1944, when the Barnet band played at the Strand Theatre in New York City, Dizzy Gillespie joined the orchestra briefly as a substitute. Acquaintance was quickly made and the trumpeter invited Marmarosa home to a private jam session where he introduced him to Charlie Parker.

During his time with Charlie Barnet, Marmarosa's recording career got its "official" start [10] with a path-breaking piece of modern jazz piano playing. On

---

8. Ira Gitler, "Swing To Bop", New York 1987, p.209-210
9. John Kuehn, "Buddy De Franco", p.48
Recordings of the Stuff Smith trio from November 1943 reveal Jones indeed as a surprisingly modern accompanist. He makes almost no use of stride-piano but plays either half-note chords behind the soloist or "strums" the four beats like a guitar, much in the style that Erroll Garner began to use at the time. Occasionally he even "comps" freely with offbeat chords, as they should become customary in bebop-accompaniment. This all lends more fluency to the performance of a tune by avoiding the Swing-typical accentuation on beats two and four of the bar. In his solos, Jones features single-note lines in his right hand with sparse accompaniment by left hand chords, but his harmonic alterations sound more moderate in comparison to Marmarosa's efforts with Barnet (esp. *The Moose* from October 1943). Obviously Marmarosa's admiration for the playing of Jimmy Jones was no one-sided affair, as a remark by Barry Ulanov in a contemporary feature article on Jones reveals: "He likes Dodo Marmarosa's work and Dodo is crazy about his." (METRONOME, November 1945, p.23)
10. His first transcribed piano solo stems from a private air-check of February 1943, when Gene Krupa's Orchestra was performing at the famous Hotel Sherman in Chicago. Poor sound quality drowns much of the pianist's playing on "Buster's Last Stand," but the recording nevertheless allows us to recognize and appreciate youthful exuberance combined with spontaneous creativity, a modern single line approach, and virtuoso command of the keyboard.

the orchestra's recording session for DECCA from October 21, 1943, two takes of a concertante-like setting for piano and swing orchestra by composer and arranger Ralph Burns were made. Titled *The Moose*, which was a nickname Barnet used for Marmarosa, it features the pianist as main soloist in constant alternation with light and unpretentious but effectively conceived passages by the band. The fast tempo and the effortless flow of the performance as a whole give it a modern appearance, enhanced by Marmarosa's use of almost exclusively single-note lines and the at times strikingly dissonant melodic exposure of chord alterations or inversions. His predominant focus on the linear display of harmonical changes, neglecting almost entirely motivic techniques of melodic design, makes this recording sound rather "abstract" in comparison to common riff-oriented instrumental or romantically melodious ballad arrangements of the Swing era. Even if Marmarosa's rhythmic conception here is not yet that of a typical bop line, he anticipated (at only 17 years of age) essential characteristics of the fully developed bebop piano style of the years to come.[11]

When Charlie Barnet disbanded in March 1944, the DeFranco-Marmarosa team joined Tommy Dorsey's aggregation, but split not long thereafter, for Marmarosa left Dorsey again in October 1944. Unfortunately Dorsey allowed his young pianist less room to unfold his talents and ambition, although Marmarosa had his moments also with the trombonist's orchestra. Fun lay at any rate outside the regular work as Marmarosa recalled in his 1995 interview with Robert Sunenblick: "Buddy Rich, he was something else...he'd just gotten out of the Marines. He was hard to make friends with or something, but we got to be real good friends. We drove around in his car. He used to take me out in his convertible. Mel Tormé was with us. We used to go out to the beach, drive around, you know." The musical side of these pleasure trips is illustrated by pianist Billy Taylor's recollections in Shapiro and Hentoff's "Hear me talkin' to ya": "I remember once on the Coast, when Buddy Rich, Dodo Marmarosa and Buddy DeFranco were all with Tommy Dorsey, they used to come into the clubs and cut everybody." [12]

A glimpse of this exuberant trio (with the addition of Sid Block on bass) can be seen in a short jam session sequence of the M-G-M musical comedy

---

11. Referring to this period in the pianist's playing, Cecil Taylor for example stated in a 1961 DOWN BEAT interview: "The first modern pianist who made any impression on me was Dodo Marmarosa with Barnet."

12. Nat Shapiro and Nat Hentoff, *Hear Me Talkin' To Ya*, first edition, New York, 1955: "Billy Taylor"

Thrill of a Romance, in which the Tommy Dorsey Orchestra participated in summer 1944. Marmarosa's playing in this scene as well as his recordings with Barnet, a few solos with Dorsey, and especially six trio performances - three from Dorsey broadcasts and three from a May 4, 1944 V-Disc recording session - for which the pianist was joined by Buddy DeFranco on clarinet and Rich's predecessor Gene Krupa on drums - underline Marmarosa's early reputation as a highly virtuoso pianist with a brilliant technique and self-assured harmonic progressiveness. To illustrate these qualities, probably no recording is suited better than the trio version of the title *Hodge Podge* from the above-mentioned V-Disc session. Dorsey had added the Krupa-DeFranco-Marmarosa trio as an extra attraction to the live performances of his orchestra, serving above all as a showcase for the extraordinary abilities of each of its three musicians. The music of the trio was presented in a brilliant and highly stylized manner with ensemble passages being carefully arranged to integrate all three instruments. Enough room was left for solo statements, however, and Marmarosa used Krupa's V-Disc date to give definite samples of his stunning art. The pianist's three-quarter chorus on *Hodge Podge* shows all the virtues and characteristics of his playing of the period. His melodic language is decidedly progressive in its use of a bop-oriented vocabulary with the typical eighth note triplets as pickups, interval leaps as phrase endings, and a strictly harmony-derived melodic line with shifting rhythmic accents. Technically Marmarosa's execution is of fascinating certainty when he alternates freely and with ease between passages of eighth notes, triplets, and sixteenths, finally leading in the bridge to a sequence of block chords as prime examples of his accomplished harmonic versatility. Marmarosa's virtuoso command of this modern musical approach appears startlingly uncompromising, as if there had never been another way to play the piano. If he acted similarly on those club contests remembered by Billy Taylor, it must certainly have been difficult to find anyone his peer in terms of technical and harmonic prowess. There was at least one person, however, who did not approve of such modern ambitions. As Peter J. Levinson in his biography "Tommy Dorsey: Livin' in a Great Big Way" suggests, it was mainly Dorsey's dislike for the modern elements in his pianist's playing that caused to his dismissal in October 1944.

Clarinettist Artie Shaw immediately seized the opportunity and engaged Marmarosa into the rhythm section of his newly formed orchestra the following month. Shaw intended to respond to contemporary developments in the jazz field, and, besides fellow musicians Barney Kessel and Herbie Steward, Marmarosa was one of the key men to bring an incipient bop-flavour to the band. He did so not only in his solos with their increasing use of a bebop-oriented melodic vocabulary, but also in his way of comping which brings a perceptively modern rhythmic concept to the band. It also gives evidence of a new understanding of the pianist's role in a big band setting. The way Marmarosa fills open spots in the ensemble passages with tiny piano inventions is certainly indebted to Count Basie, but their special sense of adapting ideally to the whole and at the same time contrasting the written parts with small rays of individualism, is strictly Marmarosa's own. The overall relaxation of Shaw's band that can be felt throughout many of its recordings, is to a considerable degree generated by its pianist's supplements to the preconceived course of the tunes.

Vice versa the relaxed musical climate of the Shaw band may also be partly responsible for a change in Marmarosa's solo style during his stay with the clarinettist. His improvisations on his first session with Shaw still seem to set their primary stress on exuberant virtuoso exposure of his stunning technical brilliance and harmonic advancement. But then in some of the following recordings a gradual shift towards a more deliberate use of these devices in favour of poised melodic and formal shaping becomes perceptible. As if the pianist began to listen to his harmonic inventions and to discover a musical palette of colours in them, he more and more uses their potential for making melodically characteristic statements, which sometimes can even take on an impressionistic flavour. His solos on *I'll Never Be the Same* (January 9, 1945), *Summertime* (April 17, 1945), *No One But You* (July 20, 1945), or *They Didn't Believe Me* (July 21, 1945) are fine examples of this tendency.

Interestingly, this change led away from the orthodox aesthetic principles of bebop playing as soon as Marmarosa had made them his own.[13] Although he adopted the innovative harmonic ideas of Gillespie and Parker [14], he did not retain their way of generating intensity of rhythm and time partly through speed and density of the notes played. The chords

---

13. Marmarosa's recording of *The Moose* with Charlie Barnet (Oct. 1943) is seen by some critics as the first manifestation of bebop-piano playing on record.

and melodic lines Marmarosa invents need time and space to unfold their harmonic colours and musical sense. While his articulation and basic principles of motivic design remained clearly those of bebop playing, he began to conceive the architecture of his improvisations in a way other than most of the bebop musicians did with their long streams of notes. His melodic sequences are composed of shorter sections in mostly symmetrically built periods, and their coherence as a whole evolves out of motivic elaboration in the sense of repetition, variation, or development, using pauses as structural elements. Where bebop lines in a strict sense still occur in his work, he likes to use their melodically rather abstract and sometimes asymmetric appearance as a contrasting device, often enhancing the effect by playing them in octave runs. This approach to the musical organization of form and time, after being of course a personal artistic feature, is in a way also a recourse to aesthetical categories of swing music.[15] In this respect then his approach can be understood as an anticipation of the bebop and swing-derived style which a few years later should be labelled as "West Coast jazz"—except that Marmarosa had left the scene even before this 'cool'-movement began to show its first signs of existence. In his following recordings, Marmarosa frequently returned to virtuoso playing and in swing-oriented contexts would feature occasional stride basses or other devices of swing piano. But in most of his work there is a predominance of this individual modern conception, the tone of which is defined by a new more thoughtful and mellow strain.[16] At least for the time until 1948 it marks the essence of his art and distinguishes his playing distinctly from that of other pianists of early bebop.

Meanwhile, the jazz world increasingly began to recognize the pianist's talents and individual voice. While former colleagues and friends praised his abilities [17], bandleader Artie Shaw spoke of Marmarosa as one of his fa-

---

14. Occasionally Marmarosa even goes a step or two further in terms of overt deviation from the harmonic roots of a tune. In his *Tone Paintings* (1947) he partly leaves the spheres of tonality.

15. It may have been on the same kind of notion, that Len Lyons in his book *The Great Jazz Pianists* characterized Marmarosa mainly as a *"melodic"* improviser. In a more general sense such an approach can also be seen as a characteristic feature of traditional European concert music which determined to a large extent Marmarosa's early musical background.

16. In a lengthy and sensitive essay entitled *"Un oiseau rare: Dodo Marmarosa"* the French writer and jazz critic Jacques Réda from another point of view comments in detail on this dichotomy in the pianist's work.

vourite players, from whom even he was able to learn a few things. With the public Marmarosa's popularity had increased to a point that he was voted 6th popular pianist in DOWN BEAT's readers poll in late 1945. This popularity was not only based on his big band recordings, but also on his work in Artie Shaw's Gramercy Five. The latter's combo setting had provided more space for the pianist's improvising talents than the piano chair of the big band, and the Gramercy Five's preserved live performances as well as its studio recordings clearly show that Marmarosa did not have to hide his talent behind those of star soloists Roy Eldridge on trumpet and Shaw himself. On the combo's first recording, *The Grabtown Grapple*, one has only to listen to Marmarosa's pianistic suggestions of Johnny Guarnieri's harpsichord playing of the original Gramercy Five or on *The Sad Sack* to follow the melodic exploitation of the extended harmonies in his lines to comprehend the technical and expressive potential of his creative mind. The delicate harmonical tensions on *The Gentle Grifter* are all Marmarosa's own and are mainly generated by his widely spread voicings in his solo bits as well as in his accompaniment (especially behind Barney Kessel's brief guitar solo). Obviously such "chamber jazz" arrangements suited the pianist's musical intentions in a certain way and stimulated his inventiveness to special heights. These performances belong to the best of Marmarosa's work on record. When Artie Shaw finally disbanded in November 1945, Marmarosa looked for more of such artistically rewarding fields.

Still while being with Shaw's mostly California based band, the pianist had begun to immerse himself into the flourishing scene along Los Angeles' Central Avenue. For a short while during and after World War II it represented a kind of western counterpart to New York City's 52nd street, and attracted first-rate jazz musicians of all styles. One of the more popular of these at the time was guitarist and vocalist Bulee "Slim" Gaillard, who secured himself Marmarosa's pianistic talents for some twenty titles recorded in December 1945 (and several more in the two years to follow). The stylistic setting of Gaillard's spontaneous musical ventures was an ideal playground for

---

17. Barney Kessel, for example, who played next to Marmarosa in Shaw's rhythm section, stated some thirty years later: "He was one of the most brilliant musicians I met during that entire period."
Art Tatum, when asked in the mid-forties to single out the most promising of his young piano colleagues, named Red Garland and Dodo Marmarosa (see liner notes by Mark Gardner to the album *Red Garland Revisited!* Prestige PR 7658).

the pianist's now fully developed colourful range of expressivity. His contributions to the guitarist's fabulous nonsense-creations range in all varieties from stunning stride-virtuosity (*Slim's Riff*, probably recorded in 1946) through orientalistic exoticism (*Dunkin' Bagels*) and delicately quiet, almost classically inspired counterpoint inventions (*Jumpin' at the Record Shop*) to modern cascades of bebop-piano (*Minuet in Vout*). Purists might criticize such pluralism as lack of artistic identity, but in Marmarosa's case, the stimulus seems to lie elsewhere. Not exclusively in his solos on Gaillard's tunes, but here without doubt most extrovertly and perhaps also most humourously comes to light the ability of the pianist to make more than an average jazz-solo out of each of his improvisations, to do more than 'just' a convincing realization of orthodox stylistic categories. Inspired by his notion of the musical and sometimes putative extra-musical character of a tune, he invents meaningful statements which are at the same time personal as well as integrant to a general level of expression of each individual tune. The result on the Gaillard sides is a highly charming variety of miniature tone paintings, which show Marmarosa's own world of perception [18], painted in the pianist's individual tinge of swing, bebop, and elements of classical piano music, and yet never crossing the border of genuine jazz improvisation. It is not in the least this sincerity about his art, the avoidance of any kind of self-complacency in these inventions, which makes them so appealing.[19]

Two further sessions of the period contain similar, but somewhat 'straighter' examples for Marmarosa's particular ability to adapt his playing to a given musical context. By introducing him into the ranks of the major protagonists of American jazz they also proved of greater historical significance than his Gaillard escapades.

---

18. Marmarosa's raised receptivity to sounds in general is well illustrated by Ross Russell, who described a few of the unusual habits of the pianist: "Every sound had a secret meaning for him. Certain sounds issued imperious orders. If he were walking down the street and a cathedral began chiming vespers he would stop and listen, rooted to the spot until the sounds stopped and he was released from their spell. One of his favourite things was to stay up all night so that he could stand barefoot on the dewy plot in front of the house, listening to the cries of the birds as they awakened to the California dawn."

19. A remark by Artie Shaw about his former pianist, that he "had an utter purity about him," probably referred to the same kind of notion.

Another pianist, who frequently showed a similar variety of expressive colours in genuine jazz playing, is Marmarosa's former schoolmate Erroll Garner. Despite all the obvious differences in their approach, which have been rightly pointed at, it might nevertheless be an equally rewarding task, to look for correspondences in their expressive techniques.

In mid-December 1945, Lester Young chose the pianist for his first recording session after his release from the army. "Pres dug Dodo very much", remembers Red Callender, who played bass at the session, and says himself about Marmarosa: "He was very inventive, a genius in his own way".[20] Marmarosa's contributions to the four titles of the session are an ideal amalgam of his modern harmonic and melodic conception with a more traditional rhythmic feeling that keeps him in line with the swing-oriented beat of Young's drummer Henry "Tucker" Green. The pianist's chorus on *Jumpin' At Mesner's*, for example, opens each section with decidedly modern, rhythmically even single-note lines, only to adapt in the endings to Green's more heavily pronounced rhythm, the last A-section eventually being entirely played in stride. The gem of the session, of course, is Young's famous version of *These Foolish Things*, opened by a short, highly atmospheric piano introduction of a few broken chords, which beautifully lead into the chorus by a repeated rhythmic anticipation of the first three-note figure of the theme. They remain, though, the only quotation of the song as Young starts to improvise on his very first note, accompanied by Marmarosa in perfect sympathetic understatement.

A second occasion of historical dimension for Marmarosa was his first opportunity to record with Charlie Parker and Dizzy Gillespie. The session was another one of Slim Gaillard's spontaneous undertakings and must have occurred in the second half of the same month. Gillespie and Parker had just arrived on the Coast with a sextet to play a six-week engagement at Billy Berg's Swing Club in Hollywood, and Slim Gaillard was alternating sets with them. Parker, who would stay in Los Angeles for more than a year, later gave Marmarosa two more significant opportunities to accompany him in a recording studio. Their first recording meeting here, however, is rather disparate in its stylistic scope. Surrounded by a fine yet imperturbably traditional rhythm section (Zutty Singleton is the drummer), the modernistic playing of Parker and Gillespie here stands out as if they had flown in from another world. Only Marmarosa seizes again the opportunity of an informal musical setting to fill the gap with plenty of humourous and strikingly dissonant piano fantasies. Their omnipresence and surprising inventiveness made the English jazz

---

20. cited after Bob Eleff, "The Mystery Of Dodo Marmarosa", Coda, Sept./Oct. 1993, p.20-24

critic Owen Peterson accurately comment on the session: "It is as an accompanist that Marmarosa's particular talents are most effectively displayed on this recording [*Popity Pop*]. In his unique way he dominates the performance from first to last. ... Everything he does is arresting and magical, constantly diverting the listener from the surface to another level of musical endeavour; deeper and infinitely meaningful."

Behind such creative energy, one is tempted to presume an artist's will to give everything and even the tiniest accompanying figure a special meaning beyond its pure functional task, a definite place in a superior musical context. Marmarosa's unusual improvisatory inventiveness and intelligence in this respect are discernible in many of his recorded performances of the period, but such aesthetic demands may also lead a musician to seek perfection beyond the spontaneity of improvisation. Consequently the attentive listener will also find examples of the pianist's playing, which reveal themselves as precast and thus repeatable musical conceptions.

Every now and then such moments occur, when Marmarosa, once content with the shape of an improvisation, kept to it and repeated it on occasions, where the same arrangement of a tune was played again. A few examples of this can be found when comparing studio recordings with air-checks of the Boyd Raeburn Orchestra, which Marmarosa joined in December 1945 as a substitute for pianist/arranger George Handy. Temporarily forced to function more or less as a rehearsal band at that time, the ranks of Raeburn's orchestra were filled with the most skilled and dedicated players of the Los Angeles scene, interpreting unusual and highly demanding scores mainly by George Handy and Ed Finckel. Both arrangers wrote in an avant-garde style, which combined elements of bebop with loans from European concert music, especially the works of Igor Stravinsky. The complex and dissonant ensemble textures and the ambitious modernism, apparent in the project as a whole, blended ideally with Marmarosa's own interests in this field, and his contributions in solos as well as in his accompaniments stand out among the many excellent statements from other soloists such as Lucky Thompson, Ray Linn or Britt Woodman.

Still a bit modest at his first recording date in December 1945 with this new company, a highlight of Marmarosa's activities with Raeburn emerged out of a composition by Ed Finckel, which left much room for the pianist's own modernistic ideas. The tune was titled *Boyd Meets Stravinsky* and was first recorded by AFRS at one of its "Jubilee" shows, probably at the end of January 1946. Formally based on the 12 bars of the blues, the considerably fast piece contains a through-composed middle section 'à la Stravinsky,' which sets a percussive ostinato-riff in the trombone section against reeds and trumpets. Whereas the "Jubilee" version contains only two improvised choruses by Marmarosa with some of his most bop-like piano playing, in a studio recording for JEWELL only a few days later he takes two more choruses and plays an unusual bass figure behind the end of the second trumpet chorus. Alternating bars of half-note triplets with regular quarter notes, it lends a peculiar kind of suspension to the rhythmic flow of the short passage where it occurs. In a third version of the title, recorded also in February 1946 for STANDARD, this bass figure returns more prominently behind the trumpet chorus, briefly at the beginning of the trombone solo and finally once more at the end of the piece. Moreover, it is joined by other ostinato-like elements in Marmarosa's accompaniment, which even find entrance into his third and fourth solo chorus, where the pianist alternates at length two overtly dissonant chord structures. Viewed against the through-composed middle section of the arrangement, these inventions by Marmarosa function as a kind of improvised anticipation of the rhythmic suspension and ostinato structure found in this section. In addition to this, they bear as obviously a streak of 'construction' as does the 'Stravinsky' part of the tune. Again Marmarosa shows his extraordinary ability to bring his improvisations into line with the composition and arrangement they refer to, and it is interesting to see how he constantly works out his ideas from one session to another, the last version here being near to a stroke of genius.[21]

Boyd Meets Stravinsky is not singular as an example for the pianist's abundant inventiveness in decorating Raeburn's band book. There were many other excellent contributions by Marmarosa to tunes like *Tonsillectomy, Two Spoos in an Igloo, Boyd's Nest,* and others on which he played brilliantly. But as was already mentioned, one may also find titles in the Raeburn programs on which the pianist repeats originally improvised solos literally over the six months he performed them with the orchestra.[22] One

---

21. Three later versions of the title from the summer of 1946 contain still new ideas on this subject by the pianist.

of these titles is *I Don't Know Why*, of which five versions from February to late July 1946 show a kind of 'frozen in' quarter chorus by Marmarosa. It is a variation of the theme, that bears his typical orderly handwriting with its extremely clean and economical legato-playing, delicate embellishments, and the characteristic octave runs in the ending. It is not a spectacular solo and moreover a rather brief statement, but it nevertheless leaves a very harmonious impression in itself as well as in relation to the tune as a whole. Its repetition then is just another variant to secure the concordance of a solo and its musical surrounding.

The final step in striving to fulfil such aesthetic standards in the realm of jazz, of course, leads to composing in combination with arranging. From Marmarosa only two recorded ventures into this field are known. One was written for the orchestra of Boyd Raeburn and transcribed in early February 1946 by STANDARD under the significant title *Amnesia*. The piece shows strong influences from the musical language of bebop with characteristic figures and passages for all sections, which at times even for the brilliantly skilled players of the Raeburn ranks seem to have been difficult to execute. A reason for this may be the transfer of rather pianistically conceived ideas to the writing for horns. Nevertheless, Marmarosa's score offers interesting harmonical sequences, attractive backings by the band for solos and a fine dramatic sense in the varied use of the horn sections for the overall conception of the piece. With its uncompromising commitment to the stylistics of bebop (underlined also by rhythmic irritation in the introduction and a very sudden ending), it could easily have been part of the band book of Dizzy Gillespie's 1946 big band.

Marmarosa's other recorded arrangement was part of a studio session for the small label ENCORE, which had taken place already two months earlier in mid-December 1945. Ray Linn was leading a combo with five horns and rhythm then and seized the opportunity to record part of its modern repertory with arrangements by Tommy Todd, Sonny Burke, and Marmarosa. In terms of progressiveness, Marmarosa's contribution cer-

---

22. Further almost identically repeated choruses by Marmarosa can be heard in comparing the studio recording of *Lucky Number* (Artie Shaw a. h. Orchestra, June 14, 1945) to a 'live' version of the same title from a "Coca Cola Spotlight Bands" broadcast (Sept. 12, 1945), or Tommy Dorsey's *Opus One* recording for Lang-Worth transcriptions (May 12, 1944) to the version played on an AFRS "Command Performance" show from ca. October 1944.

tainly was the most modern sounding of the four recorded items. The structure of his composition titled *Escape*[23] resembles Dizzy Gillespie's *A Night in Tunisia*. Harmonically elaborated, but rather static 'A'-sections of an 'AABA' formal scheme are combined with a more conventional bridge. While for the first chorus of the score the horns state the melodic outline of Marmarosa's theme, they return in the last chorus with the focus on the chord structures of its 'A'-sections, which are presented in widely spread and markedly dissonant voicings, producing an unusually provocative tone colour for the time. Such writing for combo was new then and did not fail to make some stir. Jazz critic Barry Ulanov wrote in a review of the session for the March 1946 issue of METRONOME magazine: "So was Dodo Marmarosa's *Escape*, like *Caravan* [arrangement by Sonny Burke] daring in its use of jazz horns, unlike anything I've heard in its fullness of sound out of a couple of hands-ful of instruments. ... As a result of it, the angular little pianist has been swamped with arranging offers from Coast leaders..." Despite such positive reactions to his composing efforts, Marmarosa obviously continued to prefer performing to arranging. At least on record, no other examples of his writing for larger ensembles are known.

The most promising opportunities for a jazz musician to pursue his own artistic ideas are probably those in which he is allowed to determine the setting and outline of his performance by himself. For Marmarosa such an opportunity materialized on January 11, 1946 in the form of a first recording session under his leadership. With Ray Brown on bass and Jackie Mills on drums in a trio and with the addition of tenor-saxophonist Lucky Thompson for two quartet sides, the pianist definitely had a team of his own choice. Surrounded by these stylistically advanced musicians and without having to make concessions to someone else's conceptions, one expects Marmarosa to develop and realize his very own musical thoughts freely. The result is convincing, and especially one of the pianist's own tunes, a medium-tempoed trio feature entitled *Mellow Mood*, remains a masterpiece of piano trio recording to date. Significantly, the main accent of the performance lies not on showing facility with the newest developments in bebop. Marmarosa's thirty-two-bar theme is very simple and rather conventional in its melodious outline. Based essen-

---

23. Marmarosa recorded it himself in trio formation in December 1947.

tially on a descending three-note sequence stated in half notes, it derives its charm entirely from its linear harmony, moving in the first two bars from the major seventh to the sixth and third of the key, and from its vertical harmonization in close-harmony block chords, whose colours create the melancholy mood heralded by the title of the tune. The main features of the recording being these harmonies and a certain feeling of counterpoint in the pianist's constant alternation between his right and left hand, it is especially Marmarosa's chord formations that require a closer look. Thoroughly versed in the extended harmonic vocabulary of contemporary jazz [24], he shows little interest in its linear display, which is characteristic for bebop improvisation. For the harmonic possibilities of the piano, it means an unnecessary limitation. Marmarosa thus prefers the enriched sound qualities of extended harmonies when played at once in the form of chords and obviously likes to seek and utilize expressive values in their dissonant overtones. To leave still no doubt here about his modernistic ambition, he takes up such dissonant devices as parallel seconds, ostentatiously pointed out in the bridge of his solo-chorus on *Mellow Mood*, which certainly sounded quite provocative in those times. On the other hand, he does not shy away from opening his solo with four bars of traditional stride piano, concluding it, however, with a six-bar line of pure bebop-phrasing with its characteristic shifting accents. Typically for Marmarosa this line is played in octaves, which gives it a certain artificiality, as though it were inserted especially for demonstrative purposes. In all this a kind of overt independency of the pianist's playing from stylistic tendencies around him becomes apparent. "It was a nice record. It wasn't real modern or anything," Marmarosa characterized the record himself in his 1995 interview. In demonstrating that he was able to play in several styles simultaneously and that he liked to draw on them freely, according to his different expressive purposes, he documented a self-confident emancipatory attitude towards the main streams of stylistical development of the time.[25] Yet such experiments seldom affected the distinctive homogeneity of Marmarosa's playing, and it is

---

24. Any pianist who is familiar with romantic and post-romantic classical piano literature will be at ease with the harmonic principles of bebop. Interviewed by DOWN BEAT in the spring of 1943 as a member of Gene Krupa's orchestra, Marmarosa denoted Chopin, Stravinsky, Debussy, and Ravel as some of his favourite composers.

above all the wonderfully relaxed mood of this recording, the excellent inter-play of all three musicians, and the effortless flow of Marmarosa's inventions, paired with a marvellous sense of balancing contrasting devices of musical design, which make *Mellow Mood* an outstanding performance.

Later on we will discuss a few more of Marmarosa's own small group sessions, among which one may find examples of his most individual work. The majority of his recording activities, however, have been cap-tured in the groups of others, among them the already mentioned Charlie Parker, a young avant-garde arranger named Tom Talbert and such major bop (or near-bop) stars as trumpeter Howard McGhee, tenor saxophon-ists Lucky Thompson and Wardell Gray, or guitarist Barney Kessel.[26] Tal-bert, for years a West Coast stalwart, wrote for ensembles in an exceptional modern style, that then was rather known to musicians only. In late 1946 he had been asked by producer and owner of the ATOMIC label Lyle Grif-fin to write a special solo feature for Marmarosa, who in those years was 'pianist in residence' and the star of Griffin's little record company. Talbert years later recalled that he had been very pleased with the task. "Lyle Grif-fin, who owned Atomic Records, wanted me to record a big band piece fea-turing Dodo. I was thrilled as he had been one of my favorite pianists right from the time I heard him with Artie Shaw's band in San Diego."[27] The orchestra, which was formed on the recording date of November 4, 1946, combined musicians of Talbert's rehearsal band with a few stars of the lo-cal scene including Lucky Thompson on tenor saxophone. Despite a very pathetic introduction, which according to Talbert was meant as a parody on Hollywood movie openings, the recorded piece itself evolves into a less ambitious and happy swinging affair. *Flight of the Vout Bug*, as Griffin later titled the recording for release, shows off Marmarosa's talents well, and it is difficult to decide, whether his pianistic contributions are written out or

25. Obviously this kind of individualism was not confined to Marmarosa's music alone as tenor saxo-phonist Teddy Edwards remembered in an interview for JAZZ JOURNAL in 1982: "Dodo was a fine pianist. During that time he was close to genius. He had his own way, his own attitude about life and everything."
26. It is interesting to see, that with the exception of Benny Carter, Lester Young, and perhaps Wardell Gray, Marmarosa seems to have rarely if ever worked in public with any of the leaders he recorded with. The time between the numerous calls for recording sessions he spent playing in big bands (esp. Boyd Raeburn and Tommy Pederson), at jazz concerts, as a soloist in nightclubs (he appeared as a solo feature at Billy Berg's and the 400 Club in Hollywood), or jamming after hours.
27. Cited after Bruce Talbot, "Tom Talbert – His Life and Times", p.76

improvised, as they are well integrated into the musical surroundings of the orchestra. The pianist will most certainly have had a sketch of Talbert's arrangement in advance to be able to work out his solo part, and Talbert recalled, that "this piece was a joy to write and record. The written parts of the score contain a lot of two-hand octaves and Dodo came to the session prepared to play".[28] The including of a few pianistic virtuoso devices typical for classical piano studies or etudes in the solo line and the use of ritornellos for the orchestra suggest the intention of both Marmarosa and Talbert to create a kind of "condensed" concertino with a leaning toward classical formal concepts, as was typical also for the "progressive" music played by Boyd Raeburn or Stan Kenton at the time. The overall result is humorous and charming, even if the time limit of three minutes did not allow for much of a formal extension.

In the context of bebop groups, Marmarosa had to submit his creative freedom somewhat to the more narrowly defined rules of this style, these restrictions not necessarily impairing his expressive spirit. To the contrary, some of his most appealing work emerges out of moments where he manages to combine his individualistic ideas with the stylistic conformity of bop-improvisation, and occasionally this brings a unique colour to the respective performances One of the most original of such moments was caught on a recording Marmarosa did as guest with a working group of trumpeter Howard McGhee for the label DIAL on October 18, 1946. The piece was given the allusive title *Dialated Pupils* and is based on the standard *I Got Rhythm*. Taken at a fast tempo, Marmarosa keenly starts the first solo after the theme with a series of prominently exposed and fluently executed classical finger studies, before changing to a more bop-like idiom. This alien element lends a peculiar and unexpected touch of artificiality to his statement without impairing in any way the natural flow and unity of the performance as a whole.[29] It is, of course, also a humorous reference to the fact that there is actually no harmonical movement to be found in the first sixteen bars of *I Got Rhythm*.

Other, perhaps better-known examples of such individualistic manifestations of Marmarosa's inventiveness can be found on some of the takes from

---

28. Liner notes to Sea Breeze SB-2069, "Tom Talbert - Jazz Orchestra 1946-1949"
29. The fifth take of the title contains similar, but less convincingly executed ideas by Marmarosa

Charlie Parker's two DIAL-sessions, on which he chose Marmarosa to be his piano player. The first session took place on March 28, 1946, and the story of how Marmarosa came to replace Parker's regular pianist Joe Albany a day or two before the session has been told by Ross Russell in his Parker biography, "Bird lives".[30] It seems, however, that Marmarosa was at ease with most of the recorded material from frequent jamming at the Club Finale where Parker was working at the time. Of the first title, *Moose the Mooche*, which will be the only one we discuss here at length, three takes were made on the session, the third one being the most interesting as far as Marmarosa's ideas are concerned. He opens each of the takes with an eight-bar introduction based on the theme of the tune, yet does it a bit differently every time. The third version is the most daring one in that, in bars 5 to 8, he fans out linearly over two octaves an augmented chord based on *e*-natural, which finally leads as a guide tone into the first note *f* of the theme. While pushing beautifully forward with its rhythmic shape, this whole-tone structure generates a kind of dissonant standstill in terms of harmonic progression, constantly building up tension over the four bars and thus enhancing and, at the same time, contrasting its final resolution into the theme. This is a fine example of how Marmarosa uses harmonic ideas not-then-common in modern jazz as a contrasting and ornamenting device in the context of bop. For a few bars of his otherwise conventional bebop solo on this take he once more takes up the same idea, forming a link in character between the solo and his introduction. Equally unusual is his comping behind the first statement of the theme. With heavily pronounced chords in the lower register of the piano, he forms a kind of prominent counterpart to the horn-unison, playing a variety of rhythmic patterns, which partly follow the accents of the theme and partly are set against it. The addition of this second level to the polyrhythmic texture of the theme and the use of the unusual harmonic character of whole-tone elements in introduction and solo give this third rendition of Parker's tune a special Marmarosan flavour. That he played much more discretely on the two other takes of *Moose the Mooche* is a sign of the occasional spontaneity, if not to say "unpredictability" of the pianist's imagination, as Barney Kessel once observed. Nevertheless, Marma-

---

30. Joe Albany himself gave a detailed description of the event in an interview with Ira Gitler for DOWN BEAT in October 1963.

rosa did not play himself into the foreground with such inventions. But he most certainly knew how to use his limit as an accompanist more exhaustively and more effectively than any other pianist of his time. For the French jazz-critic Alain Tercinet he was just "an ideal partner for Parker; on the trail of his leader: never imposing nor effacing himself." [31]

As Miles Davis suggested in his autobiography, it was Marmarosa's remarkable work on the above session which mainly led to his election as "New Star" of the piano category by a board of experts voting for the magazine ESQUIRE's poll in January 1947. Davis and Lucky Thompson, who also had participated on the session, won their respective categories. About a month later, Marmarosa was once more in the recording studio with Parker. Of the four titles recorded on the 26th of February 1947, *Relaxin' at Camarillo* is especially notable for its piano introduction. The pianist develops it over the course of the session from an ending he plays on take one of the title. It is built of two equal parts of four bars, setting a three-eighth meter in both hands over the fourths of the ride cymbal in the first two bars and a series of syncopated bass notes in bars three and four. Both features function as a kind of anticipation of the polyrhythmics of Parker's theme, which begins equally syncopated as Marmarosa's eight bars end. This introduction (and ending) has since become almost as much a classic as the tune itself.[32] It is again an example for Marmarosa's extraordinary ability to contribute to the performance of a tune with ideas that are more than passing inventions of routine improvisation, and interestingly it is often in such minor or subordinated parts as introductions or accompaniment that one finds some of the pianist's most meaningful statements, not necessarily in his solos.

Generally speaking of Marmarosa's playing with Parker, its emotional quality seems fundamentally different from that of his other accompanists like, for example, Bud Powell or Al Haig. In his solos Marmarosa articulated eighth and sixteenth notes with an almost perfect rhythmic preci-

---

31. Alain Tercinet, "Be-bop", Paris 1991, p.178
32. On a broadcast from the Royal Roost from November 1948, Hank Jones plays a virtual copy of Marmarosa's introduction as an opener for the tune *Heat Wave*, sung by Ella Fitzgerald.
It is still cited by Alan Broadbent in a rendition of *Relaxin' at Camarillo* by the Charlie Haden Quartet from July 30/August 1, 1993.

sion, a feature absolutely common to the performance of classical piano music, but not necessarily for the bebop-pianist as Bud Powell's highly intensive and in its creative impetus often a bit sloppy playing exemplifies. Against Powell's feverish haste, Marmarosa's even articulation conveys a notion of order and control, but also a certain lightness through its effortless flow. The latter is enhanced by a more legato-like linking of the notes in Marmarosa's case, whereas Powell's playing is more percussive. Marmarosa replaced this articulatory intensity often found in the playing of bop-musicians with the finesse and subtlety of his harmonic inventions and the distinction of his formal conceptions. While in his solos he thus shows an outward calm atypical in the circles of bop, Marmarosa's comping is, on the contrary, extraordinarily tight and pressing in its rhythmic presence as well as in the abundant inventiveness of its accentuating. Compared, for example, to Bud Powell's comping on Parker's SAVOY session from May 8, 1947 or the accompaniments of Duke Jordan on the Parker DIAL recordings from the fall of the year, Marmarosa plays with decidedly more complexity and drive on the *Relaxin' At Camarillo* recordings. His most exciting exercise in this field, however, can be found on a date with Wardell Gray from November 1946.

The bebop boom in Los Angeles did not last forever. A few weeks after his *Relaxin' at Camarillo* session, Charlie Parker left the West Coast again for New York. The scene in L. A. continued for a while without him and there still were highlights like Gene Norman's first two "Just Jazz" concerts from April 29 and June 23, 1947, during which Marmarosa was prominently featured in different stylistic contexts. At the period he also worked with the "part-time" orchestra of trombonist Tommy Pederson, who featured the pianist as one of his main soloists over the year. Recording opportunities, however, became less, and in December 1947 Ross Russell with his record company DIAL, who had done much for the documentation of Los Angeles' blooming avant-garde circles, also headed for New York and its more rewarding events in the field of modern jazz. Yet he did not neglect his long-standing plan to produce a Dodo Marmarosa recording session. The project had failed in the beginning because of the pianist's doubts about his abilities as a soloist. As Russell remembers, Marmarosa had an unexpected excuse when he was first offered a date for DIAL: "He was almost on the verge of tears. He said, "Man, I don't have the hands for it. Look at these tiny little hands. They're just too small. I can't do anything with them." [33] Marmarosa's favourite drummer and close associate Jackie Mills gained a deeper insight into the origins for such scruples when he was Marmarosa's fellow-lodger in 1946 and 1947: "Dodo was the most dedicated of players. He practiced an incredible amount of hours all day long. He wouldn't stop to eat. He would eat at the piano with one hand and keep playing with the other." And Mills continues: "He never allowed anything but the piano to be important to him. The piano was his life. He heard things in his head that he wasn't able to play and it frustrated him. Once, he got mad at the old upright piano we had and chopped it up with an axe." [34] When Marmarosa finally agreed to do the session for Russell, Mills was on the team, as well as Harry Babasin, who besides his bass brought a cello to the date.

The overall impression of the session, which took place on November 12, 1947, matches the picture drawn by Jackie Mills of the pianist's attitude towards his music. Of five titles recorded on the day there were cut twenty-nine takes altogether, which makes an average of nearly six takes per title. As Ross Russell put it in the liner notes for a later LP-reissue of the session, "the perfectionist in Marmarosa's nature compelled him to try again and again." And perhaps not too surprisingly, if one compares the different issued takes of a title to each other, they seem to differ only in shades. There is a slightly faster or slower tempo here and there or Marmarosa plays a theme more legato on a second try, but in his improvisations there are only minor variations in character or quality of execution audible.[35] The pianist seems to have taken his business more than seriously on this session, but even if such an over-sensitive perfectionism might have impaired to a certain extent Marmarosa's spontaneity in improvising, one should nevertheless regard the remarkable output of this session as an integral artistic statement on a very high level.

---

33. Martin Williams, *Dial Days: A Conversation with Ross Russell* in "Jazz Changes", New York 1992, p.40-54
34. cited after Bob Eleff, "The Mystery Of Dodo Marmarosa", p.22
35. The high standard of at least eleven of the takes led to their release at different times by DIAL and other record companies, causing some confusion for the discographer to discern 'which take of what title has been reissued *where*' over the course of time.

A closer look at Marmarosa's choice of tunes and the way he interprets them reveals a deliberate approach to making up a session of his own. It seems that he took the opportunity to respond to contemporary developments in jazz piano playing as well as to some of its roots. The first title *Bopmatism* bears most certainly a grammatical reference to Jay McShann's *Swingmatism*, which is known for one of Charlie Parker's early influential solos on a recording from 1941. Marmarosa's title thus puts the emphasis on <u>Bop</u>-matism, the tune belonging to it being very likely intended as a study in bebop. Compared to the other titles of the session it shows in fact the strongest traits of bop, in its theme as well as in the improvised parts. Marmarosa's single-note lines almost organically flow out of his right hand, and he accompanies them with chord progressions in his left, which now and then take on a melodic shape of their own. From this kind of 'two-line' playing and its prevailing minor key the tune derives a special charm, and even though one might miss a bit the final spark of spontaneity found in others of the pianist's solos, the beautiful conception and execution on both issued takes nevertheless make them one of Marmarosa's finest trio performances on record.

The assumption that *Dodo's Dance* might be named after *Dee Dee's Dance* by Denzil Best[36] is to a certain extent confirmed by a comparison of the themes and tempo of both tunes. There is a resemblance between the former's series of descending eighth-note figures and the latter's repetition of an ascending eighth-note motif, but this is already where the similarities end. Marmarosa's "Dance" is a showcase for his brilliant facility in up-tempo playing, the whole performance being kept in breathtaking double-time. It has much in common with a fast riff-tune, and its traditional outline is further enhanced by the pianist's stride-accompaniment to his own single-note lines. Like two solo performances from 1946, it is strongly influenced by the pianistics of Art Tatum, and though musically the least rewarding title of the session, it may after all be understood as a reference to one of Marmarosa's greatest idols.[37]

---

36. A recording of the title, which Marmarosa might have known, was made by Clyde Hart's All Stars, including Denzil Best, on December 19, 1944 for the label SAVOY. At any rate, he would have been familiar with the title from jamming with followers of the modern jazz scene.

The semantic connotation of "Dary Departs" is not known. Musically it recalls in several ways Marmarosa's *Mellow Mood* from 1946. There is the same relaxed medium-tempo and a similar outline in the harmonic progression of the theme, though realized with a different motif here, the bridge nevertheless calling to mind the melody of the A-sections in the earlier composition. Both tunes present their themes in block chords and for the improvised parts draw equally on stride piano as well as on the modern single-note style. Even the peaceful and somewhat pensive character of *Dary Departs* is much the same as that of *Mellow Mood*. But, whereas all three issued takes here are beautifully executed, with the seventh take showing a slightly different character through its faster and more fluent tempo, they do not seem to be entirely carried by the spirit that enhances *Mellow Mood*.

Lover, which was given the title *Cosmo Street*[38] on a second issue on LP, comes closer in terms of creative energy. Taken at a considerably fast tempo, Marmarosa accompanies the theme and his improvisations with swaying left hand chords in half notes, stretching a little the first half of each bar compared to the second and thus maintaining a reminiscence of the waltz-feel of the original tune. In his improvisations, especially on the slower take four, the pianist expresses himself with ease, building up a symmetrical structure through constantly complementing two bars with two others in a scheme of opening and closing melodic shape. This regular course adds to the waltz-like flow of the performance and is skilfully prevented from becoming tedious by the creation of larger thematic correspondences and a lively touch of rubato in the pianist's playing. Apart from the interesting task to convert a waltz tune into a four beat-performance, one is tempted to seek other motives for the inclusion of this title into the program of the session. By the end of 1947, the four beat-version of Richard Rodgers' composition had presumably become a frequently played tune in jam sessions. But what may have made it a challenge for Marmarosa is the fact that other

---

37. Already in early 1946, when he was allowed two solo performances during an AFRS "Jubilee" show as member of Boyd Raeburn's orchestra, Marmarosa had not sought to dwell on his inside reputation as one of the leading avant-garde pianists. Instead he took a bow to Art Tatum in re-tracing two of the master's famous solo recordings from 1939, *Tea for Two* and *Deep Purple*.
38. This title probably refers to Cosmo Street, a short road between Hollywood Boulevard and Selma Avenue in Hollywood, CA, not far from the famous intersection of Sunset Boulevard and Vine Street.

pianists had already included the title into their repertoires, the rendition which might have first and foremost served here as a model being that of Erroll Garner from the afore-mentioned "Just Jazz" Concert from April 1947. While the keyboard texture and the formal layout of both performances are much the same, Marmarosa takes his interpretation at a decidedly faster tempo, converting Garner's famous four-beat 'strumming' into the afore-mentioned half bar-chords. Also, against the fast but unobtrusive and unaccented four-beat playing of Mills and Babasin, Marmarosa's chords become more perceptible than Garners's strumming, which is completely embedded into the playing of his rhythm section. Thus, as already observed in *Bopmatism*, Marmarosa wins an intermediary level between his right hand and the basic rhythm, which enables him to complement independently his melodic lines through the playing of his left hand. The pianist's intelligent use of the keyboard and the careful avoidance of repetitive patterns in his right-hand improvisation make his rendition clearly the more elaborate of the two, but on the other side it does not quite show the spontaneous and playful vigour from which Garner's performance earns a significant amount of its appeal.

Finally Marmarosa had also included a ballad into his program for DIAL. Again there are indications that the pianist obtained part of his inspiration from a performance by Erroll Garner, this time the trio recording of Red Callender's *Pastel* for the same company from February 1947. We do not know who conceived the title *Trade Winds* for Marmarosa's recording [39], nor do we know the motivation behind this choice. The basis for the pianist's playing here is clearly the standard *You Go To My Head*, and whatever title one may choose [40] for this performance, it is a real gem (the first take sounding still a bit more definite than the third). From Garner's famous recording, Marmarosa adopted the particularly slow pace, the transparent keyboard texture, and the interplay between bass and piano for introduction and ending. He takes, however, considerably long eight bars to set with his introduction the slow beat and the 'pastel'-like sonority for the piece, ideally supported by the light pizzicato of Harry Babasin's cello and a very decent cymbal

---

39. In the early 1950s, Harry Babasin owned a club of the same name in Los Angeles' Inglewood neighbourhood, where he organized regular jam sessions.
40. The later issue of the first take on a DIAL-LP was given the standard's title.

timbre from Jackie Mills.[41] This configuration returns once again as a coda and thus beautifully frames one simple chorus of highly intimate ballad playing. It is perhaps the virtual absence of any kind of customary embellishments which is responsible for this climate of intimacy here, laying bare at such a slow pace the melodic and harmonic inventions of the pianist. In his playing, he touches the original melody of the tune only occasionally at a few characteristic points. The space in between is filled with transparent chord-structures in both hands, from which Marmarosa now and then frees his right hand to carry out a linear spreading of his harmonic ideas, the performance living entirely on the perfect balancing and rhythmic variation of horizontally and vertically displayed harmony and the addition of a few intriguing and very personal dissonant dots. Quantitatively speaking, it is the unpretentious proof that less can be (much) more, which raises this recording clearly above the level of conventional entertaining piano music. It remains one of Marmarosa's best trio sides.

As his DIAL session reveals, even at times when the bebop movement had firmly established itself, Marmarosa still took no definite position toward its stylistical implications. He pairs performances that conform with the new style with others in which he blends bop-specific elements with more traditional features, maintaining in one case even an exclusively swing-oriented stride accompaniment. He does so in a session for the leading company of its day in recording modern jazz. His efforts therefore received mixed critiques at the time of their first release. From today's point of view, however, it seems that stylistical opportunism prevented the view on an overall excellent pianistic elaboration and execution in these performances and the nevertheless apparent currency in their individual artistic approach. That they do not convey completely the freshness and nonchalance of Marmarosa's experiments in his earlier solo and trio performances may have been the result of a kind of 'over'-elaboration or the wish to make everything perfect on such an occasion.

Seen against the otherwise slow entertainment business in the Los Angeles area, the city's recording studios once more saw an unequalled boost

---

41. Unfortunately on all later LP and CD reissues of the session such decent elements in the accompaniment are drowned by poor sound quality. To get a full impression of the sensitive work of Mills and Babasin, one has to turn, if possible, to LP releases from the early 1950s!

of activity at the end of 1947. This was due to the American Federation of Musicians' announcement of a second ban directed against the country's major record companies, which was set to begin on January 1, 1948. Everyone—but primarily the record companies—hurriedly sought to produce a sufficient reserve of recorded music to be released during the time of nonrecording. As it seems, Dodo Marmarosa seized the opportunity to get some of his more unorthodox ideas on wax. In the last two months of the year he played three more recording sessions under his name, of which at least two show a decidedly more experimental approach than had his abovementioned DIAL session.

On a recording date, which was probably done for the label ATOMIC on November 1, 1947, Marmarosa began these experiments with two explorative solo pieces. Although they seem to be without parallel in the field of early modern jazz piano, they nevertheless belong to a category of piano fantasias, which have a small but continuous tradition in the history of jazz. Since Bix Beiderbecke's *In a Mist*, a study in impressionistic harmonic language recorded in 1927, other pianists have occasionally used solo recordings as an experimental field. Jess Stacy's *Ain't Goin' Nowhere* and *Ec-Stacy* from 1939 adhere to this tradition, as well as some of Erroll Garner's private recordings for the Danish baron Timme Rosenkrantz in 1944 or Mary Lou Williams' solo movements from her suite *Signs of the Zodiac* of the year following, to name a few. Marmarosa's two studies are simply called *Tone Paintings I* and *II*[42], of which at least the second had already been conceived in December 1946, when it served as an object of analysis for Sharon Pease in DOWN BEAT. Marmarosa then introduced it as a "mood picture" under the dedicatory title *Miles' Influence*. A closer look at *Tone Paintings II* reveals that the piece is mainly built on a two-bar motif introduced in bar fifteen, which at least in its rhythmic shape is repeated constantly in the course of the composition and, together with a kind of parodied stride-rhythm, gives it coherence. The peculiar 'mood' of this 'sound picture' emerges from a strange discrepancy between the happy and joyful character of its rhythm and the 'lamento' effect of chromatic downward steps while sequencing its main motif. Framed by two brief episodes of undefined tonality

---

42. This title may be a later publisher's invention. A tag of some fifty seconds, audible on the recording of *Tone Paintings II*, seems to be a fragment not belonging originally to this piece, but most certainly was recorded on the same date.

and enhanced through dissonant chord structures, the combination of these opponent emotional qualities results in a quasi-suggestive atmosphere, in the creation of an unusual and striking mood.

Tone Paintings I depicts basically the extension in time of a somewhat gloomy area of chordal sounds with only minor variations, freely following a stream of associations without any fixed structure of rhythm. Only once does a concretely shaped element show in the form of a brightening little melody, which for six bars introduces rhythm and a symmetrical order into the run of events, before it also disappears in the darkness of sound.[43] A listener accustomed to the formal and rhythmic self-evidence of traditional music will once more be irritated by this contrast of seemingly 'real' and 'unreal' musical elements and may sense a kind of suggestive aura around them, not unlike the imaginative stimulation one may find in music written for a silent movie or, for example, in the kind of images used by the painters and writers of surrealism. It seems that Marmarosa's interest in improvisation or musical creativity in general often had a certain tendency to explore such associative potentials in the forming of musical time through harmony and rhythm. But nowhere else does he allow such artistic leanings to express themselves as freely as in these two solo studies. That he himself did not give away them for release may have been a sign of own discontent with the outcome of his musical experiments or of mistrust in the ability or will of public audiences to appreciate and understand them.[44]

The second more experimental session under Marmarosa's name followed on December 24, 1947. As the previously mentioned recordings, it is supposed to have originally been intended for release on the small ATOMIC label, but the plan to publish the ten trio sides recorded on this day as an album called "Tone Paintings" was never carried out.[45] Remarkable about these titles at first sight is their varying length. While each of the

---

43. This little episode bears a certain resemblance in character to thematic inventions in piano works of Maurice Ravel, for example his *Jeux d'eau* or the first movement of his *Sonatine*.
Also seen in general Marmarosa's impressionistic ventures might have gained part of their inspiration from the piano music of Ravel.
44. *Tone Paintings I* and *II* for the first time were released on a British SPOTLITE LP in the mid-1970s.

four included ballads runs up to the usual two and a half or three minutes of duration, most of Marmarosa's six originals, being held in a modern medium or up-tempo vein, come only short of two minutes. An imaginable reason for this could have been the possible intention to offer these recordings to radio stations as a kind of intermission music. As to the performances themselves, it is the fact that Marmarosa leaves nearly all of the improvisational spots to Barney Kessel's guitar and thus confines himself to the interpretation of his themes, which makes them comparatively short in time. Along with this segregation of duties also goes a diverging stylistic approach on Kessel's and Marmarosa's side. Where the guitarist displays a decidedly modern and clearly bop-rooted language in his improvisations, Marmarosa's approach is more diverse. In his ballad playing, he features a harmonically enriched and melodically highly inventive but all in all conventional style of cocktail piano music with the use of a full keyboard and a bundle of customary embellishments. Reciting the themes of his originals, though, he comes closer to Kessel's style, as they are almost all composed in a modern style. Moreover Marmarosa's comping behind Kessel's solo lines in its rhythmic variety and incentive attack is a prime example of uncompromising modern jazz accompaniment. The only solo he takes on the modern tracks, however, typically avoids such stylistic directness: On his original *Compadoo* he follows Kessel's half-chorus in bebop with a somewhat different solo of his own, which demonstrates their diverging musical references on this session. While Kessel keeps beautifully in line with the patterns developed by the creators of bop, Marmarosa picks up one of these motifs played by Kessel as the closing figure of his solo and makes it the starting point of a series of variations. Its isolation transforms this three-note figure from a common bebop ending to a statement of its own, on which Marmarosa throws light from changing melodic and tonal corners by gradually interweaving it into longer phrases, leading at the climax of his solo to an up- and down of whole-tone scales, which seem to decompose completely the once clearly set figure. In addition to this, he enhances the climatic points of the solo in slowing down or accelerating his playing

---

45. At least this is what George Hoefer says in his article, "The recorded Flights of Dodo," published in DOWN BEAT magazine's issue of December 29, 1966. Instead the titles were released in two portions within the MacGregor Transcription Library series in spring and summer 1948.

over the steady beat of guitar and bass.

It may have been such musically explorative statements as well as the romantically inclined cocktail style, which made Barney Kessel reflect upon Marmarosa's playing as being handicapped by a lack of modernism some 25 years later in an interview with Leonard Feather: "Dodo's early experience did not logically equip him for bop. After the classical training he went into the world of dance bands, and he came to bop as a dance band pianist. I always felt that he didn't have a chance to evolve fully in the new jazz."[46]

Judging from this statement, Kessel obviously never questioned the stylistic direction, which most of the aspiring jazz musicians of the later 1940s believed to be the way to go. Marmarosa, however, and possibly also other pianists of the time including Jaki Byard, who once made the significant remark, that he could not "sit there and just play single lines all night and go away satisfied,"[47] seem to have been more reluctant to approve of the one-dimensional character of bebop stylistics. For the multi-layered possibilities of the piano in comparison to melodic instruments like horns or the guitar played in the single-note tradition of Charlie Christian it meant an unnecessary restriction. As he had already shown before, for Marmarosa the language of bebop consequently remained just one of several colours in the palette for painting a modern musical picture.

Thus on this recording session it is the direct contrasting of more popular traditional elements with the abstraction of modern bebop phrasing which forms an experimental component and leads to a mutual enhancement in the outline of the character and virtues of both styles. The strict assignment of roles helps to emphasize the effect, while the superb comping of both Marmarosa and Kessel and the light but impeccably even and sonorous beat of Gene Englund form the brackets which hold the experiment in a nevertheless overtly modern frame.

The convincing realization of the concept through perfect integration of the two diverging approaches, presented with marvellous execution on the side of all three musicians, moreover suggests, that the recorded titles

---

46. Liner notes to Prestige PCD-24021-2 "Jug & Dodo"
47. Jaki Byard in: Dan Morgenstern, *Ready, Willing, and Able: Jaki Byard* (DOWN BEAT magazine, October 1965, p.18)

had been developed and elaborated as part of a concert repertory, and that the trio at the time of recording had not merely been a studio but a working group. Little as they are known, these ten trio sides belong to the most appealing and musically rewarding piano trio recordings of the decade, and one can only regret, that more did not follow.

Besides his own dates, the recording boom in the year's end procured Marmarosa his participation in two more sessions with Slim Gaillard as well as in two studio groups of a more modern conception led by Lionel Hampton and Red Norvo, respectively. Marmarosa did not continue for long his activities in Los Angeles, however, leaving for his hometown Pittsburgh in the spring of 1948. A few weeks before, in early February 1948, he had once more been transcribed at an AFRS "Jubilee" show as the pianist of an All-Star line-up, which included clarinettist Stan Hasselgard and tenor saxophonist Wardell Gray. Although his playing on this occasion still shows bits of his unique inventiveness[48], seen on the whole it seems "strangely pensive and a little detached," as one commentator on the session expressed it. Certainly no one, including Marmarosa himself, guessed at the time that this would be the last recorded document of his first and most extensive period of public appearance on the national stage.

Illness dictated that he stay in his hometown of Pittsburgh for the rest of the year, where he continued to perform mainly in trios. He reappeared in April 1949 as a member of Johnny 'Scat' Davis' orchestra, with whom he had begun his professional career seven years earlier. Again due to illness, Marmarosa left Davis in early summer 1949 and once more returned to Pittsburgh. In the fall he accepted an offer from Artie Shaw to join his newly formed orchestra as a substitute for pianist Gene DiNovi. The line-up of this band was a who's who of modern big band musicians, but whereas Shaw asked arrangers like Johnny Mandel, Tadd Dameron or Eddie Sauter to write advanced charts for the band, he conceded to DOWN BEAT in September 1949 that he would "play whatever the public wants," including his old hit tunes from the *Begin The Beguine* period. Marmarosa joined the orchestra in New York in September 1949 and stayed on tour with Shaw

---

48. Listen, for example, to the pianist's highly original chord voicings for a short introduction to Frances Wayne's vocal rendition of *Who's Sorry Now*.

possibly until early November for an engagement at the Blue Note in Chicago, IL. During this engagement the pianist's uncompromising nature was at odds with Shaw's programming policy. After one request too many for the tune *Frenesi*, Marmarosa left the piano chair without saying a word and did not return.[49] Unfortunately this happened before most of the band's book was transcribed for THESAURUS in December 1949 and January 1950.

The fifties proved to be a discouraging decade for Dodo Marmarosa. In July 1950 he recorded four titles with a trio for the label SAVOY in Pittsburgh, which offer but an echo of his exciting playing of the forties. They remained his only visit to a recording studio of renown for the next ten years. In that time the pianist married and became the father of two daughters. With his new family in tow, he returned to California in 1952. The marriage failed, however, and Marmarosa returned again to Pittsburgh in the fall of that year. In 1953 he went on the road for a few months with Charlie Spivak's band. A brief and unkind stint in the army followed in 1954, after which he did not appear publicly for more than a year. Starting with a concert in March 1956 he began to play again in local orchestras and with a trio of his own in clubs and restaurants of his hometown Pittsburgh.

A private recording of Marmarosa's trio playing at Pittsburgh's Midway Lounge in March 1958 allows insight into the pianist's style of the period. This tape, recorded and guarded by Marmarosa's long-time friend Danny Conn until its release on CD in 1997, clearly documents that Marmarosa had kept an excellent form over the years. "Dodo was playing so beautiful", Conn remembered, but explained his motivation to tape the event: "hardly anyone, except his friends, were paying attention."

Ten years of absence from the national scene had been long enough for the name of Marmarosa to sink into obscurity. Nevertheless already a brief glance at the eleven released transcriptions from the Midway Lounge is sufficient to leave the impression with the listener that here one of the true masters of jazz piano playing is giving samples of his rare art. Marmarosa had lost none of the virtues of his earlier style. The elegance and facility of execution combined with a superior technical command that enabled him

---

49. At least this is the version of Marmarosa's break with Shaw as it is told by some of the relevant sources. In his 1995 interview with Robert E. Sunenblick the pianist declared, that he got fired because of his untenable behaviour while being drunk.

to transpose everything that came to his mind onto the keyboard at once, are still there, as well as the abundance and conclusiveness of ideas and (above all) his harmonic sophistication. Backed by a discrete but always alert rhythm of bass and drums, Marmarosa has no limitations to express his thoughts freely. He responds to this freedom with the spontaneous use of a variety of pianistic devices in the form of frequent phrase modulations or changes of texture from single note lines to interplay between both hands and block chord passages. On the interpretative side he seems to have retained a different and individual approach for each of the standard tunes he chose to play on the occasion. Listen, for example, to the pianist's beautifully varied melodic line and the colourful voicings of his chord progressions on the fragmentary transcription of *Body And Soul*, or the stunning stream of motivic inventions on the considerably fast and fluent *Cherokee*. That not each of the eleven interpretations transcribed on the date shows the same elaborate level of compelling thought, may be due to the fact, that the engagement had been played on a rather informal basis with possibly little preparatory arrangements, that it had been "just an impromptu thing", as Marmarosa put it in his own words.[50] Moreover the limited sound quality provided by a small tape recorder slipped under the piano seems to drown some of the instrument's registers. Thus the 1958 transcriptions form a most welcome documentation of Marmarosa's music of the period, but they do not convey a completely satisfying impression of all levels of his playing and leave the wish to hear more. Luckily this wish found its fulfilment with the results of Marmarosa's long overdue return to the recording studios some three years after the Pittsburgh transcriptions had been made.

When in 1962 his comeback LP with the matching title "Dodo's Back!" was finally released, the jazz public had not heard Marmarosa for more than ten years. For those who had still in mind his work from the era of early bebop, this was a somehow different Marmarosa, for the others, who heard him for the first time, there was nothing spectacular about this LP in comparison to the newest developments in jazz. Some critics therefore

---

50. Spoken introduction to the release on CD of the 1958 transcriptions, taped in June 1995 by producer Robert Sunenblick.

were not interested enough to listen carefully to these recordings, and the trio set got mixed reviews. Someone to plead for a more thorough study was the English jazz critic Max Harrison, who wrote in an excellent review of the LP for the British magazine JAZZ MONTHLY in 1962: "One hearing of this record would be enough to show conclusively, to all but the most careless listener, that throughout the long years of neglect Marmarosa has been working very hard on his music. Each further hearing reveals more, until the listener realises the disc has so much to offer that it is difficult to know where to begin discussing."

We confine ours to a short study of the newly recorded *Mellow Mood* as an example for the high standard of the titles on this record in general. In comparison to Marmarosa's earlier version from 1946 there are several features which immediately strike the listener's ear. The pianist had tightened his light and elegant approach to the keyboard to a harder and more energetic touch, his even, classically derived articulation had given way to a more rhythmically pronounced, jazz-oriented playing, and, above all, his musical personality seemed still more determined and coherent than it had already been in former times. This shows, for example, in the convincing development of an improvisational whole over three full choruses on *Mellow Mood*. The pianist draws on just a few ideas derived from the basic motif of the theme, which he binds through intelligent variety of texture, rhythm and melodical sequences into "one line of thought" over the whole performance, as Harrison described it in his review. While this 'line of thought' is basically a melodic one through the constant citing of the above-mentioned motif, it is, on the other hand, interspersed with idiomatic bebop runs. The ever-changing texture of the motif and its effective combination with bop lines make the choruses in their entirety seem a spontaneous and organic flow of ideas that never seems to lose its connection to the theme of the tune and its particular character. Such conceptual thinking had already been a feature of Marmarosa's earlier playing, but now, freed from the limitation of time on the old 78rpm records, he was able to develop it to full extension.

Technically, as Max Harrison stated, "the variety of keyboard devices at his command" had even grown since his earlier days. However, as Harrison also pointed out rightly, Marmarosa's methods on these recordings were "essentially orthodox and even conventional". There lies no depreci-ation of the pianist's work in this statement for Harrison continues: "This music presents us, in fact, with one of the most difficult things to bring off in art: the significantly personal use of exclusively traditional material and procedures." Marmarosa himself in his 1995 interview explained his approach to this particular session as follows: "It's not real modern or any-thing like that. I was trying to be a little on the commercial side you know. Sometimes you play too far out and people don't understand it." This is perhaps the point, why several commentators on the pianist's music pre-ferred his early work to his recording of the sixties. In the context of early bebop Marmarosa's approach and its diverse sources emanated a kind of exotic appeal, from which his music derived at least part of its particular charm. In the early sixties, musical progressiveness in the jazz field was de-fined by totally different aspects, and Marmarosa's playing, at least on his recordings, showed no longer the experimental boldness it used to have some fifteen years before.

As his trio recordings from 1961 nevertheless reveal, Marmarosa had advanced his musical as well as his technical skills during his absence from the national scene. Seen from a point of view beyond consideration of the newest stylistic developments in jazz, he was probably still one of the most capable pianists of his time. His interest, however, to give phonographic tastes of his new art seems to have been limited. Besides some informally recorded titles from already 1960, which show him as an ingenious ac-companist for the singer Johnny Janis, he did only two more sessions for the Chicago-based ARGO label. One of them he shared in May 1962 with tenor saxophonist Gene Ammons, and it produced in a quartet and again in trio configuration equally convincing results, as had the session from the year before. At the time of the recordings, however, Ammons still was under contract with the PRESTIGE label. The session therefore had to be handed over to this company and unfortunately was not released before 1972. The last date was realized in November 1962 in a quartet with trum-peter Bill Hardman and remained unissued until six of the seven originally produced titles appeared for the first time on an Italian LP release as late as 1988! Again Marmarosa excels throughout. Once more the combina-tive task of accompaniment and soloing shows off the versatility of the pianist's talents. One only has to listen to the melodically beautifully conceived introductory chorus to his blues composition *Analysis* and the way he continues the thus-set groove through his comping, solo-choruses and the delicate accompaniment for Richard Evans' bass solo, to appreciate besides the ever present melodious inventiveness and technical facility also his unique sense of time. Other pianistic highlights of the session emerge out of the intriguing harmonies of Marmarosa's block chord passages on *Gone with the Wind* or his improvisatory ideas on the crisp and hard-driving *Dodo's Tune*, which he binds into some of the most compelling uptempo playing of his later period.

Although, as these albums clearly document, Marmarosa in the early sixties played better than ever, his comeback remained short-lived. After two years of recording and performing in Chicago, he continued for a while to play in both cities, Chicago and Pittsburgh, mainly as a soloist in clubs and restaurants until ca. 1975, when he ceased to appear publicly. As longtime friends and colleagues remembered, he went on playing the piano in the basement of his parents' home in Glenshaw near Pittsburgh and finally on instruments at the Army Veteran's Medical Center in Lincoln Lemington, PA, to which he had moved for the last years of his life.

In December 1988 a first group of musicians was raised into the Pittsburgh Jazz Society's newly inaugurated Hall of Fame, among them Earl Hines, Billy Eckstine, Ahmad Jamal and Dodo Marmarosa. He did not attend the ceremony, however. In July 1991 DOWN BEAT's Detroit correspondent reported of the pianist's visit to a local concert. After the concert Marmarosa tried the house piano and exchanged voicings on Cole Porter's *Where Are You* with Eliane Elias. But such occasions had become rare, and it was in the 1980s and 1990s, as it had been with too few exceptions already in the two decades before: most of Marmarosa's music since had been heard by anyone but himself. One exception from this rule emerged, at least verbally, when Robert E. Sunenblick interviewed the pianist in June 1995 for the already mentioned release of a CD with unissued and mainly private recordings of Marmarosa from 1956 to 1962. It seems that at that time he had a tremor in his right hand, which finally prevented him from playing professionally any longer, but nevertheless allowed little jam sessions or impromptu concerts for the personnel at the VA Medical Center, whenever friends from

Pittsburgh like trumpeter Danny Conn or trombonist Joe Dallas visited him.

Marmarosa died of a heart attack on September 17, 2002. As his sister Doris Shepherd was cited in a local newspaper obituary [51], in the hours before his death he had still played a small organ at the Center's building were he lived. It seems that through his long time of musical reclusiveness and despite the growing health problems that had overshadowed his later years, playing the keyboard had remained until his last day one of the central things in life to Michael "Dodo" Marmarosa. After all he still was, just like his friend and colleague of earlier times Jackie Mills once had to say, "the most dedicated of players."

Fabian Grob

---

51. Nate Guidry, "Obituary: Michael "Dodo" Marmarosa / Legendary jazz pianist" in: Pittsburgh Post-Gazette, Friday, September 20, 2002.

Performing with Charlie Barnet at New York City's Strand Theatre, January 1944, back row from l. to r.: Dodo Marmarosa, unknown, Turk Van Lake, Harold Hahn, unknown, Jimmy Pupa, Al Killian, unknown (Art House?), Peanuts Holland; front row from l. to r.: Danny Bank, Andy Pino, Ray De Greer, Buddy DeFranco, Kurt Bloom (hidden), Charlie Barnet, Claude Murphy, Tommy Pederson, Porky Cohen, prob. Ed Fromm.

The Tommy Dorsey Orchestra performing „Song Of India" in a scene from the M-G-M musical comedy "Thrill Of A Romance", Hollywood, ca. July/August 1944, including Sid Block (b), Dodo Marmarosa (p), Bob Bain (g), Buddy Rich (d), leader Dorsey, Doris Briggs (harp).

The full Tommy Dorsey Orchestra in a publicity still from the M-G-M musical comedy
"Thrill Of A Romance", Hollywood, ca. July/August 1944; standing in front
are vocalists Bob Allen, The Sentimentalists, and Bonnie Lou Williams.

Posing for the photographer in the garden of Artie Shaw's Hollywood
home, during the new band's rehearsal period in early November 1944.
From l. to r.: Dodo Marmarosa, Lou Fromm, Barney Kessel, Artie Shaw.

Performing with Artie Shaw's Gramercy Five at New York City's Strand Theatre, ca. February 1945, from l. to r.: Dodo Marmarosa, Roy Eldridge, Artie Shaw, Barney Kessel, Morris Rayman.

Recording for the label Sunset with Lem Davis, Los Angeles, October 20, 1945.

Recording for Billy Berg with Slim Gaillard, Los Angeles, early December 1945, from l. to r.:
Bam Brown, Dodo Marmarosa, Slim Gaillard, Billy Berg, Zutty Singleton.
By permission of Getty Images, Inc.

Recording for the
first time under
Marmarosa's own
name: Atomic
recording session,
Radio Recorders,
Hollywood, January
11, 1946, from l.
to r.: Ray Brown,
Jackie Mills, Dodo
Marmarosa.

Rehearsing with Boyd Raeburn's vocalist Ginny Powell at Raeburn's recording session for Standard Transcriptions, Hollywood, February 1946.

At Slim Gaillard's recording session for the label Four Star, Los Angeles, late March 1946.

Discussing the music of "Cartaphilius (The Wandering Jew)" with Boyd Raeburn's composer/arranger George Handy, at the piano of the Club Morocco, Hollywood, ca. July 1946.

Four famous members of the sensational 1946 Boyd Raeburn Orchestra glancing at the piano score of George Handy's controversial composition "Dalvatore Sally", Hollywood, Club Morocco, ca. July 1946, from l. to r.: leader Raeburn, Dodo Marmarosa, drummer Jackie Mills, trumpeter Ray Linn.

Recording for the label
Dial probably with Howard
McGhee, at Hollywood's
Universal Recorders, October
18, 1946.

Recording in Chicago, 1961.

Final preparations for the recording of „Flight Of The Vout Bug", at Radio Recorders, Hollywood, November 4, 1946, from l. to r.: Atomic label owner and producer Lyle Griffin, Dodo Marmarosa, composer/arranger Tom Talbert. By kind permission of Betty Talbert and Bruce Talbot.

Talking over the book for Peggy Lee's appearance at the first of the famous Gene Norman "Just Jazz" concerts, Pasadena Civic Auditorium, Pasadena CA, April 29, 1947, from l. to r.: singer Lee, producer Norman, Dodo Marmarosa.

Posing with other performers around the grand piano at the second "Just Jazz" concert, Pasadena Civic Auditorium, Pasadena CA, June 23, 1947, from l. to r.: Dodo Marmarosa, Barney Kessel, Willie Smith, André Previn, Nat King Cole, co-producer Eddie Laguna, Johnny Miller, producer Gene Norman, Charlie Shavers, Louie Bellson, Red Norvo, Stan Getz, Oscar Moore, Red Callender. By permission of GNP Crescendo.

In the studio at the South Dakotan radio station KSOO with singer Pat Lockwood and Artie Shaw during the Shaw band's 1949 theatre tour, early October 1949.

DISCOGRAPHY

CHRONOLOGY OF THE YEARS BEFORE DISCOGRAPHICAL LISTING

December 12, 1925 :   Born <u>Michael Marmarosa</u> in Pittsburgh, Pa.

Marmarosa's parents had emigrated from Italy to the
U.S.A.
The family lived on Paulson Avenue in the East
Liberty district of Pittsburgh, Pa.
The nickname "Do-Do" was how Marmarosa
used to call himself as a child.
Marmarosa began to take classical piano lessons
with neighbourhood teachers at the age of nine.
Two sisters, Audrey (elder) and Doris (younger), the
latter also playing piano.

ca. 1936 - 1940 :   Five years of piano lessons with Evelina Palmieri.

Marmarosa went to Peabody High School in
Pittsburgh, Pa. (which is not the school attended by
Billy Strayhorn, Jimmy Pupa, and Erroll Garner, as is
often stated).

Befriended with Billy Strayhorn (10 years older),

Jimmy Pupa (6 years older), and Erroll Garner (4 years older).

Marmarosa used to hold piano sessions together with Erroll Garner and a local player named Tootsie Davis.

Pianist Johnny Guarnieri remembers having met Marmarosa during jam sessions at the social hall of the Pittsburgh Musicians Union, Local 60, early in 1939.

1940 :   Marmarosa worked in local dance bands in Pittsburgh, Pa., including Brad Hunt's society orchestra.

Participation in a jam session at Billy Kretchmer's on Ransted Street in Philadelphia, Pa.; Buddy DeFranco plays on the same session.

1941 :   Marmarosa worked in vocalist/guitarist Bill Yates' territory band.

late 1941/1942 :   The Pittsburgh column in *Down Beat* magazine of February 1, 1942 praises Marmarosa as star of a local jam session.

In summer 1942 (possibly July or August) Dodo Marmarosa began to work with the orchestra of trumpeter/vocalist/actor **Johnny "Scat" Davis** through a recommendation by Jimmy Pupa. In Davis' band the pianist also met Buddy DeFranco, who according to *Down Beat* magazine of June 15, 1942 had joined Davis around that time. Pupa, DeFranco, and Marmarosa should remain together for more than a year, changing later from Davis to the bands of Gene Krupa and Charlie Barnet.

For July until early September 1942 the following engagement of the "Scat" Davis Orchestra was listed in *Down Beat* magazine:

early July - early September 1942   : Sea Girt, N.J., Sea Girt Inn

During its stay at the Sea Girt Inn the orchestra was regularly broadcast on Saturdays and Sundays over the Mutual Broadcasting System. To our knowledge none of these broadcasts has been preserved on transcriptions or "air-checks".

JOHNNY "SCAT" DAVIS AND HIS ORCHESTRA   PARAMOUNT SOUNDTRACK RECORDINGS

unknown band personnel, including:

Jimmy Pupa + two unknown (tp), Herbie Harper + unknown (tb), Buddy DeFranco (as) + four unknown (reeds), Dodo Marmarosa (p), unknown (b), Gordon Heiderich (dm), Gloria Van, Johnny „Scat" Davis (voc)

ca. September / October 1942, probably Paramount Studios, New York

REDWING (JSDv) ( )
NOBODY (JSDv) ( )
WONDER WHEN MY BABY'S COMING HOME (GVv) ( )
PRAISE THE LORD AND PASS THE AMMUNITION (JSDv) ( )

Note:

The above recordings were made for a musical short entitled "Paramount Headliner: Johnny "Scat" Davis and his Orchestra". This short band·feature was directed by Leslie Roush and produced for Paramount Pictures in 1942.

Subsequent *Down Beat* listings of "Scat" Davis engagements for 1942 were:

mid September - ca. mid October 1942	: Baltimore, Md., Summit Ballroom
mid October - early November 1942	: "On Tour" [one-nighters]
November 6 - 12, 1942	: Chicago, Ill., Oriental Theatre
November 20 - 26, 1942	: Milwaukee, Wisc., Riverside Theatre
December 4 - 6, 1942	: Davenport, Iowa, Orpheum Theatre
December 7 - 15, 1942	: "One-Nighters"

JOHNNY "SCAT" DAVIS AND HIS ORCHESTRA

VICTORY PARADE OF SPOTLIGHT BANDS NO. 83/-11 RADIO BROADCAST

unknown band personnel, including:

Dodo Marmarosa (p), Gordon Heiderich (dm), Gloria Van, Johnny „Scat" Davis (voc)

December 25, 1942, Army Air Base, Salina, Kansas

9:20 SPECIAL ( )
DAYBREAK (GVv) ( )
EVERY NIGHT ABOUT THIS TIME ( )
HIP HIP HOORAY (JSDv) ( )
DAY DREAMING ( )

Note:

From November 1941 until May 1942 the Coca Cola Company had sponsored a radio program series under the original headline of "Coca Cola Spotlight Bands". The series then reappeared in a revised format in September 1942 with the new title "Victory Parade of Spotlight Bands". It featured big bands performing mainly at military installations all over the U.S.A. in programs of 25 minutes duration, which were broadcast on six days a week over NBC's Blue Network.

Additionally the performing bands were generously paid by the Coca Cola Company to continue their playing after broadcast time for the military audiences at the sites from where the shows were transmitted.

On December 25, 1942 the program series provided the frame for a special radio event presented by the Coca Cola Company in coordination with the U.S. War Department. For twelve hours from 43 different military institutions 43 bands were broadcast in a non-stop radio marathon headlined as "Uncle Sam's Christmas Tree of Spotlight Bands". Within the series the program was assigned its regular number '83', the succession of bands being indicated with an additional tag to this number. "Scat" Davis' orchestra thus was the eleventh band to perform on that day's program. Duration of each band's broadcast performance was 15 minutes.

At the period Gene Krupa had begun to lure away several members of the "Scat" Davis Orchestra starting with saxophonists Buddy DeFranco and Jimmy Rudge already in November 1942. Dodo Marmarosa probably joined the drummer's band in early January 1943.

NOTE: On January 8, 1943 the Johnny "Scat" Davis Orchestra once more appeared on a program (No. 95) within the Coca Cola Company's "Victory Parade of Spotlight Bands" series. An excerpt probably stemming from this broadcast presents an instrumental version of the title *Hip Hip Hooray*, on which Marmarosa seems to have been no longer present.[1]

The **Gene Krupa** Orchestra had closed a six week engagement at the Hollywood Palladium on December 29 and went on a month's tour of one-nighters, including stays in San Diego, at the Golden Gate Theatre in San Francisco (January 18/19, 1943), and at Los Angeles' Orpheum theatre, before heading east and opening in late January 1943 at the Hotel Sherman in Chicago, Illinois. During this tour two appearances of the orchestra in the "Victory Parade of Spotlight Bands" series were broadcast on radio. At latest on these broadcasts Marmarosa seems to have been definitely present.[2]

---

1   This title has been released on a 6 CD box set "Victory Parade of Spotlight Bands" by The Audio File.

2   Some sources antedate Marmarosa's debut with Krupa to late 1942. However, bits and pieces of audible piano playing on earlier broadcast transcriptions from December 1942 seem more likely to stem still from the hands of Marmarosa's predecessor Joe Springer. These transcriptions originate from the "Coca Cola Victory Parade of Spotlight Bands" series (December 18 and 25) and from Krupa's regular radio broadcasts from the Hollywood Palladium (December 20). Releases are on Fanfare LP 44-144 and Jasmine 2515 (LP).

GENE KRUPA   VICTORY PARADE OF SPOTLIGHT BANDS NO. 96
AND HIS ORCHESTRA   RADIO BROADCAST

band personnel probably:

Roy Eldridge (tp,voc), Mickey Mangano, Joe Triscari, William Stanley Kent (tp), Herbie Harper, Babe Wagner, Tommy Pederson (tb), Buddy DeFranco (cl,as), Jimmy Rudge (as), Charlie Ventura, Jerry Field (ts), Rex Roy Sittig (bs), Dodo Marmarosa (p), Remo „Ray" Biondi (g,arr), Ed Mihelich (b),Gene Krupa (dm), Penny Piper, Ray Eberle (voc), Toots Camarata, Elton Hill, Bert Ross, Jimmy Mundy, Sam Musiker, Fred Norman, Chappie Willet (arr)

<u>January 9, 1943, unknown location, probably California</u>

MOONLIGHT MOOD (REv) (/)
BUGLE CALL RAG (/)
ROCKIN' CHAIR (/)
JERSEY BOUNCE ( )
I HAD THE CRAZIEST DREAM (REv) (/)
WHO (/)
SOMEONE ELSE'S SWEETHEART (PPv) ( )

Note:
Initially no official recordings of the "Victory Parade of Spotlight Bands" program series were made. Preserved programs or excerpts from this period as the above titles mostly stem from privately made transcriptions of the original radio transmissions.
LP reissue:
MOONLIGHT MOOD, BUGLE CALL RAG, I HAD THE CRAZIEST DREAM, and WHO on Fanfare LP 44-144.
CD reissue:
BUGLE CALL RAG and ROCKIN' CHAIR on The Audio File DVSB450.

<u>NOTE</u>:   Charles Garrod in his Gene Krupa Discography (revised edition, Zephyrhills 1996) lists an appearance of the Krupa orchestra performing WIRE BRUSH STOMP on the Fred Allen Show of January 10, 1943.
There is no such appearance on this particular show, which featured Jack Benny as guest star. Krupa, however, guested with WIRE BRUSH STOMP on the Edgar Bergen show of the very same date, accompanied not by his own but by the program's resident orchestra of Ray Noble.

GENE KRUPA AND HIS ORCHESTRA   VICTORY PARADE OF SPOTLIGHT BANDS NO. 100 RADIO BROADCAST

band personnel same as before

<u>January 14, 1943, unknown location, probably California</u>

BLUE SKIES (Roy Eldridge -voc) (/)
I HEARD YOU CRIED LAST NIGHT (REv) (/)
CHALLENGING THE CHALLENGER (/)
I WANT A BIG FAT MAMA (Roy Eldridge -voc) (/)
PRAISE THE LORD AND PASS THE AMMUNITION (RE&Ens v) (/)

Note:

The listed titles of the above program have been preserved as a privately made "off the air" transcription only. There were no official recordings of the "Spotlight Bands" broadcast shows made at the period.

LP reissue:

All titles on Fanfare LP 44-144.

NOTE: Several discographies list the Gene Krupa Orchestra again for a January 21, 1943 appearance within the Coca Cola Company's "Victory Parade of Spotlight Bands" series (program No. 106) without giving any further details. Possibly this appearance was scheduled, but as it seems, the Krupa Orchestra for unknown reasons was not able to fulfil its obligation. A preserved transcription disc of unknown origin features Spotlight Bands program No. 106 (clearly identified by the announcer as "Victory Night" No. 106) as a performance of George Olsen and his Orchestra from the Merritt Island Navy Yard in California.

For January/February 1943 the following engagement of the Gene Krupa Orchestra was listed in the trade papers (Anita O'Day returned as vocalist replacing Penny Piper for the first week of the engagement only):

January 29 - February 25, 1943 : Chicago, Ill., Hotel Sherman (Panther Room)

During the above engagement the band was broadcast four times a week over the NBC 'Blue' network.

The *Down Beat* issue of March 1, 1943 mentioned the below appearance of the Gene Krupa Orchestra at a students war chest drive in Madison, Wisc., shortly after finishing their cross-country tour from the West Coast to Illinois:

ca. early February 1943 : Madison, Wisc., University of Wisconsin, Field House

---

GENE KRUPA AND HIS ORCHESTRA   NBC RADIO BROADCAST
(BLUE NETWORK)

---

band personnel probably same as before; Bob Davis (voc) replaces Ray Eberle

February 7, 1943, Chicago, Ill., Hotel Sherman (Panther Room)

I HAD THE CRAZIEST DREAM (BDv) (/)	Jazz Hour JH-1044 (CD)
WIRE BRUSH STOMP (/)	–
SLENDER, TENDER AND TALL (Roy Eldridge -voc) (/)	–
BLUE RHYTHM FANTASY (ending only) (/)	–
THEME (THAT DRUMMER'S BAND) (/)	–

Note:

Other titles of the above broadcast unknown.

The CD release of the above titles was made from private "off the air" transcriptions.

GENE KRUPA AND HIS ORCHESTRA   *NBC RADIO BROADCAST*
(BLUE NETWORK)

band personnel same as before

<u>February 8, 1943, Chicago, Ill., Hotel Sherman (Panther Room)</u>

DRUM BOOGIE (Ens -voc) (s)	Jazz Hour JH-1044 (CD)
BUSTER'S LAST STAND (s)	–

Note:

Other titles of the above broadcast unknown.

BUSTER'S LAST STAND is a composition and arrangement by Gil Evans.

The CD release of the above titles was made from private "off the air" transcriptions.

GENE KRUPA AND HIS ORCHESTRA   *NBC RADIO BROADCAST*
(BLUE NETWORK)

band personnel same as before

<u>February 9, 1943, Chicago, Ill., Hotel Sherman (Panther Room)</u>

KNOCK ME A KISS (Roy Eldridge -voc) (/)	Jazz Hour JH-1044 (CD)
(YA' CAN'T GET) STUFF IN YOUR CUFF (Roy Eldridge -voc) (/)	–

Note:

Other titles of the above broadcast unknown.

The CD release of the above titles was made from private "off the air" transcriptions.

GENE KRUPA AND HIS ORCHESTRA   NBC RADIO BROADCAST
(BLUE NETWORK)

band personnel same as before

<u>February 11, 1943, Chicago, Ill., Hotel Sherman (Panther Room)</u>

MOONLIGHT MOOD (BDv) ( )

Note:
Other titles of the above broadcast unknown.

For the time from the end of February until early April 1943 the following engagements of the Gene Krupa Orchestra were listed in the trade papers:

<u>late February - March 4, 1943</u>	: Chicago Ill., Oriental Theatre
<u>March 9 - 11, 1943</u>	: Columbus, Ohio, Palace Theatre
<u>March 12 - 18, 1943</u>	: Cleveland, Ohio, Palace Theatre
<u>March 19 - 22, 1943</u>	: Akron, Ohio, Palace Theatre
<u>March 23 - 25, 1943</u>	: Youngstown, Ohio, Palace Theatre
<u>March 26 - April 1, 1943</u>	: Pittsburgh, Pa., Stanley Theatre
<u>April 2 - 8, 1943</u>	: Philadelphia, Pa., Earl Theatre

GENE KRUPA   VICTORY PARADE OF SPOTLIGHT BANDS NO. 170
AND HIS ORCHESTRA   RADIO BROADCAST

band personnel probably:

Roy Eldridge (tp,voc), Mickey Mangano, Joe Triscari, Jimmy Pupa (tp), Ferdy Von Verson, Babe Wagner, Tommy Pederson (tb), Buddy DeFranco (cl,as), Johnny Bothwell (as), Charlie Ventura, Andy Pino (ts), Lynn Allison (bs), Dodo Marmarosa (p), Remo „Ray" Biondi (g,arr), Ed Mihelich (b), Gene Krupa (dm), Gloria Van, Gene Howard (voc)

<u>April 6, 1943, unknown location around Philadelphia, Pa.</u>

AS TIME GOES BY ( )   (AFRS) Spotlight Bands No. 14 [?]

Note :

In March 1943 the radio section of the U.S. War Department's "Special Services Division" (later to be called "Armed Forces Radio Service" or "AFRS") began to transcribe the "Victory Parade of Spotlight Bands" broadcast series for rebroadcast purposes. The original transmissions of 25 minutes duration were shortened to programs of 15 minutes, featuring normally five to six titles of music of the recorded band. As such they were released on 16 inch 33rpm transcription records and distributed for transmission via AFRS stations all over the U.S.A. and the conflict areas.

Other titles of the above program unknown.
A portion (15 min.) of the original broadcast program (25 min.) used on (AFRS) Spotlight Bands No. 14.

For mid April 1943 the following engagement of the Gene Krupa Orchestra was listed in the trade papers:

<u>April 9 - ? , 1943</u>   : Newark, N.J., Frank Dailey's Terrace Room

GENE KRUPA   VICTORY PARADE OF SPOTLIGHT BANDS NO. 179
AND HIS ORCHESTRA   RADIO BROADCAST

band personnel probably similar as before

<u>April 16, 1943, unknown location around Newark, N.J.</u>

DRUM BOOGIE ( )   (AFRS) Spotlight Bands No. 23 [?]

Note :

Other titles of the above program unknown.

A portion (15 min.) of the original broadcast program (25 min.) used on (AFRS) Spotlight Bands No. 23.

GENE KRUPA AND HIS ORCHESTRA   CBS RADIO BROADCAST

band personnel probably similar as before

<u>April 18, 1943, unknown location around Newark, N.J.</u>

ST. LOUIS BLUES ( )
BUGLE CALL RAG ( )

Note:

Other titles of the above broadcast unknown.

In a May 1943 *Metronome* magazine review of the Terrace Room engagement Marmarosa gets the following mention by jazz critic Leonard Feather:

"Dodo Marmarosa, a new star from Pittsburgh, is a highly promising pianist in the single-note style. It's good to know he'll be around at least a few months more (he's 17)."

For the first half of May 1943 the following engagement of the Gene Krupa Orchestra was listed in the trade papers:

May 6 - 12, 1943   : Boston, Mass., RKO Theatre

On May 10, 1943, during the above engagement, Gene Krupa flew to San Francisco to appear in court in the matter of two related drug delinquencies, which had already occurred on January 18 of the year, when the band was playing in San Francisco. Contrary to his expectations of simply a fine, in the first trial Krupa was sentenced to 90 days detention. The second trial on the other, more serious charge led to a sentence of one to six years. A pending appeal brought about his release on August 9, 1943, but the charges on him were not dropped completely before a final trial of more than a year later.
To carry out the orchestra's obligations, Roy Eldridge became nominal leader of the band. Drummer Harry Yaeger replaced Gene Krupa for a few evenings of the following engagements. When Yaeger was not available, Eldridge played drums:

May 18 - late May, 1943   : Atlantic City, N.J., Steel Pier

early June - June 12, 1943   : Philadelphia, Pa., Metropolitan Ballroom

It was on the early morning of June 10, 1943, after finishing their work with the Gene Krupa Orchestra at Philadelphia's Metropolitan Ballroom, that Buddy DeFranco and Dodo Marmarosa became the victims of an altercation. While they were waiting for their subway train to go home, a group of five sailors came across the rail tracks and started provoking them. In a following fight both were knocked down and Marmarosa suffered from a serious head injury, which kept him in a coma for several days. According to DeFranco Marmarosa mentally never wholly recovered from this incident.

After the above engagements the Gene Krupa Orchestra disbanded.

Jimmy Pupa, Buddy DeFranco, and Dodo Marmarosa together with Joe Triscari (tp) and Nick De Luca (ts) from the Gene Krupa Orchestra soon joined the orchestra of **Ted Fio Rito** for at least one month during July and August 1943. According to the memories of Buddy DeFranco in Fabrice Zammarchi's DeFranco biography Marmarosa was hired as a second pianist besides Fio Rito to play on the band's ordinary numbers, while Fio Rito confined his playing to a few special features of his pianistics. This edition of the Fio Rito band seems not to have been documented on recordings or transcriptions. At the beginning of Fio Rito's Roseland Ballroom engagement in New York City (September 15 - November 29, 1943) Marmarosa was no longer present.

In September 1943, about three weeks after his friends and colleagues Jimmy Pupa and Buddy DeFranco, Dodo Marmarosa joined the orchestra of **Charlie Barnet** for an engagement at the Cocoanut Grove atop New York City's Park Central Hotel. He took the place of pianist/arranger Ralph Burns who concentrated on writing arrangements for the band. The band was due to stay from September 23 until October 20, 1943 and was broadcast four times a week over the Mutual net. Marmarosa probably joined already on September 21 for two days of rehearsals.

Leonard Feather reviewed the Barnet orchestra at its Park Central engagement for the November 1943 issue of *Metronome* and included the following note on Marmarosa:
"Another ex-Krupa man who makes an exciting addition to the Barnet bunch is pianist Marmaroso [sic], who has a splendid light swing style."

CHARLIE BARNET AND HIS ORCHESTRA

**MBS OR CBS
RADIO BROADCAST**

Al Killian, Jimmy Pupa, Lyman Vunk (tp), Peanuts Holland (tp,voc), Bob Swift, Eddie Bert, Ed Fromm, Claude Murphy (or Trummy Young who was replaced by Murphy during the above engagement) (tb), Charlie Barnet (ss,as,ts), Ray De Greer (as), Buddy DeFranco (cl,as), Kurt Bloom, Mike Goldberg (ts), Danny Bank (bs), Dodo Marmarosa (p), Turk Van Lake (g), Russ Wagner (b), Harold Hahn (dm), George Siravo (arr)

probably October 1943, New York City, Cocoanut Grove

MY IDEAL (/)   AFRS Yank Swing Session No. 92

Note :

The AFRS "Yank Swing Session" program series featured half hour compilations of swing music taken from various sources like commercial studio recordings, transcriptions of 'live'-performances or excerpts of other AFRS programs ("One Night Stand", "Spotlight Bands", etc.) with the original source not always being indicated.

Bob Crosby, leading through the program on "Yank Swing Session" No. 92, makes no statements to the origin of the different 'live' performances, which had been assembled by AFRS for the above edition of the show.
Dan Mather in his Charlie Barnet biography assumes the origin of the above title to be one of Charlie Barnet's regular radio broadcasts from the Cocoanut Grove.

CHARLIE BARNET AND HIS ORCHESTRA   MBS OR CBS
RADIO BROADCAST

band personnel same as before, add Virginia Maxey (voc)

probably October 1943, New York City, Cocoanut Grove

unknown titles   AFRS News From Home No. ?

Note :

The "News From Home" program series had been designed by AFRS to bring memories of their home country to American soldiers fighting overseas via reports of cultural events from all over the United States. Some of the programs also contained transcriptions of musical performances. Only very few program issues of this series seem to have survived.

Dan Mather in his Charlie Barnet biography mentions the above issue of a set of unknown titles from one of Charlie Barnet's regular radio broadcasts from the Cocoanut Grove.

CHARLIE BARNET AND HIS ORCHESTRA
DECCA RECORDING SESSION

Al Killian, Jimmy Pupa, Lyman Vunk (tp), Peanuts Holland (tp,voc), Bob Swift, Eddie Bert, Claude Murphy, Ed Fromm (tb), Charlie Barnet (ss,as,ts), Ray De Greer (as), Buddy DeFranco (cl,as), Kurt Bloom, Mike Goldberg (ts), Danny Bank (bs), Dodo Marmarosa (p), Turk Van Lake (g), Russ Wagner (b), Harold Hahn (dm), Virginia Maxey (voc), Ralph Burns, Howard McGhee, Billy Moore (arr)

<u>October 21, 1943, New York City</u>

71460-A	STROLLIN' (s)	Decca 18585
71461-A	THE MOOSE (s)	Brunswick 03601
71461-	THE MOOSE (s)	MCA2-4069
71462-A	POW-WOW (/)	Coral 60029
71463-A	SITTIN' HOME WAITIN' FOR YOU (VMv) (s)	Decca 18585

Note :

THE MOOSE was originally titled DICK TRACY LIQUIDATES 88 KEYS in an arrangement written by Ralph Burns to feature himself as a pianist. To shorten the title of the tune for release on record, it was renamed "THE MOOSE", which was a nickname Charlie Barnet used to call Dodo Marmarosa.

Matrix 71461-A of THE MOOSE was first issued in England on Brunswick 03601. First issue in the United States seems to have been on a 45rpm record Decca ED 725

The version of THE MOOSE on MCA2-4069 (LP) is definitely an alternate take to matrix 71461-A.

LP reissues:

The alternate take of THE MOOSE released on MCA2-4069 has also been reissued on Affinity AFS 1012.

STROLLIN' and POW-WOW also on Affinity AFS 1012.

All titles, except alternate take of THE MOOSE, also on Ajax-140.

CD reissues:

Alternate take of THE MOOSE also on Topaz TPZ 1028.

Matrix 71461-A of THE MOOSE and POW-WOW also on MCA GRP 16122.

STROLLIN', matrix 71461-A of THE MOOSE, and POW-WOW also on Jazz Archives CD 85.

Matrix 71461-A of THE MOOSE also on Living Era CD-AJA-5288.

From the end of October until December 1943 the Charlie Barnet Orchestra was on a ten-week theatre tour from which the following engagements are known:

October 22 - 28, 1943 : Baltimore, Maryland, Royal Theatre

November 5 - 8, 1943 : Akron, Ohio, Palace Theatre

November 9 - 11, 1943 : Youngstown, Ohio, Palace Theatre

November 12 - 18, 1943 : Chicago, Ill., Oriental Theatre

November 19 - 24 (?), 1943 : Omaha, Nebraska, Orpheum Theatre

November 25 - 28, 1943 : Des Moines, Iowa, Paramount Theatre

November 30 - December 2, 1943 : Rock Island, Ill., Joliet Theatre

December 3 - 5, 1943 : Fort Wayne, Ind., Palace Theatre

December 10 -16, 1943 : Milwaukee, Wisc., Riverside Theatre

December 17 -23, 1943 : Pittsburgh, Penns., Stanley Theatre

NOTE: For this period several discographers (Garrod, Raben, Lord) list soundtrack recordings of the Barnet Orchestra for a United World film short titled "Redskin Rhumba." This film was directed by Will Cowan and released by Universal in their "Name Band Musical" series in 1948. Stylistical comparisons, however, make it doubtful that the soundtrack was actually recorded in the 1943/1944 period. The pianist most certainly is not Marmarosa, but sounds very much like Claude Williamson. This as well as the overall sound of the band after all hint at a recording date in 1948. Four out of six titles recorded for the soundtrack are released on Joyce LP-3001.

Already in the October 1943 issue of *Metronome* the following engagement of the Barnet band had been advertised:

Dec. 31, 1943 - February 3, 1944   : New York City, Strand Theatre

(Dizzy Gillespie temporarily replaced ill trumpeter Lyman Vunk during this engagement)

A photograph of the Strand Theatre bandstand shows the orchestra with five trumpets including black trumpeters Al Killian and Peanuts Holland, Buddy DeFranco playing alto sax and Dodo Marmarosa at the piano.

CHARLIE BARNET AND HIS ORCHESTRA   FITCH BANDWAGON SHOW NBC RADIO BROADCAST

---

band personnel as before, but add Art House (tp); Tommy Pederson (tb) replaces Eddie Bert, Andy Pino (ts) replaces Mike Goldberg, and Harriet Clarke (voc) replaces Virginia Maxey. NBC file card indicates a guest conductor replacing Barnet for this broadcast, possibly George Auld.

January 23, 1944, New York City, Strand Theatre

unknown titles   AFRS Bandwagon No. ?

Note :

The "Fitch Bandwagon" radio program series had been sponsored by the manufacturers of Fitch Shampoo since 1933 with several changes of format over the years. It could be heard over the NBC radio net on Sunday evenings at 7:30 p.m. with a duration of 30 minutes. By 1944 usually a name band was featured along with other prominent musical guests. AFRS transcribed the shows, renamed them "Bandwagon", and edited them with shortened duration of 15 minutes for rebroadcast over their radio net.

Dan Mather in his Charlie Barnet biography mentions the above radio appearance of the Barnet orchestra.

From February to March 1944 the following dates of the Barnet band are known:

February 4 - February 11, 1944	: one-nighters
February 11 - 17, 1944	: New York City, Apollo Theatre
February 18 - March 9, 1944	: Newark, N.J., Frank Dailey's Terrace Room
intermission: February 22, 1944	: N. Y. C., New York City Center Ballroom

CHARLIE BARNET AND HIS ORCHESTRA   DECCA
RECORDING SESSION

Roy Eldridge, Art House, Lyman Vunk, Jimmy Pupa, Charlie Zimmerman (tp), Porky Cohen, Tommy Pederson, Ben Pickering, Ed Fromm (tb), Charlie Barnet (ss,as,ts), Ray De Greer (as), Buddy DeFranco (cl,as), Kurt Bloom, Andy Pino (ts), Danny Bank (bs), Dodo Marmarosa (p), Turk Van Lake (g), Andy Ricardi (b), Harold Hahn (dm), Gwen Tynes (voc), Ralph Burns, Ralph Flanagan, Andy Gibson, Billy Moore (arr)

<u>February 23, 1944, New York City (World studios)</u>

N-1748	BAKIFF	World 6289/6293
71792	WEST END BLUES (/)	AFRS Downbeat No. 128
71793-A	THOUGHTLESS (NOWHERE) (/)	unissued ?
71794-A	IN THERE (s)	World 6289/6293
71795-A	SALTIN' AWAY MY SWEET DREAMS (GTv) (/)	Decca 18601, World 6279/6283
71796-A	BABY WON'T YOU PLEASE COME HOME (GTv) (/)	World 6289/6293
71797-A	THE GREAT LIE (s)	Decca DL 8098, World 7114/7118

Note :

Double numbers of World releases refer to transcription records containing five titles on each side. The numbers given in discographies denote first and last issue number of the titles either on one side (5) or both sides (10) of a record.

All titles, except THOUGHTLESS and THE GREAT LIE, also on AFRS "Downbeat" program No. 128.

The version of THOUGHTLESS reissued on Ajax-147 and Swing Era 1019 LP's as from the above date is identical to the take on Circle CCD-112, released as being recorded on July 28, 1942 for Lang-Worth Transcriptions. The latter date is probably correct. If THOUGHTLESS was ever recorded on the above date, it remained unissued.

LP reissues:

All titles, except BAKIFF, THOUGHTLESS, and WEST END BLUES also on Ajax -147.

THE GREAT LIE also on MCA2-4069 and on Affinity AFS 1012.

BAKIFF, WEST END BLUES, and IN THERE also on Fanfare LP 38-138.

BAKIFF and IN THERE also on Swing Era LP-1019.

CD reissues:

THE GREAT LIE also on MCA GRP 16122 and Jazz Archives CD 85.

BAKIFF, IN THERE, and THE GREAT LIE also on Hindsight HCD 264.

CHARLIE BARNET AND HIS ORCHESTRA · DECCA RECORDING SESSION

band personnel same as before

February 24, 1944, New York City (World studios)

	THE JEEP IS JUMPIN' (s)	World 7114/7118
N-1754	BLUE MOON (s)	World 6289/6293
N-1755	IN A MELLOTONE (/)	World 6279/6283
71798-A	MY HEART ISN'T IN IT (GTv) (/)	Decca 18601, World 6279/6283
71799-A	DROP ME OFF IN HARLEM (s)	Decca 18810, World 6279/6283
71800-A	GULF COAST BLUES (/)	Decca 18810, World 6279/6283
71801-A	FLAT TOP FLIPS HIS LID (/)	World 7114/7118

Note :

Dan Mather in his Charlie Barnet biography assumes the title THE JEEP IS JUMPIN' to have been recorded on the above recording session although it is given a 1946 recording date by many discographers. Mather's assumption is verified by the presence of DeFranco and Marmarosa as soloists.

Some sources (Jepsen, Bruyninckx, Lord) give matrix no. 71791 for FLAT TOP FLIPS HIS LID.

GULF COAST BLUES also on V-Disc 218.

BLUE MOON, IN A MELLOTONE, and GULF COAST BLUES also on AFRS "Downbeat" No. 128.

LP reissues:

All titles, except THE JEEP IS JUMPIN' and IN A MELLOTONE also on Ajax -147.

BLUE MOON and IN A MELLOTONE also on Swing Era LP-1019.

BLUE MOON, IN A MELLOTONE, and GULF COAST BLUES also on Fanfare LP 38-138.

DROP ME OFF IN HARLEM and GULF COAST BLUES also on MCA2-4069.

DROP ME OFF IN HARLEM, GULF COAST BLUES, and FLAT TOP FLIPS HIS LID also on Affinity AFS 1012.

THE JEEP IS JUMPIN' also on Ajaz 201 and Big Band Archives BBA 1209.

CD reissues:

DROP ME OFF IN HARLEM and GULF COAST BLUES also on MCA GRP 16122 and on Jazz Archives CD 85.

FLAT TOP FLIPS HIS LID also on Living Era CD-AJA-5288.

THE JEEP IS JUMPIN', BLUE MOON, IN A MELLOTONE, DROP ME OFF IN HARLEM, and GULF COAST BLUES also on Hindsight HCD 264.

Dan Mather in his Barnet biography states that Barnet disbanded already after the preceding World recording sessions. He does not mention the band's engagement at Frank Dailey's Terrace Room in Newark, N.J., which would have lasted until March 9, 1944, if it was actually carried out and not only remained a planning status, prematurely published by the music press. Barnet at latest in early March moved to Hollywood to work with studio musicians on RKO's movie "Music In Manhattan".

Dodo Marmarosa went back to Pittsburgh, Pa., for a short vacation.

A few weeks after his friend and colleague Buddy DeFranco, Marmarosa received an offer to join the orchestra of **Tommy Dorsey**. He accepted and, as a member of the Dorsey band, soon was on the road again...

NOTE: Several discographies list Dodo Marmarosa already in the personnel of the Tommy Dorsey Orchestra for three earlier broadcasts out of the "Victory Parade of Spotlight Bands" program series (Spotlight Bands No. 473 of March 24, 1944, No. 475 of March 27, 1944, and No. 485 of April 7, 1944). Preserved AFRS transcriptions of these programs (AFRS Spotlight Bands No. 318 for March 24, 1944, and AFRS Spotlight Bands No. 330 for April 7, 1944), however, reveal the pianist on these broadcasts still to be Marmarosa's predecessor Milt Raskin (a few titles of the March 24, 1944 broadcast have been reissued commercially on Manhattan LP 501).

Marmarosa most certainly gave his debut with Dorsey's orchestra at the below engagement. Although METRONOME magazine's May 1944 issue still mentions Raskin in a review of the orchestra being broadcast on radio from the Terrace Room on April 14, 1944, we believe Marmarosa to have played already on that date. Both could easily have been mistaken for each other in their similar ways of supporting Dorsey's band. The subsequent entry for April 17, 1944 denotes Marmarosa's first recorded performance with Tommy Dorsey.

For the second half of April 1944 the following engagement of the Tommy Dorsey Orchestra was advertised in the trade papers:

April 14 - 27, 1944   : Newark, N.J., Terrace Room

TOMMY DORSEY   VICTORY PARADE OF SPOTLIGHT BANDS NO. 493
AND HIS ORCHESTRA   RADIO BROADCAST

George Seaberg, Pete Candoli, Sal La Perche, Dale Pearce (tp), Tommy Dorsey (tb,arr), Tommy Pederson, Tex Satterwhite, Walter „Red" Benson (tb), Buddy DeFranco (cl,as), Sid Cooper (as), Gail Curtis, Al Klink (ts), Bruce Branson (bs), Dodo Marmarosa (p), Dennis Sandole (g), Sid Block (b), Gene Krupa (dm), Leonard Atkins, Alex Beller, Bernard Tinterow, Ruth Rubinstein, Joseph Goodman, Manny Fiddler (vl), David Uchitel, Sheppard Lehnoff (viola), Fred Camelia, Howard Reich (cello), Bob Allen, The Sentimentalists (voc), Sy Oliver (arr); Georgia Gibbs and Morton Downey (voc) appeared as guest stars

Note :   The Sentimentalists are the former "Clark Sisters" consisting of Jean, Ann, Mary, and Peggy Clark.

April 17, 1944, New York City, Carnegie Hall

dress rehearsal :

VP 622	AND SO LITTLE TIME (MDv) (/)	V-Disc 206
VP 622	PRETTY KITTY BLUE EYES (MDv) (/)	V-Disc 206
VP 623	PARAMOUNT ON PARADE (/)	V-Disc 206
VP 625	NOT SO QUIET, PLEASE (/)	V-Disc 220
VP 626	THE MINOR GOES A-MUGGIN' (p-intro)	V-Disc 220
VP 627	TESS' TORCH SONG (GGv) (/)	V-Disc 227
VP 632	IRRESISTIBLE YOU (BA&TSv) (/)	V-Disc 227
VP 638	WAGON WHEELS (/)	V-Disc 222
VP 651	T.D. CHANT (HAWAIIAN WAR CHANT (/)	V-Disc 222

broadcast :

THEME (Spotlight Bands signature tune) (/)
THE MINOR GOES A-MUGGIN' (p-intro) AFRS Spotlight Bands No. 338
I DREAM OF YOU (BAv) (/)   AFRS Spotlight Bands No. 338

VP 627	MILKMAN, KEEP THOSE BOTTLES QUIET (GGv) (/)	
		V-Disc 227, AFRS Spotlight Bands No. 338
VP 632	I NEVER KNEW (TSv) (/)	V-Disc 227, AFRS Spotlight Bands No. 338
	AND SO LITTLE TIME (MDv) (/)	AFRS Spotlight Bands No. 338
	SONG OF INDIA (/)	AFRS Spotlight Bands No. 338
VP 626	LOSERS WEEPERS (/)	V-Disc 220, AFRS Spotlight Bands No. 338
	THEME (I'M GETTING SENTIMENTAL OVER YOU) (/)	
	THEME (Spotlight Bands signature tune) (/)	

Note :

The above "Spotlight Bands" appearance of the Dorsey orchestra was a concert for invited service men and women at New York's famous Carnegie Hall, specially arranged by the Coca Cola Company and the AFRS for V-Disc recordings.

The announcer of "Spotlight Bands" program No. 493 points to the fact, that several V-Disc titles had already been recorded in a rehearsal prior to the broadcast

A selection of the above broadcast titles (probably as indicated) also used for AFRS Spotlight Bands No. 338.

I DREAM OF YOU, THE MINOR GOES A-MUGGIN' (broadcast take), LOSERS WEEPERS, and SONG OF INDIA also used for BML P-104. SONG OF INDIA also used on AFRS "G.I. Jive" No. 621 and AFRS "Sound Off" No. 357.

PARAMOUNT ON PARADE is the Paramount newsreel theme THE EYES AND EARS OF THE WORLD.

LP reissue:

PARAMOUNT ON PARADE and NOT SO QUIET, PLEASE also on Joyce LP-2004.

CD reissues:

PARAMOUNT ON PARADE, TESS'S TORCH SONG, IRRESISTIBLE YOU, WAGON WHEELS, T.D. CHANT, and complete broadcast, except AND SO LITTLE TIME, but including THEMES also on Hep CD 40.

PARAMOUNT ON PARADE, TESS' TORCH SONG, IRRESISTIBLE YOU, WAGON WHEELS, T.D. CHANT, THE MINOR GOES A-MUGGIN' (broadcast, not V-Disc take!), MILKMAN, KEEP THOSE BOTTLES QUIET, I NEVER KNEW, and LOSERS WEEPERS also on "V-Discs: Tommy Dorsey".

AND SO LITTLE TIME (broadcast take) also on Sandy Hook CD S.H. 2001.

TOMMY DORSEY   AFRS "ONE NIGHT STAND"
AND HIS ORCHESTRA   RADIO BROADCAST

band personnel similar as before

April 22, 1944, Newark, N.J., Terrace Room

HAWAIIAN WAR CHANT (/)	AFRS One Night Stand No. 218
I DREAM OF YOU (BA&TSv) (/)	–
YOU'RE MINE YOU (/)	–
IRRESISTIBLE YOU (BA&TSv) (/)	–
PARAMOUNT ON PARADE (/)	–
MANDY, MAKE UP YOUR MIND (s)	–
MY FIRST LOVE (BA&TSv) (/)	–
WELL, GIT IT! (faded) (/)	–

Note :

The AFRS "One Night Stand" program series had started in late September 1943 and featured half hour broadcasts of name band 'live'-performances from the sites, where these bands were regularly playing at the time of recording. These performances were transcribed and released in edited versions for rebroadcast on the Armed Forces' radio net.

The above was Tommy Dorsey's first appearance within the "One Night Stand" series. As Mackenzie and Polomski in their "One Night Stand"-discography remark, it is insofar unusual, as there is no applause audible, except for the opening of the broadcast and after the title OPUS ONE, which had been dubbed in from the AFRS "Spotlight Bands" program series (see below). Possibly the audience at the Terrace Room, which judging by the audible background noises is nevertheless present, had been asked not to applaud between the titles for the recording.

The AFRS opening signature on the above program is not played by Dorsey, but probably by an AFRS orchestra. The above program release by AFRS also contained a performance of OPUS ONE, which was dubbed from AFRS Spotlight Bands Program No. 344 (see April 24, 1944).

The above version of MANDY was also used on AFRS Yank Swing Session program No. 107.

The above version of YOU'RE MINE YOU also used on AFRS One Night Stand program No. 391 (see October 14, 1944).

TOMMY DORSEY
AND HIS ORCHESTRA

FITCH BANDWAGON SHOW
NBC RADIO BROADCAST

band personnel same as before

<u>April 23, 1944, New York City</u>

I NEVER KNEW (TSv) (/)	AFRS Bandwagon No. 98
I DREAM OF YOU (BAv) ( )	–
EVERYTHING HAPPENS TO ME (Celeste Holm -voc) ( )	–
LEAVE US FACE IT (Celeste Holm -voc) ( )	–

Note:

The Tommy Dorsey Orchestra and Broadway singer Celeste Holm appeared as guests on this program. Tom Reddy acted as host and the announcer was Jack Costello. More details on the show are unknown.

AFRS Bandwagon No. 98 was mastered for release by AFRS sound engineers on July 23, 1944.

I NEVER KNEW also used as fill-in on AFRS "Your All Time Hit Parade" transcription No. 38 (see July 2, 1944).

TOMMY DORSEY   VICTORY PARADE OF SPOTLIGHT BANDS NO. 499
AND HIS ORCHESTRA   RADIO BROADCAST

---

band personnel similar as before, but Mickey Mangano (tp) replaces Pete Candoli and
Charles Small (tb) replaces Tommy Pederson

<u>April 24, 1944, Atlantic City, N.J., Naval Air Station</u>

THEME (Spotlight Bands signature tune) (/)	AFRS Spotlight Bands No. 344
OPUS ONE (s)	–
THIS I LOVE ABOVE ALL (BAv) (/)	–
WAGON WHEELS (/)	–
only DeFranco, Marmarosa, Krupa (plus full orchestra on final chord):	
I GOT RHYTHM (s)	–
full orchestra again :	
SWING HIGH (/)	–

Note :

Additional titles of the original Coca Cola Spotlight Bands broadcast program (25 minutes duration) unknown.

Titles as above used on AFRS Spotlight Bands No. 344 (15 minutes duration).

Closing theme (Spotlight Bands signature tune) on AFRS release played by other band than Dorsey's.

OPUS ONE here is a shortened version of the arrangement as it was usually played by Dorsey.

The above version of OPUS ONE also used on AFRS One Night Stand program No. 218 (see April 22, 1944).

LP reissue:

WAGON WHEELS, I GOT RHYTHM, and SWING HIGH on Manhattan 501.

For April/May 1944 the following engagement of the Tommy Dorsey
Orchestra was advertised in the trade papers:

<u>April 28 - May 18, 1944</u>   : Chicago, Ill., Hotel Sherman, Panther Room

TOMMY DORSEY AND HIS ORCHESTRA   VICTORY PARADE OF SPOTLIGHT BANDS NO. 505 RADIO BROADCAST

band personnel similar as before,

<u>May 1, 1944, unknown location around Chicago, Ill.</u>

MANDY, MAKE UP YOUR MIND (s)	AFRS Spotlight Bands No. 350
NOT SO QUIET, PLEASE (/)	–
WELL, GIT IT! (/)	–

Note :

The other titles played on this program by the Tommy Dorsey band are unknown.

A portion of the above program (five to six titles) used on AFRS Spotlight Bands No. 350.

CD reissue:

Above three titles on Jass JCD 14.

GENE KRUPA TRIO   V-DISC RECORDING SESSION

Buddy DeFranco (cl), Dodo Marmarosa (p), Gene Krupa (dm)

<u>May 4, 1944, Chicago, Ill., NBC studios</u>

VP 660	LIZA (s)	V-Disc 253
VP 660	HODGE PODGE (s)	V-Disc 253
	HOW HIGH THE MOON (s)	V-Disc unissued
	THE MAN I LOVE ( )	V-Disc unissued ?

Note :

The Gene Krupa Trio was a prominently featured extra attraction during 'live' performances of the Tommy Dorsey Orchestra in April, May, and June 1944, before Krupa left the trombonist's orchestra.

THE MAN I LOVE is a title usually not mentioned in discographical references to this session. Marmarosa, however, remembered in a 1995 interview with Robert E. Sunenblick, that originally four titles had been recorded on the above date, and he recalled THE MAN I LOVE as one of these.

LP reissues:

LIZA and HODGE PODGE also on Giants Of Jazz LP-1006.

All titles, except THE MAN I LOVE, on Aircheck 35.

CD reissue:

LIZA and HODGE PODGE also on Classics CD 1096.

TOMMY DORSEY   VICTORY PARADE OF SPOTLIGHT BANDS NO. 511
AND HIS ORCHESTRA   RADIO BROADCAST

band personnel similar as before, including strings and harp

<u>May 8, 1944, Joliet, Ill., Seabees Navy Docks</u>

THEME (Spotlight Bands signature tune) (/)	AFRS Spotlight Bands No. 356
SOMEBODY LOVES ME (TSv) (/)	–
I DREAM OF YOU (BAv) (/)	–
THE MINOR GOES A-MUGGIN' (p-intro)	–
WHEN THEY ASK ABOUT YOU (BLWv) (/)	–
only DeFranco, Marmarosa, Krupa:	
LIZA (s)	–
full orchestra again :	
IRRESISTIBLE YOU (BA&TSv) ( )	

Note :

Additional titles of the original Coca Cola Spotlight Bands broadcast program (25 minutes duration) unknown.
Titles as above, except IRRESISTIBLE YOU, used on AFRS Spotlight Bands No. 356 (15 minutes duration).
Closing theme (Spotlight Bands signature tune) on AFRS release played by other band than Dorsey's.

TOMMY DORSEY AND HIS ORCHESTRA

LANG-WORTH RECORDING SESSION

Mickey Mangano, George Seaberg, Dale Pearce, Sal La Perche (tp), Tommy Dorsey (tb,arr), Walter „Red" Benson, Nelson Riddle, Tex Satterwhite (tb), Joe Park (tuba), Buddy DeFranco (cl,as), Sid Cooper (as), Gail Curtis, Mickey Sabol (ts), Bruce Branson (bs), Dodo Marmarosa (p), Dennis Sandole (g), Sid Block (b), Gene Krupa (dm), Alex Beller, Leonard Atkins, Bernard Tinterow, Robert Konrad, Manny Fiddler, Ben Blackman, Royal Johnson, Ruth Rubinstein, Joseph Goodman, Peter Vinitranes, Paul Kahn (vl), David Uchitel, Sheppard Lehnhoff (viola), Fred Camelia, David Greenbaum (cello), Doris Briggs (harp) Bonnie Lou Williams, Bob Allen, The Sentimentalists (voc), Sy Oliver (arr)

May 12, 1944, Chicago, Ill.

YTC 1581	I'M GETTING SENTIMENTAL OVER YOU ( )	Lang-Worth AS 76
	(with spoken introduction by Tommy Dorsey)	
	WAGON WHEELS (/)	–
	DO NOTHIN' 'TIL YOU HEAR FROM ME (BLWv) (/)	–
	ON THE SUNNY SIDE OF THE STREET (TSv) (/)	–
YTC 1582	YOU BROUGHT A NEW KIND OF LOVE TO ME (BLWv) (/)	
		Lang-Worth AS 82
	I NEVER KNEW (TSv) (/)	–
	YOU'RE DRIVING ME CRAZY (TSv) (s)	–
	THE MINOR GOES A-MUGGIN' (p-intro)	–
YTC 1583	OPUS ONE (s)	Lang-Worth LWT 1020
	I'M IN LOVE WITH SOMEONE (BAv) (/)	–
	WHEN YOU PUT ON THAT OLD BLUE SUIT AGAIN (TSv) (/)	–
	AMOR (/)	–
YTC 1584	SWING HIGH (s)	Lang-Worth LWT 1040
	I DREAM OF YOU (BAv) (/)	–
	WELL, GIT IT! (/)	–
	LOSERS WEEPERS (/)	–

Note :

The exact date and location of this recording session, not to be found with any of the reissues, were kindly conveyed by Harry Mackenzie and are taken from the yet unpublished Tommy Dorsey discography written by Ken Seavor.

LP reissues:

OPUS ONE, I'M IN LOVE WITH SOMEONE, SWING HIGH, WELL, GIT IT!, and LOSERS WEEPERS also on Movietone MT S 4005.

WAGON WHEELS, ON THE SUNNY SIDE OF THE STREET, I NEVER KNEW, THE MINOR GOES A-MUGGIN', OPUS ONE, I'M IN LOVE WITH SOMEONE, AMOR, SWING HIGH, WELL, GIT IT!, and LOSERS WEEPERS also on Philips 6641 170.

CD reissues:

WAGON WHEELS, ON THE SUNNY SIDE OF THE STREET, THE MINOR GOES A-MUGGIN', OPUS ONE, I'M IN LOVE WITH SOMEONE, AMOR, SWING HIGH, WELL, GIT IT!, and LOSERS WEEPERS also on Jasmine JASMCD 2537.

TOMMY DORSEY AND HIS ORCHESTRA   VICTORY PARADE OF SPOTLIGHT BANDS NO. 517 RADIO BROADCAST

band personnel similar as before

<u>May 15, 1944, Great Lakes, Ill., U.S. Naval Hospital</u>

THEME (Spotlight Bands signature tune) (/)	
IT'S LOVE, LOVE, LOVE (TSv) (/)	AFRS Spotlight Bands No. 362
THIS I LOVE ABOVE ALL (BAv) (/)	AFRS Spotlight Bands No. 362
SONG OF INDIA (/)	AFRS Spotlight Bands No. 362
DO NOTHIN' 'TIL YOU HEAR FROM ME (BLWv) (/)	
HAWAIIAN WAR CHANT (/)	AFRS Spotlight Bands No. 362
I DREAM OF YOU (BAv) (/)	
LOSERS WEEPERS (/)	AFRS Spotlight Bands No. 362
THEME (I'M GETTING SENTIMENTAL OVER YOU) (/)	AFRS Spotlight Bands No. 362
THEME (Spotlight Bands signature tune) (/)	

Note :

Titles as indicated used on AFRS Spotlight Bands No. 362 (15 minutes duration).

The above performance of SONG OF INDIA also used on AFRS One Night Stand No. 391 (see October 14, 1944).

For the mid of May 1944 the following engagement of the Tommy Dorsey Orchestra was listed in the trade papers:

<u>May 19 - May 25, 1944</u>   : Detroit, Mich., Downtown Theatre

---

TOMMY DORSEY   **VICTORY PARADE OF SPOTLIGHT BANDS NO. 528**
AND HIS ORCHESTRA   **RADIO BROADCAST**

---

band personnel similar as before

<u>May 27, 1944, Chicago, Ill., Chicago Stadium</u>

THEME (I'M GETTING SENTIMENTAL OVER YOU) (/)
SAN FERNANDO VALLEY (TSv) (/)   AFRS Spotlight Bands No. 373
I DREAM OF YOU (BAv) (/)   AFRS Spotlight Bands No. 373
          only DeFranco, Marmarosa, Krupa (plus full orchestra on final chord):
I GOT RHYTHM (s)   AFRS Spotlight Bands No. 373
          full orchestra again :
THIS I LOVE ABOVE ALL (BAv) (/)   AFRS Spotlight Bands No. 373
I'LL GET BY (BLWv) (/)   AFRS Spotlight Bands No. 373
SWING HIGH (/)   AFRS Spotlight Bands No. 373
THEME (I'M GETTING SENTIMENTAL OVER YOU) (/)

Note :

The above program was played before an audience of Western Electric workers.

Titles as indicated used on AFRS Spotlight Bands No. 373 (15 minutes duration). The opening bars of I'LL GET BY have been edited out by the AFRS sound engineers when mastering the program for release.

AFRS Spotlight Bands No. 373 also contains an excerpt of LOSERS WEEPERS as closure, which has been dubbed and filled in from Dorsey's performance of the title on Victory Parade of Spotlight Bands No. 517 (see May 15, 1944).

TOMMY DORSEY AND HIS ORCHESTRA

VICTORY PARADE OF SPOTLIGHT BANDS STANDBY PROGRAM

band personnel similar as before

<u>ca. May 1944, probably Chicago, Ill. (or Chicago area)</u>

THEME (Spotlight Bands signature tune; faded) (/)	
SONG OF INDIA (/)	AFRS Spotlight Bands No. 529
I DREAM OF YOU (BAv) (/)	AFRS Spotlight Bands No. 529
THE MINOR GOES A-MUGGIN' (p-intro)	AFRS Spotlight Bands No. 529
ON THE SUNNY SIDE OF THE STREET (TSv) (/)	AFRS Spotlight Bands No. 529
HAWAIIAN WAR CHANT (/)	
THIS I LOVE ABOVE ALL (BAv) (/)	
WELL, GIT IT! (/)	AFRS Spotlight Bands No. 529
THEME (I'M GETTING SENTIMENTAL OVER YOU) (/)	
THEME (Spotlight Bands signature tune) (/)	

Note :

If ever, the above program was possibly broadcast within the Coca Cola "Victory Parade of Spotlight Bands" series as substitute for the originally scheduled program No. 684 on November 25, 1944. The presence of Bob Allen, Dodo Marmarosa, and Gene Krupa among the featured soloists, however, hints at an earlier date of transcription, most likely in May 1944.

Tommy Dorsey greets the audience at the site of performance as follows: "This is Tommy Dorsey pinch-hitting for the band you expected to hear. Although we're sorry at these Spotlight misconnections, we're glad to be on hand to carry on with the music." This was probably a faked announcement to allow the transcription to be used as a substitute program for possible future needs. The above titles most certainly were recorded after one of Dorsey's regular "Spotlight Bands" broadcasts, when the band continued to play "off the air" for the local audience, a normal practice to gain so called "standby" programs for the "Spotlight Bands" series.

SONG OF INDIA, I DREAM OF YOU, THE MINOR GOES A-MUGGIN', WELL, GIT IT!, and ON THE SUNNY SIDE OF THE TREET in this partly revised title order used on AFRS Spotlight Bands program No. 529.

On May 30, 1944 the Tommy Dorsey Orchestra started for a tour of concerts, departing from Chicago, and ending in San Antonio, Texas, on the 11th of June. The individual stations of the tour are given below:

May 30, 1944	: Evansville, Ind., Auditorium
May 31, 1944	: Louisville, Ky., Auditorium
June 1, 1944	: St. Louis, Mo., Municipal Auditorium
June 2, 1944	: Kansas City, Mo., Auditorium
June 3, 1944	: Tulsa, Oklahoma, Fairgrounds Park
June 4, 1944	: Oklahoma City, Oklahoma, Blossom Heath Inn
June 6, 1944	: Fort Worth, Texas, Lake Worth Casino
June 7, 1944	: Shreveport, La., Auditorium
June 8, 1944	: Dallas, Texas, Plantation Club
June 9, 1944	: Austin, Texas, Auditorium
June 10, 1944	: Houston, Texas, Coliseum
June 11, 1944	: San Antonio, Texas, Auditorium

TOMMY DORSEY AND HIS ORCHESTRA

YOUR ALL TIME HIT PARADE NBC RADIO BROADCAST

band personnel similar as before, but Cappy Lewis (tp), Bob Bain (g), and Buddy Rich (d) replace Sal La Perche, Dennis Sandole, and Gene Krupa; Bing Crosby (voc) appears as guest star

June 18, 1944, Hollywood, Calif., NBC studios

dress rehearsal:

VP 773	SMALL FRY (Bing Crosby -voc) (/)	V-Disc 269
VP 786	PENNIES FROM HEAVEN (Bing Crosby -voc) (/)	V-Disc 287
VP 787	SOMEBODY LOVES ME (TSv) (/)	V-Disc 282

broadcast (4:00 to 4:30 PM):
THEME (I'M GETTING SENTIMENTAL OVER YOU) ( )

SOMEBODY LOVES ME (TSv) ( )
SMALL FRY (Bing Crosby -voc) ( )
LONG AGO AND FAR AWAY (BLWv) ( )
I KNOW THAT YOU KNOW ( )
I'LL NEVER SMILE AGAIN (BA&TSv) ( )
LOUISE (Bing Crosby -voc) ( )
MARIE (BA&Ens -voc) ( )
THEME (I'M GETTING SENTIMENTAL OVER YOU) ( )

Note :

The "Your All Time Hit Parade" radio show series, sponsored by the Lucky Strike tobacco company, had started in February 1943 and was to feature current and older hit songs once a week, bearing the name "Your All Time Hit Parade" in analogy to the other then popular radio show sponsored by Lucky Strike which was called "Your Hit Parade" and featured solely current popular songs.

Dorsey's affiliation with the program started on the above date and lasted for fifteen shows until September 24, 1944.

Some of the recordings coming from Tommy Dorsey's "Your All Time Hit Parade" shows were actually made in two different takes: AFRS recorded the broadcast programs for rebroadcast (AFRS "All Time Hit Parade" transcriptions), as they had already done with earlier shows in this series, and additionally made recordings of a selection of titles during the dress rehearsals prior to the 'live' shows, many of which were used for release on V-Disc, BML and other series of AFRS popular music programs like "G.I. Journal", "G.I. Jive", or "Sound Off". For later editing of their "All Time Hit Parade" transcriptions AFRS took out the commercials from the original broadcasts and added transcribed titles from other of Dorsey's "Your All Time Hit Parade" broadcasts or older Dorsey programs to fill out the time gaps. This AFRS practice is the reason why there often exist two versions of the "Your All Time Hit Parade" shows among collectors: First the original broadcasts containing "Lucky Strike Cigarettes"-commercials, which were presented over the NBC radio network; and second the AFRS rebroadcast programs containing only announcements and music of the original NBC broadcasts plus the above mentioned musical fill-ins in place of the cut out commercials. These rebroadcast programs were sent overseas by AFRS for use on their radio stations. As far as Dorsey's "Your All Time Hit Parades" are concerned, AFRS release obviously began with AFRS "All Time Hit Parade" transcription No. 38 taken from the July 2, 1944 program (see below), the shows of June 18 and 25, 1944 (program Nos. 36 and 37) possibly having been transcribed by AFRS, but seemingly not issued.

A version of MARIE with Bob Allen as vocalist was released on AFRS Basic Musical Library P-202. It was probably taken from the above program.

CD reissues:

All three dress rehearsal takes also on Hep CD 40.

SMALL FRY and SOMEBODY LOVES ME (dress rehearsal takes) also on "V-Discs: Tommy Dorsey".

In an interview with Robert E. Sunenblick in 1995, Dodo Marmarosa recalled, that after Buddy Rich's return into the Dorsey ranks, Dorsey used to feature him, Buddy DeFranco, Sid Block, and Rich in a quartet in live performances (a glimpse of this quartet can be seen in a jam session sequence of MGM's movie "Thrill Of A Romance", see September 11, 1944).

TOMMY DORSEY   YOUR ALL TIME HIT PARADE
AND HIS ORCHESTRA   NBC RADIO BROADCAST

band personnel similar as before, Gracie Fields (voc) appears as guest star

June 25, 1944, Hollywood, Calif., NBC studios

	dress rehearsal:	
	STARDUST (BA&TSv) (/)	GI Journal No. 50
	IT HAD TO BE YOU (BLWv) (/)	BML P-123
	TOP HAT, WHITE TIE, AND TAILS (TSv) (/)	GI Journal No. 50
	BLUE SKIES (BA&Ens -vocal) (/)	GI Journal No. 50
VP 804	I NEVER CRIED SO MUCH (Gracie Fields -voc) (/)	V-Disc 579
	broadcast (4:00 to 4:30 PM):	
	STARDUST (BA&TSv) ( )	
	IT HAD TO BE YOU (BLWv) ( )	
	TOP HAT, WHITE TIE, AND TAILS (TSv) ( )	
	BLUE SKIES (BA&Ens -vocal) ( )	
	I NEVER CRIED SO MUCH (Gracie Fields -voc) ( )	

Note:

Dress rehearsal takes of STARDUST, IT HAD TO BE YOU, TOP HAT, WHITE TIE, AND TAILS, and BLUE SKIES also used for Basic Musical Library P-123.

Dress rehearsal take of BLUE SKIES also used on AFRS G.I. JIVE program No. 705.

CD reissue:

TOP HAT, WHITE TIE, AND TAILS (dress rehearsal take) also on Hep CD 39, although indicated there as from August 20, 1944. Kiner / Mackenzie (BML-Discography) give the above recording date, which is probably correct.

On June 27, 1944 the Tommy Dorsey Orchestra was scheduled to open at the Casino Gardens Ballroom in Santa Monica's Ocean Park, Calif. Dorsey then was in negotiations with the management of the Ballroom to buy it and operate it as a joint venture by bandleaders Harry James, Jimmy Dorsey and himself. These plans soon materialized and Dorsey's band played there on three consecutive weekends starting either on June 30/July 1 or July 7/8, 1944. It was followed by Harry James' band on July 28, 1944.

NOTE: Harry Mackenzie in his discography on the AFRS "Command Performance" program series lists program No. 127 (mastering date July 1, 1944) with, among others, participation by Tommy Dorsey, but gives no further details as to the kind of his performance. Aural verification reveals a guest appearance of Jimmy and Tommy Dorsey accompanied by the program's resident AFRS orchestra. Dorsey's own orchestra was not involved in this production.

For further information on the AFRS "Command Performance" program series see the corresponding entry for late October 1944.

TOMMY DORSEY AND HIS ORCHESTRA

YOUR ALL TIME HIT PARADE NBC RADIO BROADCAST

band personnel similar as before, Frances Langford (voc) appears as guest star

<u>July 2, 1944, Hollywood, Calif, NBC studios</u>

	dress rehearsal:	
	HEAT WAVE (TSv) (/)	GI Journal No. 51
VP 787	INDIAN SUMMER (BAv) (/)	GI Journal No. 51, V-Disc 282
VP 786	I'M IN THE MOOD FOR LOVE (Frances Langford -voc) (/)	V-Disc 287
	I'LL BE SEEING YOU (BLWv) (/)	Hep CD 39
	AS TIME GOES BY (Frances Langford -voc) (/)	Hep CD 39
	HAWAIIAN WAR CHANT (/)	GI Journal No. 51

broadcast (4:00 to 4:30 PM):	
THEME (I'M GETTING SENTIMENTAL OVER YOU) (/)	
	AFRS All Time Hit Parade No. 38
HEAT WAVE (TSv) (/)	–
INDIAN SUMMER (BAv) (/)	–
I'M IN THE MOOD FOR LOVE (Frances Langford -voc) (/)	–
I'LL BE SEEING YOU (BLWv) (/)	–
AS TIME GOES BY (broadcast) (Frances Langford -voc) (/)	–
HAWAIIAN WAR CHANT (/)	–
THEME (I'M GETTING SENTIMENTAL OVER YOU) (/)	–

Note :

AFRS "All Time Hit Parade" transcription No. 38 was the first of the "Your All Time Hit Parade" programs with Dorsey participation to be released by AFRS for rebroadcast (transcription No. 50 taken from the Sept. 24, 1944 broadcast being the last show in the series featuring the Dorsey orchestra).

AFRS "All Time Hit Parade" transcription No. 38 also contained dubbed in versions of SONG OF INDIA, I FOUND A NEW BABY, and SLEEPY LAGOON (introduction and part of theme only) from AFRS "Tommy Dorsey Show" No. 36 (September 8, 1943), and THE WORLD IS WAITING FOR THE SUNRISE and I GOT RHYTHM from AFRS "Tommy Dorsey Show" No. 35 (September 1, 1943), all of which were performed without the participation of Dodo Marmarosa. Milt Raskin played piano with Tommy Dorsey in 1943.

One further dubbed in performance of I NEVER KNEW was derived from AFRS "Bandwagon" No. 98 (see April 23, 1944). This program was mastered for release by AFRS sound engineers on July 23, 1944.

HEAT WAVE (dress rehearsal take) also used for BML P-123, HAWAIIAN WAR CHANT (dress rehearsal take) also used for BML P-145, INDIAN SUMMER (dress rehearsal take) also used for BML P-256.

HEAT WAVE *(dress rehearsal take) also used for AFRS Sound Off program No. 414.*

HAWAIIAN WAR CHANT *(dress rehearsal take) also used for AFRS Down Beat program No. 106.*

LP reissues:

THEME, HEAT WAVE, I'LL BE SEEING YOU, AS TIME GOES BY, *and* HAWAIIAN WAR CHANT *(broadcast takes) also on Sunbeam SB-220. The recording date given for this reissue (March 12, 1944) is not correct.*

INDIAN SUMMER *as dress rehearsal take also on Joyce LP-2004.*

CD reissues:

HAWAIIAN WAR CHANT *as dress rehearsal take also on Jazz&Jazz CD-614.*

INDIAN SUMMER *as dress rehearsal take also on "V-Discs: Tommy Dorsey".*

I'M IN THE MOOD FOR LOVE *and* INDIAN SUMMER *as dress rehearsal takes also on Hep CD 40.*

I'll BE SEEING YOU, AS TIME GOES BY, *and* HAWAIIAN WAR CHANT *as dress rehearsal takes also on Hep CD 39.*

TOMMY DORSEY	**YOUR ALL TIME HIT PARADE**
AND HIS ORCHESTRA	**NBC RADIO BROADCAST**

---

band personnel similar as before, Cass Daley (voc) and Bob Burns (bazooka, voc) appear as guest stars

<u>July 9, 1944, Hollywood, Calif., NBC studios</u>

	dress rehearsal:	
	MARGIE (TSv) (/)	BML P-162
VP 1289	PLEASE DON'T TALK ABOUT ME WHEN I'M GONE	
	(Cass Daley -voc) (/)	V-Disc 477
	WHISPERING (BLWv) ( )	unissued V-Disc
	broadcast (4:00 to 4:30 PM):	
	THEME (I'M GETTING SENTIMENTAL OVER YOU) (/)	
		AFRS All Time Hit Parade No. 39
	MARGIE (TSv) (/)	–
	PLEASE DON'T TALK ABOUT ME WHEN I'M GONE	
	(Cass Daley -voc) (/)	–
	I'LL BE SEEING YOU (BAv) (/)	–
	WHISPERING (BLWv) (/)	–
	YOU ARE MY SUNSHINE (Cass Daley, Bob Burns, TSv) (p-intro)	–
	MANDY (opening bars only) (/)	–
	DARK EYES (opening bars only) (/)	–
	SONG OF INDIA (/)	–
	THEME (I'M GETTING SENTIMENTAL OVER YOU) (/)	–

Note :

Dress rehearsal take of PLEASE DON'T TALK ABOUT ME WHEN I'M GONE also issued on V-Disc 579.

On YOU ARE MY SUNSHINE Bob Burns also plays bazooka.

WHISPERING was planned for release on V-Disc, but remained unissued.

NOTE: In the July 15, 1944 issue *Down Beat* reports of the Dorsey Orchestra working at the MGM studios in Culver City (Los Angeles). The band was to appear in the musical comedy "Thrill Of A Romance" starring Esther Williams, Van Johnson and Lauritz Melchior, produced by Joe Pasternak, directed by Richard Thorpe. Some of the orchestrations were written by Calvin Jackson and Fred Norman.

Work on this film obviously endured until the end of September 1944.

As to the participation of Dodo Marmarosa, see list of soundtrack-recordings further below.

TOMMY DORSEY
AND HIS ORCHESTRA

YOUR ALL TIME HIT PARADE
NBC RADIO BROADCAST

band personnel similar as before, Rudy Vallee (voc) appears as guest star

<u>July 16, 1944, Hollywood, Calif., NBC studios</u>

dress rehearsal:

VP 870	SWEET AND LOVELY (BAv) (/)	V-Disc 320
	SLEEPY LAGOON ( )	BML P-131

broadcast (4:00 to 4:30 PM):

THEME (I'M GETTING SENTIMENTAL OVER YOU) (/)

AFRS All Time Hit Parade No. 40

I NEVER KNEW (TSv) (/)	–
DEEP NIGHT (Rudy Vallee & Ens -voc) (/)	–
I'LL BE SEEING YOU (BLWv) (/)	–
SWEET AND LOVELY (BAv) (/)	–
THE MAINE STEIN SONG (Rudy Vallee -voc) (/)	–
SLEEPY LAGOON (/)	–
THEME (I'M GETTING SENTIMENTAL OVER YOU) (/)	–

Note :

Dress rehearsal take of SWEET AND LOVELY also used for BML P-131 and AFRS Down Beat program No. 106.

Raben ("Jazz Discography") lists SLEEPY LAGOON as reissued on Déjavu 2019 (LP). The version on the LP, however, is the RCA-Victor studio-recording from March 9, 1942.

CD reissues:

SWEET AND LOVELY as dress rehearsal take also on Jazz&Jazz CD-614, Hep CD 40, and "V-Discs: Tommy Dorsey".

TOMMY DORSEY AND HIS ORCHESTRA   *M-G-M*
SOUNDTRACK RECORDINGS

Mickey Mangano, George Seaberg, Dale Pearce, Cappy Lewis (tp), Tommy Dorsey (tb,arr), Walter "Red" Benson, Nelson Riddle, Tex Satterwhite (tb), Joe Park (tuba), Buddy DeFranco (cl,as), Sid Cooper (as), Gail Curtis, Al Klink (ts), Bruce Branson (bs), Dodo Marmarosa (p), Bob Bain (g), Sid Block (b), Buddy Rich (dm), Doris Briggs (harp) plus strings, Bonnie Lou Williams, Bob Allen, The Sentimentalists (voc)

<u>July 20, 1944, Culver City, Los Angeles, Calif., M-G-M studios</u>

    SONG OF INDIA (/)   Rhino R 2 75283 (CD)
    YOU DEAR (/)   –

Note:

The above titles were recorded for the M-G-M musical comedy "Thrill Of A Romance" (see "note" on previous page).

YOU DEAR, given by all sources on the film soundtrack as "unidentified instrumental", was composed by Ralph Freed and Sammy Fain and also played by Harry James in the 1944 M-G-M musical film "Two Girls And A Sailor".

Both Rhino reissues are complete versions of the originally recorded titles before editing for the film and dubbing of dialogue.

TOMMY DORSEY	**YOUR ALL TIME HIT PARADE**
AND HIS ORCHESTRA	**NBC RADIO BROADCAST**

---

band personnel similar as before, Al Jolson (voc) appears as guest star

<u>July 23, 1944, Hollywood, Calif., NBC studios</u>

dress rehearsal:

	LITTLE WHITE LIES (s)	BML P-162
VP 845	MA BLUSHIN' ROSIE (Al Jolson -voc) (/)	V-Disc 306
	YOU BROUGHT A NEW KIND OF LOVE TO ME (BLWv) (/)	BML P-256
VP 845	APRIL SHOWERS (Al Jolson -voc) (/)	V-Disc 306

broadcast (4:00 to 4:30 PM):

THEME (I'M GETTING SENTIMENTAL OVER YOU) (/)

AFRS All Time Hit Parade No. 41

LITTLE WHITE LIES (/)	–
MA BLUSHIN' ROSIE (Al Jolson -voc) (/)	–
I'LL BE SEEING YOU (TSv) (/)	–
YOU BROUGHT A NEW KIND OF LOVE TO ME (BLWv) (/)	–
APRIL SHOWERS (Al Jolson -voc) (/)	–
BODY AND SOUL (/)	–
THEME (I'M GETTING SENTIMENTAL OVER YOU) (/)	–

Note :

LITTLE WHITE LIES and BODY AND SOUL (broadcast takes) also dubbed in on AFRS "All Time Hit Parade" transcription No. 43 (see August 6, 1944) and No. 48 (LITTLE WHITE LIES only, see September 10, 1944 below).

LP reissue:

MA BLUSHIN' ROSIE and APRIL SHOWERS (dress rehearsal takes) also on Totem LP 1006.
All titles (broadcast takes) also on Totem LP 1030.

TOMMY DORSEY AND HIS ORCHESTRA   *M-G-M*
SOUNDTRACK RECORDING

Mickey Mangano, George Seaberg, Dale Pearce, Cappy Lewis (tp), Tommy Dorsey
(tb,arr), Walter "Red" Benson, Nelson Riddle, Tex Satterwhite (tb), Joe Park (tuba), Buddy
DeFranco (cl,as), Sid Cooper (as), Gail Curtis, Al Klink (ts), Bruce Branson (bs), Dodo
Marmarosa (p), Bob Bain (g), Sid Block (b), Buddy Rich (dm), Doris Briggs (harp) plus
strings, Bonnie Lou Williams, Bob Allen, The Sentimentalists (voc)

<u>July 29, 1944, Culver City, Los Angeles, Calif., M-G-M studios</u>

I SHOULD CARE (BAv) (/)   Rhino R 2 75283 (CD)

Note:

The above title was recorded for the M-G-M musical comedy "Thrill Of A Romance" (see "note" for July 15).
This Rhino reissue is the complete version of the originally recorded title before editing for the film and dubbing
of dialogue.

TOMMY DORSEY		***YOUR ALL TIME HIT PARADE***
AND HIS ORCHESTRA		***NBC RADIO BROADCAST***

band personnel similar as before, José Iturbi (p) appears as guest star

<u>July 30, 1944, Hollywood, Calif., NBC studios</u>

	dress rehearsal:	
	MARCH OF THE TOYS (/)	BML P-131
	AMOR (BLW & TSv) (/)	AFRS Down Beat No. 106
	THE LAMP IS LOW (BAv) (/)	BML P-319
VP 870	THE LAMP IS LOW (BAv) (/)	V-Disc 320
	BOOGIE WOOGIE (omit strings) (s)	BML P-131
VP 879	MELODY IN A (/)	V-Disc 322
	broadcast (4:00 to 4:30 PM):	
	THEME (I'M GETTING SENTIMENTAL OVER YOU) (/)	
		AFRS All Time Hit Parade No. 42
	MARCH OF THE TOYS (/)	–
	FANTAISIE-IMPROMPTU (Jose Iturbi - p-solo)	–
	AMOR (BLW & TSv) (/)	–
	THE LAMP IS LOW (BAv) (/)	–
	BOOGIE WOOGIE (omit strings) (s)	–
	MELODY IN A (/)	–
	THEME (I'M GETTING SENTIMENTAL OVER YOU) (/)	–

Note :

Jose Iturbi's solo performance on this program is the famous "Fantaisie-Impromptu" op.66 by Frédéric Chopin. On a melody from this classical piece is based the popular American song I'M ALWAYS CHASING RAINBOWS, a fact that is referred to in the announcement to Iturbi's performance.

The broadcast take of THE LAMP IS LOW is a slightly shortened performance of the arrangement as played on the dress rehearsal. This shortened version was also dubbed in on AFRS "All Time Hit Parade" transcription No. 47 (see September 3, 1944 below).

BOOGIE WOOGIE as dress rehearsal take also used for AFRS Down Beat program No. 106.

CD reissues:

BOOGIE WOOGIE and AMOR (dress rehearsal takes) are reissued on Jazz&Jazz CD JJ-614.

MELODY IN A (dress rehearsal take) reissued on "V-Discs: Tommy Dorsey".

THE LAMP IS LOW (BML P-319) and BOOGIE WOOGIE as dress rehearsal takes also on Hep CD 39.

THE LAMP IS LOW (VP 870, seemingly a second dress rehearsal take) also on "V-Discs: Tommy Dorsey". This version differs in details from the take on Hep CD 39 and also has a different ending.
MARCH OF THE TOYS and BOOGIE WOOGIE (dress rehearsal takes) also on Jass JCD 14.

NOTE: Four days later Marmarosa participated in a recording session by his former band boss Charlie Barnet, possibly as a substitute...

CHARLIE BARNET AND HIS ORCHESTRA   DECCA RECORDING SESSION

Peanuts Holland, Lyman Vunk, John Martel, Jack Mootz (tp), Gerald Foster, Dave Hallet, Burt Johnson, Chuck W. Coolidge (tb), Charlie Barnet (as,ss,ts), Hal Herzon, Joe Meissner (as), Kurt Bloom, Ed Pripps (ts), Bob Poland (bs), Dodo Marmarosa (p), Barney Kessel (g), Howard Rumsey (b), Hal Hahn (dm), Kay Starr (voc), Billy Moore, Andy Gibson (arr)

<u>August 3, 1944, Hollywood, Calif.</u>

LA-3487-A	SKYLINER (s)	Decca 18659
LA-3488-A	SHARECROPPIN' BLUES (KSv) (/)	Decca 24264
LA-3489-A	COME OUT, COME OUT, WHEREVER YOU ARE (KSv) (/)	Decca 18620
LA-3490-A	WHAT A DIFFERENCE A DAY MADE (KSv) (/)	–

LP reissues:
SKYLINER, COME OUT WHEREVER YOU ARE, and WHAT A DIFFERENCE A DAY MADE also on Ajax 147. SHARECROPPIN' BLUES, reissued on Ajax 147 as from the above session, is actually the V-Disc version recorded on July 13, 1944 without participation of Marmarosa.
SKYLINER, SHARECROPPIN' BLUES, and WHAT A DIFFERENCE A DAY MADE also on MCA2-4069.
CD reissues:
SKYLINER also on MCA CD GRP 16122, Jazz Archives CD 85, and Living Era CD-AJA-2588.
SHARECROPPIN' BLUES, COME OUT WHEREVER YOU ARE, and WHAT A DIFFERENCE A DAY MADE also on Jasmine JASCD 337/8 (2 CD-Set).

NOTE: Despite the indications of many other sources including Dan Mather's Charlie Barnet biography, the above recording session was Marmarosa's only return to Barnet. He was not with Barnet at the Casa Mañana (May-June 1944) as claimed by Charles Garrod's Barnet-discography and Raben's

Jazz Records, not on Barnet's V-Disc session (July 13 & 21, 1944) as claimed by Richard S. Sears' V-Disc-discography, nor with Barnet on the soundtrack for the Universal music featurette "Melody Parade", which was produced in Hollywood during summer 1944 (claimed among others by Scott Yanow's "Jazz On Film"). Marmarosa remained with Dorsey in Hollywood until the mid of October 1944. He was not with Barnet in New York City for a V-Disc recording session (September 11, 1944) as claimed by Garrod and Sears, nor at the Barnet Decca-recording date (October 17, 1944) as claimed by all other sources, including Garrod, Jepsen, and MCA cover information. Only Loren Schoenberg (liner notes to MCA CD GRP 16122) states correctly that on October 17, 1944 Marty Napoleon played piano.

Stylistic comparisons undoubtfully make clear that the pianist of Barnet's Casa Mañana-broadcasts is not Marmarosa and that from the July 13, 1944 V-Disc session on as well as on the soundtrack for "Melody Parade" Marty Napoleon played piano with Barnet.

NOTE: As already mentioned (see "note" for July 15, 1944), the Dorsey Orchestra worked on the music stage for M-G-M's musical comedy "Thrill Of A Romance" in July/August 1944. Some of the "pre-recordings" had probably been finished until early August.

At this time Dorsey's short tempered nature got him into one of the biggest scandals of his life. For the night of August 5 he hand his wife had invited guests to their apartment in Hollywood. Towards the end of the party an argument with the actor Jon Hall about Dorsey's wife developed into a scuffle during which Hall was injured by someone with a knife. When it became apparent that the case would finish up in court, M-G-M in fear of negative publicity dissociated from Dorsey for a while, and there were even rumours, that the studios intended to take parts of the Dorsey band sequences out of the film again. As a consequence a few titles for the soundtrack were recorded after the above mentioned short phase of resentment between Dorsey and the studios (see September 11 and 28, 1944). The completed movie picture was finally released in 1945 showing several scenes of the Dorsey band in all of which Dodo Marmarosa is present.

This proves wrong several sources on the film, who give other pianists instead of Marmarosa. So Mel Tormé in his biography of Buddy Rich ("Traps, The Drum Wonder - The Life Of Buddy Rich"), who remembers a jam session scene of the film: "with a few Dorsey men participating, among them Buddy DeFranco on clarinet and Milt Golden on piano", or Scott Yanow in his newer publication "Jazz On Film", who identifies Joe Bushkin, Dorsey's pianist of the 1940-1942 years, for "Thrill Of A Romance."

TOMMY DORSEY
AND HIS ORCHESTRA

AFRS "DOWN BEAT"
RADIO BROADCAST

band personnel approximately similar as on Tommy Dorsey's NBC Radio broadcasts from this period

<u>August (?) 1944, Hollywood, Calif.</u>

HAWAIIAN WAR CHANT ( )	AFRS Downbeat No. 96
TOP HAT, WHITE TIE, AND TAILS ( )	–
INDIAN SUMMER (BAv) ( )	–
LOSERS WEEPERS ( )	–
BLUE SKIES (BA & TSv) ( )	–
SONG OF INDIA ( )	–
WELL, GIT IT! ( )	–
MARGIE (TSv) ( )	–
WHISPERING (BLWv) ( )	–
THE MINOR GOES A-MUGGIN' ( )	–

Note :

The AFRS "Down Beat" program series featured half hour compilations of recorded music by one band, usually taken from various commercial or AFRS sources. The final program releases contained separately transcribed spoken introductions to the chosen titles by the leader of the featured band and an AFRS announcer in conversation, which gave the program the effect of a disk jockey discussing music with an invited studio guest.

The above program may have been compiled from earlier 1944-recordings with the participation of Marmarosa. TOP HAT, WHITE TIE, AND TAILS possibly stems from the June 25, 1944 "All Time Hit Parade" rehearsal.

TOMMY DORSEY AND HIS ORCHESTRA

YOUR ALL TIME HIT PARADE NBC RADIO BROADCAST

Dodo Marmarosa with Tommy Dorsey's orchestra as on July 30, 1944. Sophie Tucker (voc) appears as guest star

<u>August 6, 1944, Hollywood, Calif., NBC studios</u>

	dress rehearsal:	
VP 879	CHICAGO (TSv) (/)	V-Disc 322
	WAGON WHEELS (/)	BML P-348
VP 921	SOME OF THESE DAYS (Sophie Tucker -voc) ( )	unissued
VP 936	SOME OF THESE DAYS (Sophie Tucker -voc) (/)	V-Disc 358
	TOGETHER (BLW & BAv) ( )	unissued V-Disc
VP 891	SMOKE GETS IN YOUR EYES (/)	V-Disc 391

broadcast (4:00 to 4:30 PM):	
THEME (I'M GETTING SENTIMENTAL OVER YOU) (/)	
	AFRS All Time Hit Parade No. 43
CHICAGO (TSv) (/)	–
TOGETHER (BLW & BAv) (/)	–
I'LL BE SEEING YOU (TSv) (/)	–
WAGON WHEELS (/)	–
SOME OF THESE DAYS (Sophie Tucker -voc) (/)	–
SMOKE GETS IN YOUR EYES (/)	–
THEME (I'M GETTING SENTIMENTAL OVER YOU) (/)	–

Note :

AFRS "All Time Hit Parade" transcription No. 43 also contained dubbed in versions of LITTLE WHITE LIES and BODY AND SOUL (both broadcast takes from the July 23, 1944 show).

The title TOGETHER was planned for release on V-Disc, but not issued.

SOME OF THESE DAYS probably as a second dress rehearsal take on V-Disc 358.

TOGETHER and WAGON WHEELS (broadcast takes) were also dubbed in on AFRS "All Time Hit Parade" transcription No. 48 (see September 10, 1944 below).

SMOKE GETS IN YOUR EYES (broadcast take) was also used for AFRS "All Time Hit Parade" transcription No. 47 (see September 3, 1944 below).

CHICAGO and SMOKE GETS IN YOUR EYES (dress rehearsal takes) also on AFRS Down Beat program No. 106.

CD reissues:

CHICAGO and SMOKE GETS IN YOUR EYES (dress rehearsal takes) reissued on Jazz&Jazz CD JJ-614 and "V-Discs: Tommy Dorsey".

CHICAGO as dress rehearsal take also on Hep CD 40.

<u>NOTE</u>:   The AFRS "One Night Stand" series contain a program No. 321 from August 8, 1944, normally ascribed in discographies to Tommy Dorsey and his Orchestra. Except for two titles, however, none of the tunes of the program appears again in the Dorsey bandbook, neither before nor after this broadcast. As Harry Mackenzie and Lothar Polomski in their "One Night Stand Series"-Discography point out, the program is more typical of Freddy Martin's "One Night Stand" broadcasts of the period, with at least five of the titles of "ONS" 321 having been regularly played by Martin in 1944. Although nobody seems to have been able to check the program and clear this point definitely, we believe this broadcast to be not by Dorsey.

TOMMY DORSEY   YOUR ALL TIME HIT PARADE
AND HIS ORCHESTRA   NBC RADIO BROADCAST

Mickey Mangano, George Seaberg, Dale Pearce, Cappy Lewis (tp), Tommy Dorsey (tb,arr), Walter "Red" Benson, Nelson Riddle, Tex Satterwhite (tb), Joe Park (tuba), Buddy DeFranco (cl,as), Sid Cooper (as), Gail Curtis, Al Klink (ts), Bruce Branson (bs), Dodo Marmarosa (p), Bob Bain (g), Sid Block (b), Buddy Rich (dm), Doris Briggs (harp) plus strings, Bonnie Lou Williams, Bob Allen, The Sentimentalists (voc), add Judy Garland (voc) as guest star

<u>August 13, 1944, Hollywood, Calif., NBC studios</u>

dress rehearsal:

VP 886	OVER THE RAINBOW (JG -voc) (/)	V-Disc 335
VP 886	I MAY BE WRONG (JG -voc) (/)	V-Disc 335
	WHAT IS THIS THING CALLED LOVE (BLWv) (/)	Hep CD 39
	ON THE SUNNY SIDE OF THE STREET (TSv) (/)	AFRS Down Beat No. 106
	APRIL IN PARIS (/)	BML P-256

broadcast (4:00 to 4:30 PM):

OVER THE RAINBOW (JG -voc) ( )	AFRS All Time Hit Parade No. 44
I MAY BE WRONG (JG -voc) ( )	–
I'LL BE SEEING YOU (BAv) ( )	–
WHAT IS THIS THING CALLED LOVE (BLWv) ( )	–
ON THE SUNNY SIDE OF THE STREET (TSv) (/)	–
APRIL IN PARIS (/)	–
ROSE OF NO MAN'S LAND ( )	–

Note :
Some sources add a further title SWANEE RIVER to this program, which stems from an earlier broadcast. There is a short piano solo on this title, which is played not by Marmarosa (see following 'Note' below). SWANEE RIVER is released on RCA NL 45154 (LP).
ON THE SUNNY SIDE OF THE STREET (broadcast take, but introduction and first eight bars edited out) and APRIL IN PARIS (broadcast take) also used for AFRS "All Time Hit Parade" transcription No. 49 (see September 17, 1944 below).
ON THE SUNNY SIDE OF THE STREET (dress rehearsal take) used also for AFRS Down Beat program No.106
CD reissues:
ON THE SUNNY SIDE OF THE STREET (dress rehearsal take) reissued on Jazz&Jazz CD JJ-614.
OVER THE RAINBOW (dress rehearsal take) is reissued as V-Disc 335 on VJC-1043.

I MAY BE WRONG, WHAT IS THIS THING CALLED LOVE, ON THE SUNNY SIDE OF THE STREET, and APRIL IN PARIS as dress rehearsal takes also on Hep CD 39.

<u>NOTE</u>: There is some confusion about Dodo Marmarosa's participation on the above and the following broadcasts to be found in discographies and reissue-sleeve notes.

RCA NL 45154 liner notes give Milt Golden (p) for the one title SWANEE RIVER, released on RCA NL 45154 (see 'note' above) as from August 13, 1944. The band personnel given for this reissue, however, is identical to the personnel of the RCA-Victor studio recording session from November 14, 1944 and seems to have been anticipated by the compiler for the above date.

Raben (*Jazz Records*) and Lord (*Jazz Discography*) may have relied on this doubtful source, for they give Milt Golden (p) with Dorsey for subsequent "Your All Time Hit Parade" broadcasts from the above date on, although Raben expresses some doubt about SWANEE RIVER belonging originally to the above program. The performance of this title itself has trumpet and tenor saxophone solos by Ziggy Elman and Don Lodice and a short piano solo possibly by Milt Raskin, which would make a recording date in 1942 most likely.

Hep CD reissues and Sears (*V-Discs*) still give Marmarosa for the "Your All Time Hit Parade" programs until at least September 24, 1944. Stylistical comparisons help to confirm that Marmarosa definitely is the pianist for all titles given above on the August 13 program and that he continued to play with Dorsey until the mid of October 1944.

In mid-August 1944 a series of several jazz and dance music concerts was held at the Los Angeles Philharmonic Auditorium to raise funds for the L. A. Philharmonic Orchestra, which was in serious financial troubles during that season. According to the September 1944 issue of *Capitol News from Hollywood* among the bands who helped to save the orchestra were those of Henry King, Kay Kyser, Harry James, and Tommy Dorsey.

TOMMY DORSEY AND HIS ORCHESTRA

YOUR ALL TIME HIT PARADE NBC RADIO BROADCAST

band personnel similar as before, Phil Harris (voc) appears as guest star

<u>August 20, 1944, Hollywood, Calif., NBC studios</u>

	dress rehearsal:	
	I'M NOBODY'S BABY (BLWv) (/)	BML P-202
	AMOR (/)	Hep CD 39
	LOVER, COME BACK TO ME (/)	BML SP-42
VP 1289	THAT'S WHAT I LIKE ABOUT THE SOUTH (PH -voc) (/)	
		V-Disc 477
VP 891	SWEETHEART OF SIGMA CHI (TSv) (/)	V-Disc 391

broadcast (4:00 to 4:30 PM):	
I'M NOBODY'S BABY (BLWv) ( )	AFRS All Time Hit Parade No. 45
ALL THE THINGS YOU ARE (BAv) ( )	–
AMOR (/)	–
LOVER, COME BACK TO ME (/)	–
THAT'S WHAT I LIKE ABOUT THE SOUTH (PH -voc) ( )	–
SWEETHEART OF SIGMA CHI (TSv) ( )	–

Note :

Dress rehearsal take of THAT'S WHAT I LIKE ABOUT THE SOUTH also used for BML P-202.

Dress rehearsal take of SWEETHEART OF SIGMA CHI also used for BML P-145.

LOVER, COME BACK TO ME as broadcast take also used on AFRS "All Time Hit Parade" transcription No. 49, AMOR as broadcast take also used on AFRS "All Time Hit Parade" transcription No. 50 (see September 17 and 24, 1944 below).

I'M NOBODY'S BABY on AFRS Down Beat program No. 106 is most certainly the dress rehearsal take from the above "Your All Time Hit Parade" show.

CD reissues:

I'M NOBODY'S BABY (dress rehearsal take) also reissued on Jazz&Jazz CD JJ-614.

AMOR and LOVER, COME BACK TO ME as dress rehearsal takes also on Hep CD 39.

SWEETHEART OF SIGMA CHI (dress rehearsal take) as V-Disc 391 also on "V-Discs: Tommy Dorsey".

TOMMY DORSEY	**YOUR ALL TIME HIT PARADE**
AND HIS ORCHESTRA	**NBC RADIO BROADCAST**

band personnel similar as before, Fanny Brice and Hanley Stafford appeared as guest stars

<u>August 27, 1944, Hollywood, Calif., NBC studios</u>

dress rehearsal:

CHEEK TO CHEEK (/)	BML P-319
I'LL BE SEEING YOU (TSv) (/)	Hep CD 39
EAST OF THE SUN (BAv) (/)	BML P-145
EMBRACEABLE YOU (/)	Hep CD 39

broadcast (4:00 to 4:30 PM):

THEME (All Time Hit Parade Signature) (/)	AFRS All Time Hit Parade No. 46
THEME (I'M GETTING SENTIMENTAL OVER YOU) (/)	–
CHEEK TO CHEEK (/)	–
YOU'RE A SWEETHEART (BLWv) (/)	–
I'LL BE SEEING YOU (TSv) (/)	–
EAST OF THE SUN (BAv) (/)	–
EMBRACEABLE YOU ( )	–

Note :

The title EAST OF THE SUN was planned also for release on V-Disc, but was not issued as such.

EAST OF THE SUN and YOU'RE A SWEETHEART as broadcast takes also used on AFRS "All Time Hit Parade" transcription No. 50 (see September 24, 1944 below).

CD reissue:

CHEEK TO CHEEK, I'LL BE SEEING YOU, EAST OF THE SUN, and EMBRACEABLE YOU as dress rehearsal takes also on on Hep CD 39.

TOMMY DORSEY   YOUR ALL TIME HIT PARADE
AND HIS ORCHESTRA   NBC RADIO BROADCAST

band personnel similar as before, George Burns and Gracie Allen appeared as guest stars

<u>September 3, 1944, Hollywood, Calif., NBC studios</u>

dress rehearsal:
THE LADY IN RED (TSv) (/)   BML P-162
BLUE ORCHIDS (BAv) ( )   BML P-348

broadcast (4:00 to 4:30 PM):
THEME (All Time Hit Parade Signature) (/)   AFRS All Time Hit Parade No. 47
THEME (I'M GETTING SENTIMENTAL OVER YOU) (/)   –
THE LADY IN RED (TSv) (/)   –
BLUE ORCHIDS (BAv) (/)   –
I'LL BE SEEING YOU (BLWv) (/)   –
WHO (BAv) (/)   –
EASY TO LOVE (/)   –
THEME (I'M GETTING SENTIMENTAL OVER YOU) (/)   –
THEME (All Time Hit Parade Signature) (/)   –

Note :

AFRS "All Time Hit Parade" transcription No. 47 also contained dubbed in versions of SMOKE GETS IN YOUR EYES (broadcast take from the August 6, 1944 show), WHISPERING (broadcast take from the July 9, 1944 show), and THE LAMP IS LOW (broadcast take from the July 30, 1944 show, a shortened performance of the usually played arrangement of this title).

The title BLUE ORCHIDS was planned for release on V-Disc, but not issued as such.

THE LADY IN RED as dress rehearsal take also used for AFRS Down Beat program No. 106.

CD reissues:

THE LADY IN RED as dress rehearsal take also on Jazz&Jazz CD JJ-614 and "V-Discs: Tommy Dorsey".

TOMMY DORSEY AND HIS ORCHESTRA   V-DISC RECORDING SESSION

band personnel similar as before

<u>September 8, 1944, Los Angeles, Calif.</u>

VP 943	FOR ALL WE KNOW (BAv) (/)	V-Disc 347
VP 943	THE LADY IN RED (TSv) (/)	–
VP 999	I'M NOBODY'S BABY (BLWv) (/)	V-Disc-362
VP 999	THREE LITTLE WORDS (/)	–

CD reissues:

All titles also on Hep CD 40.

I'M NOBODY'S BABY and THREE LITTLE WORDS also on "V-Discs: Tommy Dorsey".

The versions of FOR ALL WE KNOW and THE LADY IN RED reissued on this same CD-set do not stem from the above V-Disc recording session, as one might expect, but from the dress rehearsals of the "Your All Time Hit Parade" shows of Sept. 10, 1944 (FOR ALL WE KNOW) and Sept. 3, 1944 (THE LADY IN RED).

TOMMY DORSEY   **YOUR ALL TIME HIT PARADE**
AND HIS ORCHESTRA   **NBC RADIO BROADCAST**

---

band personnel similar as before, Martha Raye (voc) appears as guest star

September 10, 1944, Hollywood, Calif., NBC studios

	dress rehearsal:	
	FOR ALL WE KNOW (BAv) (/)	BML P-162
VP 921	SHUT MY MOUTH (MR -voc) (/)	BML P-256
	DANCING IN THE DARK (/)	Hep CD 39

broadcast (4:00 to 4:30 PM):
THEME (I'M GETTING SENTIMENTAL OVER YOU) (/)

AFRS All Time Hit Parade No. 48

CRAZY RHYTHM (TSv) (/)	–
FOR ALL WE KNOW (BAv) (/)	–
I'LL BE SEEING YOU (MR -voc) (/)	–
THREE LITTLE WORDS (/)	–
SHUT MY MOUTH (MR -voc) (/)	–
DANCING IN THE DARK (/)	–
THEME (ALL TIME HIT PARADE SIGNATURE) (/)	–

Note :

AFRS "All Time Hit Parade" transcription No. 48 also contained dubbed in versions of WAGON WHEELS and TOGETHER (both broadcast takes from the August 6, 1944 show) and LITTLE WHITE LIES (broadcast take from the July 23, 1944 show).

FOR ALL WE KNOW and SHUT MY MOUTH (dress rehearsal takes) were both planned for release on V-Disc, but not issued as such.

CD reissues:

FOR ALL WE KNOW as dress rehearsal take also on "V-Discs: Tommy Dorsey".

DANCING IN THE DARK as dress rehearsal take also on Hep CD 39.

TOMMY DORSEY AND HIS ORCHESTRA   M-G-M
SOUNDTRACK RECORDINGS

Mickey Mangano, George Seaberg, Dale Pearce, Cappy Lewis, Sal La Perche (tp), Tommy Dorsey (tb,arr), Walter "Red" Benson, Nelson Riddle, Tex Satterwhite (tb), Joe Park (tuba), Buddy DeFranco (cl,as), Sid Cooper (as), Gail Curtis, Al Klink (ts), Bruce Branson (bs), Dodo Marmarosa (p), Bob Bain (g), Sid Block (b), Buddy Rich (dm), Doris Briggs (harp) plus strings, Bonnie Lou Williams, Bob Allen, The Sentimentalists (voc)

<u>September 11, 1944 (10:50 AM to 12:58 PM and 2:00 to 6:24 PM),</u>
<u>Culver City, Los Angeles, Calif., M-G-M studios</u>

	IF I HAD YOU (/)	Rhino R 2 75283 (CD)
	DeFranco, Marmarosa, Block, and Rich only:	
2044	BATTLE OF THE BALCONY JIVE (s)	Rhino R 2 75283 (CD)

Note:

The above titles were recorded for the M-G-M musical comedy "Thrill Of A Romance" (see "note" for July 15, 1944 and August 5, 1944).

BATTLE OF THE BALCONY JIVE, given by all sources as "unidentified rhythm number", is a composition by Dodo Marmarosa. The title of the tune seems to be a slightly sarcastic reference by Marmarosa to the aforementioned Dorsey-incident (see August 1944), which was dubbed "Battle of the Balcony" by the public prints (DOWN BEAT of September 1, 1944).

An A.F.M. daily return for the above soundtrack recording of BATTLE OF THE BALCONY JIVE (kindly conveyed by Ken Seavor) lists a personnel comprising Cappy Lewis (tp), Tommy Dorsey (tb), Joe Park (tuba), Buddy DeFranco (cl), Al Klink (ts), Dodo Marmarosa (p), Sid Block (b), Buddy Rich (d), and Manny Fiddler (vl). The title, however, as it has been reissued by Rhino records, is played by the quartet only (see above). On screen the extended personnel given by the A.F.M. return is joining in for the final chord on BATTLE OF THE BALCONY JIVE and accompanying the subsequently following drinking song VIVE L'AMOUR, sung by opera tenor Lauritz Melchior and a male vocal ensemble. In the A.F.M. file, however, there is no indication of the recording of this title on the above session.

Both Rhino reissues are complete versions of the originally recorded titles before editing for the film and dubbing of dialogue.

LP reissue:

BATTLE OF THE BALCONY JIVE has also been reissued on Joyce LP-3006 as "Rhythm Number". This is an edited version from the final soundtrack, which differs in various ways from the above take: the opening theme and part of the piano solo of the above performance are cut off, and it has a different drum solo and a different ending with Dorsey and a few band members joining in for the final chord (see also re-recording of the title on September 28, 1944).

The above take is a complete version with opening theme, uncut solos and a coda by the quartet only.

TOMMY DORSEY	**YOUR ALL TIME HIT PARADE**
AND HIS ORCHESTRA	**NBC RADIO BROADCAST**

band personnel similar as before, but delete Sal La Perche (tp), Frank Sinatra (voc) appears as guest star

<u>September 17, 1944, Hollywood, Calif., NBC studios</u>

dress rehearsal:

I'VE GOT RINGS ON MY FINGER (TSv) (/)	BML P-175
I CAN'T GIVE YOU ANYTHING BUT LOVE (BLWv) (/)	BML P-202
I'LL WALK ALONE (FS -voc) (/)	BML P-175
SOUTH OF THE BORDER (/)	BML P-175
IF YOU ARE BUT A DREAM (FS -voc) (/)	Hep CD 39
SUMMERTIME (/)	Hep CD 39

broadcast (4:00 to 4:30 PM):

THEME (ALL TIME HIT PARADE SIGNATURE) (/)	
	AFRS All Time Hit Parade No. 49
THEME (I'M GETTING SENTIMENTAL OVER YOU) (/)	–
I'VE GOT RINGS ON MY FINGER (TSv) (/)	–
I CAN'T GIVE YOU ANYTHING BUT LOVE (BLWv) (/)	–
I'LL WALK ALONE (FS -voc) (/)	–
SOUTH OF THE BORDER (/)	–
IF YOU ARE BUT A DREAM (FS -voc) (/)	–
SUMMERTIME (/)	–
THEME (I'M GETTING SENTIMENTAL OVER YOU) (/)	–

Note :

AFRS "All Time Hit Parade" transcription No. 49 also contained dubbed in versions of LOVER, COME BACK TO ME (broadcast take from the August 20, 1944 show), APRIL IN PARIS (broadcast take from the August 13, 1944 show), and ON THE SUNNY SIDE OF THE STREET (broadcast take from the August 13, 1944 show with introduction and first eight bars edited out).

IF YOU ARE BUT A DREAM was planned for release on V-Disc, but not issued.

CD reissue:

I CAN'T GIVE YOU ANYTHING BUT LOVE, I'LL WALK ALONE, SOUTH OF THE BORDER, IF YOU ARE BUT A DREAM, and SUMMERTIME as dress rehearsal takes also on Hep CD 39.

TOMMY DORSEY   **YOUR ALL TIME HIT PARADE**
AND HIS ORCHESTRA   **NBC RADIO BROADCAST**

band personnel similar as before, Eddie Cantor (voc) appears as guest star

<u>September 24, 1944, Hollywood, Calif., NBC studios</u>

dress rehearsal:

VP 936   HOW YOU GONNA KEEP 'EM DOWN ON THE FARM (EC -voc) (/)

                                                           V-Disc 358

         SONG OF INDIA (/)   Hep CD 39

         I'LL NEVER SMILE AGAIN (BA&TSv) (/)   BML P-175

broadcast (4:00 to 4:30 PM):

         HOW YOU GONNA KEEP 'EM DOWN ON THE FARM (EC -voc) (/)

                                         AFRS All Time Hit Parade No. 50

         SONG OF INDIA (/)   –

         I'LL NEVER SMILE AGAIN (BA&TSv) (/)   –

         I'LL WALK ALONE (BLWv) (/)   –

         I'M GONNA SIT RIGHT DOWN AND WRITE MYSELF A LETTER

                                                     (ECv) (/)   –

         SMOKE GETS IN YOUR EYES (/)   –

         THEME (I'M GETTING SENTIMENTAL OVER YOU) (/)   –

Note :

The above program was the last in a series of 15 "Your All Time Hit Parade" shows featuring the Tommy Dorsey Orchestra.

AFRS "All Time Hit Parade" transcription No. 50 also contained dubbed in versions of AMOR (broadcast take from the August 20, 1944 show), EAST OF THE SUN and YOU'RE A SWEETHEART (both broadcast takes from the August 27, 1944 show).

CD reissue:

SONG OF INDIA and I'LL NEVER SMILE AGAIN as dress rehearsal takes also on Hep CD 39.

TOMMY DORSEY AND HIS ORCHESTRA

M-G-M SOUNDTRACK RECORDINGS

Sal La Perche (tp), Tommy Dorsey (tb), Buddy DeFranco (cl), Al Klink (ts), Dodo Marmarosa (p), Sid Block (b), Buddy Rich (d)

<u>September 28, 1944, (1:00 to 2:15 PM), Culver City, Los Angeles, Calif., M-G-M studios</u>

unknown titles, possibly:
BATTLE OF THE BALCONY JIVE: Coda [?] (/)

Note :

The date of the above recording session was kindly conveyed by Ken Seavor from data researched for his forthcoming Tommy Dorsey discography.

Information on the above session comes from an A.F.M daily return, which only gives recording date and personnel, but no titles. The recording personnel, however, hints at a scene of the M-G-M musical comedy "Thrill Of A Romance", which shows a hotel bar scenery and DeFranco, Marmarosa, Block, and Rich performing the title BATTLE OF THE BALCONY JIVE. While the nucleus of this title was recorded with the quartet only (see September 11, 1944), the final soundtrack version has Dorsey and a few of his horn players joining in for the final chord. This addition probably was recorded on the above date using a method, which transcribed the music directly from the ongoing scene on the set and thus avoided any possible discrepancies between the acting of the musicians and the usual playback of the pre-recorded soundtrack. The final soundtrack performance of the title is an edited version combining material of the September 11, 1944 and the above recording session.

Trumpeter Sal La Perche, who already had left Dorsey in June 1944, obviously returned for M-G-M screening dates only (see also September 11, 1944).

Possibly also a solo-piano sequence by Marmarosa was recorded on the above date. It served as a background music fill between the two musical numbers staged in the above mentioned bar scenery.

For the final sequence of Dorsey's musical scenes in "Thrill Of A Romance" see the following entry.

<u>NOTE</u>:   Not all the titles recorded by the Dorsey band for the soundtrack of the M-G-M movie "THRILL OF A ROMANCE" have been reissued on LP or CD, coupled with exact recording documentation. We have therefore included once more a comprehensive listing of all soundtrack titles in which the orchestra or some of its members participated, although some of the titles have already been listed under the date of their recording (see July 20, July 29, September 11, and September 28, 1944). Contrary to their reissues on Rhino CD's the below listing refers to edited versions of all titles in the order in which they appear on the soundtrack.

TOMMY DORSEY AND HIS ORCHESTRA   M-G-M
SOUNDTRACK RECORDINGS

Mickey Mangano, George Seaberg, Dale Pearce, Cappy Lewis, Sal La Perche (tp), Tommy
Dorsey (tb,arr), Walter "Red" Benson, Nelson Riddle, Tex Satterwhite (tb), Joe Park (tuba),
Buddy DeFranco (cl,as), Sid Cooper (as), Gail Curtis, Al Klink (ts), Bruce Branson (bs),
Dodo Marmarosa (p), Bob Bain (g), Sid Block (b), Buddy Rich (dm), Doris Briggs (harp)
plus strings, Bonnie Lou Williams, Bob Allen, Sentimentalists (voc) add Lauritz Melchior,
Helene Stanley and Jerry Scott (voc)

July - September 1944, Culver City, Los Angeles, Calif., M-G-M studios

OPENING MEDLEY (Lauritz Melchior -voc) (/)	unissued (on LP or CD)
SONG OF INDIA (/) (background music)	Rhino R 2 75283 (CD)*
I SHOULD CARE (BLW & TSv) (/) (background music)	unissued (on LP or CD)
YOU DEAR (/) (background music)	Rhino R 2 75283 (CD)*

Dodo Marmarosa leaves piano chair to Helene Stanley :
THE GUY WITH THE SLIDE TROMBONE (Helene Stanley -voc)

Rhino R 2 75283 (CD)*

Marmarosa (p) again for Stanley :

IF I HAD YOU (part only) (/) (background music)	Rhino R 2 75283 (CD)*
I SHOULD CARE (BAv) (/) (background music)	Rhino R 2 75283 (CD)*

Dodo Marmarosa leaves piano chair again to Helene Stanley :
JEG ELSKER DIG (Lauritz Melchior -voc)   unissued (on LP or CD)

Marmarosa (p) again for Stanley :

PLEASE DON'T SAY NO (Jerry Scott -voc) (/)	unissued (on LP or CD)
BECAUSE (Jerry Scott -voc) (/)	unissued (on LP or CD)

DeFranco, Marmarosa, Block, and Rich only, plus "a few Dorsey men" in the coda :
BATTLE OF THE BALCONY JIVE (s)   Joyce LP-3006

Dodo Marmarosa (p-solo) :
improvised solo sequence of some 50 bars (background music)

unissued (on LP or CD)

DeFranco, Marmarosa, Block, Rich , and T. Dorsey plus a few band members :
VIVE L'AMOUR (Lauritz Melchior & chorus -voc) (/)   unissued (on LP or CD)

full orchestra again :
PLEASE DON'T SAY NO (Lauritz Melchior & chorus -voc) (/)

unissued (on LP or CD)

Note:

The soundtrack contains more musical numbers, in which the Dorsey orchestra does not participate.

Preceding PLEASE DON'T SAY NO (first version) the above soundtrack also contains a rendition of OPUS ONE by the Dorsey orchestra. This is an edited re-use of the version recorded but not used for the soundtrack of the M-G-M comedy "Broadway Rhythm". The recording date is June 25, 1943 and the piano solo is by Milt Raskin. The complete title can be found on Rhino CD R2 75283.

THE GUY WITH THE SLIDE TROMBONE is an adaptation from Franz Liszt's HUNGARIAN RHAPSODY No. 2 for piano solo.

The vocal of Helene Stanley on THE GUY WITH THE SLIDE TROMBONE may be dubbed by another singer, but most certainly not Bonnie Lou Williams as is suggested by most sources.

JEG ELSKER DIG (aka I LOVE YOU) is No. 3 of Edvard Grieg's songs op. 5.

BATTLE OF THE BALCONY JIVE reissued as "RHYTHM NUMBER" on Joyce LP-3006.

* All Rhino reissues are complete versions of "pre-recorded" titles before editing for the film and dubbing of dialogue. Rhino CD R 2 75283 gives soundtrack recording dates July 20, 1944 for SONG OF INDIA and YOU DEAR, July 20 and 28 for THE GUY WITH THE SLIDE TROMBONE (without Marmarosa), July 29 for I SHOULD CARE, and September 11 for IF I HAD YOU and BATTLE OF THE BALCONY JIVE.

For the end of September 1944 the following engagement of the Dorsey Orchestra was listed in the trade papers:

September 29 - October 1, 1944   : Ocean Park, Calif., Casino Gardens

TOMMY DORSEY AND HIS ORCHESTRA   NBC RADIO BROADCAST

band personnel probably same as on September 24, 1944 broadcast

<u>October 1, 1944, Ocean Park, Calif., Casino Gardens</u>

THEME (I'M GETTING SENTIMENTAL OVER YOU) ( )
OPUS ONE ( )
THE BELLS OF NORMANDY (BA&TSv) ( )
IT'S A CRYING SHAME (BLWv) ( )
SWINGIN' ON A STAR ( )
I DREAM OF YOU (BAv) ( )
AMOR ( )
WELL, GIT IT! (s)
THEME (I'M GETTING SENTIMENTAL OVER YOU) ( )

Note:
The above represents one of Tommy Dorsey's regular broadcasts from the Casino Gardens ballroom. It was aired over the NBC net and simultaneously transcribed to allow rebroadcast on the East Coast with the necessary time-shift, a practice used by NBC most certainly on more broadcasts by Dorsey and other bands of the period. Surviving original NBC Electrical Transcription-discs ("ETs") today are preserved in the RCA/BMG archives, mostly without ever having been issued commercially.

CD reissue:
WELL, GIT IT! reissued by Reader's Digest on RC7-007-1/3.

For the next October weekend the following engagement of the Dorsey Orchestra was listed in the trade papers:

<u>October 6 - 8, 1944</u>   : Ocean Park, Calif., Casino Gardens

TOMMY DORSEY
AND HIS ORCHESTRA

FITCH BANDWAGON SHOW
NBC RADIO BROADCAST

band personnel similar as before

<u>October 8, 1944, Hollywood, Calif., NBC studios</u>

unknown titles   AFRS Bandwagon No. 122

Note:

The Tommy Dorsey Orchestra and trombonist/comedian Jerry Colonna appeared as guests on this program.

The reissue of two Dorsey titles on Jass JCD 14 (CHICAGO and IT'S A CRYIN' SHAME) as coming from the above program actually belongs to the Dorsey appearance on the "Fitch Bandwagon Show" of November 19, 1944 (released on AFRS Bandwagon No. 128; information kindly conveyed by Ken Seavor). At that time Dodo Marmarosa had already been replaced by Milt Golden.

Also the discographies of Tom Lord, Erik Raben, and the Tommy Dorsey discography of Garrod/Scott/Green erroneously date the November 19, 1944 "Fitch Bandwagon" Show on October 8.

TOMMY DORSEY   VICTORY PARADE OF SPOTLIGHT BANDS NO. 645
AND HIS ORCHESTRA   RADIO BROADCAST

band personnel similar as before

<u>October 11, 1944 (6:30 to 6:55 PM), Tucson, Arizona, Davis-Monthan Field</u>

THEME (Spotlight Bands signature tune) ( )
I'M GETTING SENTIMENTAL OVER YOU (Theme) ( )
THERE'LL BE A HOT TIME IN THE TOWN OF BERLIN (TSv) (/)
I DREAM OF YOU (BAv) (/)   AFRS Spotlight Bands No. 490
Incidental Music (Flourish) (/)
HEAVENLY (BLWv) (/)   AFRS Spotlight Bands No. 490
THE BELLS OF NORMANDY (BA&TSv) (/)   AFRS Spotlight Bands No. 490
AMOR (BLW&TSv) (/)   AFRS Spotlight Bands No. 490
WELL, GIT IT! ( )   AFRS Spotlight Bands No. 490
THEME (Spotlight Bands signature tune) ( )

Note:

WELL, GIT IT!, I DREAM OF YOU, HEAVENLY, THE BELLS OF NORMANDY, and AMOR in this title order used on AFRS Spotlight Bands No. 490 (15 minutes program). The sequence of titles had been changed by AFRS as compared to the original Victory Parade of Spotlight Bands program given above.

For mid October the following engagement of the Tommy Dorsey Orchestra was listed in the trade papers:

<u>October 13 - 15, 1944</u>   : Ocean Park, Calif., Casino Gardens

---

| **TOMMY DORSEY** | **AFRS "ONE NIGHT STAND"** |
| **AND HIS ORCHESTRA** | **RADIO BROADCAST** |

---

band personnel similar as before

October 14, 1944, Ocean Park, Calif., Casino Gardens

IS YOU IS OR IS YOU AIN'T MY BABY (BLWv) (/)

AFRS One Night Stand No. 391

I DREAM OF YOU (BAv) (/)	–
THREE LITTLE WORDS (/)	–
I'LL WALK ALONE (BLWv) (/)	–
HAWAIIAN WAR CHANT (/)	–
THE BELLS OF NORMANDY (BA&TSv) (/)	–
PARAMOUNT ON PARADE (s)	–

Note:

The AFRS release of the above program contained as sixth title a rendition of YOU'RE MINE YOU, which was dubbed from AFRS One Night Stand program No. 218 (see April 22, 1944) and as last title a rendition of SONG OF INDIA, which was dubbed from AFRS Spotlight Bands program No. 362 (see May 15, 1944).

IS YOU IS OR IS YOU AIN'T MY BABY and THE BELLS OF NORMANDY also used on AFRS One Night Stand program No. 466.

LP reissue:

THREE LITTLE WORDS, I'LL WALK ALONE, and HAWAIIAN WAR CHANT also on Joyce LP-1042.

TOMMY DORSEY AND HIS ORCHESTRA   NBC RADIO BROADCAST

band personnel similar as before

October 22, 1944, Ocean Park, Calif., Casino Gardens

HEAVENLY (BLWv) ( )
I DREAM OF YOU (BAv) ( )
WELL, GIT IT! ( )
THEME (I'M GETTING SENTIMENTAL OVER YOU) ( )

Note:

The above titles form the second part of one of Tommy Dorsey's regular broadcasts from the Casino Gardens ballroom. It was aired over the NBC net and simultaneously transcribed to allow rebroadcast on the East Coast with the necessary time-shift.

The above listing follows information by the RCA/BMG archives, researched and kindly conveyed by Ken Seavor. The remaining titles of the original broadcast are unknown.

TOMMY DORSEY AND HIS ORCHESTRA   NBC RADIO BROADCAST

band personnel similar as before

October 24, 1944, Ocean Park, Calif., Casino Gardens

THEME (I'M GETTING SENTIMENTAL OVER YOU) ( )
THE ONE I LOVE (BA&TSv) ( )
I'LL WALK ALONE (BLWv) ( )
HAWAIIAN WAR CHANT ( )
THE BELLS OF NORMANDY (BA&TSv) ( )

Note:

The above titles form the first part of one of Tommy Dorsey's broadcasts from the Casino Gardens ballroom. It was aired over the NBC net and simultaneously transcribed to allow rebroadcast on the East Coast with the necessary time-shift.

The above listing follows information by the RCA/BMG archives, researched and kindly conveyed by Ken Seavor. Seavor remarks, however, that the date of October 24, 1944, as given by RCA, denotes a Tuesday. The regular schedule for Dorsey's broadcasts from the Casino Gardens foresaw airing on weekends only.

Remaining titles of the original broadcast are unknown.

TOMMY DORSEY AND HIS ORCHESTRA

AFRS "COMMAND PERFORMANCE" RADIO SHOW

probable band personnel:

Mickey Mangano, George Seaberg, Dale Pearce, Cappy Lewis (tp), Tommy Dorsey (tb,arr), Walter „Red" Benson, Nelson Riddle, Tex Satterwhite (tb), Joe Park (tuba), Buddy DeFranco (cl,as), Sid Cooper (as), Gail Curtis, Al Klink (ts), Bruce Branson (bs), Dodo Marmarosa (p), Bob Bain (g), Sid Block (b), Buddy Rich (dm), Doris Briggs (harp) plus strings, Bonnie Lou Williams, The Sentimentalists (voc), add Bob Burns (bazooka) as guest star

late October 1944, Hollywood, Calif.

THEME (I'M GETTING SENTIMENTAL OVER YOU) (/)

AFRS Command Performance No. 149

OPUS ONE (s)   –

Bob Burns (bazooka), Tommy Dorsey (tb), backed by Dorsey's rhythm section:

SWEET SUE (/)   –

full orchestra again:

ON THE SUNNY SIDE OF THE STREET (TSv) (/)   –

WHAT IS THIS THING CALLED LOVE (BLWv) (/)   –

Note :

The "Command Performance" program series had originally been created by the Bureau of Public Relations of the U.S. War department to meet demands of servicing men and women for performances of their favourite artists and bands. In late 1942 AFRS took over production of the series, which was broadcast weekly as a half hour show. The majority of the series' radio programs featured edited transcriptions of the original AFRS "Command Performance" concert shows staged at Hollywood's famous NBC and CBS studios. Some were also completed with or compiled from selections derived from other sources accessible to the AFRS.

The program dates given by Harry Mackenzie in his "Command Performance" discography usually denote the date of mastering. For AFRS Command Performance program No. 149 this was November 7, 1944. As the mastering of the individual programs usually was done about a week after transcription, the above program had most certainly been transcribed in late October 1944. This is corroborated by the presence of Dodo Marmarosa on all titles, who is reported rehearsing with Artie Shaw's new orchestra from November 1, 1944 on (see "Note" for Artie Shaw below). The above program was released in early 1945. There were other musical numbers without the participation of the Dorsey Orchestra. Claudette Colbert acted as "mistress of ceremonies". All titles, except WHAT IS THIS THING CALLED LOVE, also used for AFRS Command Performance program No. 250

TOMMY DORSEY   VICTORY PARADE OF SPOTLIGHT BANDS NO. 662
AND HIS ORCHESTRA   RADIO BROADCAST

band personnel similar as before

<u>October 31, 1944, Stockton, Calif., Ordnance Depot</u>

I DREAM OF YOU (BAv) (/)	AFRS Spotlight Bands No. 507
HEAVENLY (BLWv) (/)	–
THE BELLS OF NORMANDY (BA&TSv) (/)	–
TOGETHER (BLW&BAv) (/)	–
MIDRIFF (/)	–
STRAIGHTEN UP AND FLY RIGHT (TSv) ( )	–

Note :

Additional titles of the original Coca Cola Spotlight Bands broadcast program (25 minutes duration) unknown.
Ken Seavor assumes the title STRAIGHTEN UP AND FLY RIGHT to have also been performed on the above
program.
Titles as above, except STRAIGHTEN UP AND FLY RIGHT, used on AFRS Spotlight Bands No. 507 (15
minutes duration) with no opening theme. Closing theme (Spotlight Bands signature tune) on AFRS release
played by other band than Dorsey's.

<u>NOTE</u>:   According to Ross Russell, owner of DIAL records and one of the later promoters of Dodo Marmarosa's recording career, the pianist left Dorsey after an engagement at the Casino Gardens in Ocean Park, California (liner notes to Spotlite LP SPJ-128). In fall 1944 the Dorsey band played there throughout the month of October. Marmarosa's presence on the orchestra's "Spotlight Bands" performance still on October 31 suggests the assumption, that he continued to play with Dorsey until the very end of October 1944 and quit thereafter.

For Tommy Dorsey's first RCA-Victor date after the recording ban (November 14, 1944) Dodo Marmarosa had definitely been replaced by Milt Golden, a capable and highly talented Californian pianist who was tragically killed in a car accident at the age of 30 in August 1946.

In September 1944 **Artie Shaw** was reported to start rehearsals for a new orchestra, after being discharged from the Navy. Rumors that Kay Starr, Dave Matthews, Johnny Guarnieri, and Buddy Rich would be in the personnel proved as premature, for in October 1944 *Metronome* magazine stated that the band was still in the "paper" stage and Rich definitely had to stay with Dorsey because of his contract. The November 1944 *Metronome* issue reported that Shaw "*after several in-the-flesh rehearsals has welded together a crack combination*", (trumpet, two trombonists, and alto still missing). Of Dodo Marmarosa, who is now listed in the personnel, is said that he "*quit Tommy Dorsey*". Finally *Down Beat* of November 1, 1944 reported: "*Artie Shaw's band will go into rehearsal November 1.*" Added is the following band route information:

beginning ca. mid November 1944   : "two weeks of one-nighters"

ARTIE SHAW AND HIS ORCHESTRA   RCA-VICTOR
RECORDING SESSION

Roy Eldridge, Ray Linn, Jimmy Pupa, George Schwartz (tp), Ray Conniff, Harry Rodgers (tb,arr), Pat McNaughton, Chuck W. Coolidge (tb), Artie Shaw (cl,arr), Les Clark (Goldberg), Tommy Mace (as), Jon Walton, Herbie Steward (ts), Chuck Gentry (bs), Dodo Marmarosa (p), Barney Kessel (g), Morris Rayman (b), Louis Fromm (dm), Imogene Lynn (voc), Harry Rodgers, Johnny Thompson, Jimmy Mundy, Ray Conniff (arr)

November 22/23, 1944 (10:30 PM to 3:00 AM), Hollywood, Calif.

D4VB 1052-1	AC-CENT-TCHU-ATE THE POSITIVE (/) (ILv)	Victor 20-1612
D4VB 1053-1	LADY DAY (/)	Victor 20-1620
D4VB 1054-1	LET'S TAKE THE LONG WAY HOME (ILv) (/)	–
D4VB 1055-1	JUMPIN' ON THE MERRY-GO-ROUND (s)	Victor 20-1612

LP reissue:

All titles also on Bluebird AXM2-5579.

CD reissues:

LADY DAY and JUMPIN' also on RCA CD ND 89914.

All titles also on Hep CD 70(3) and Classics CD 1242.

For the time from the end of November 1944 until early January 1945 the following engagements of the Artie Shaw Orchestra were listed in the trade papers:

November 23 - 26, 1944	: San Diego, Calif., Pacific Square Ballroom
December 1 - 7, 1944	: Minneapolis, Minn., Orpheum Theatre
December 8 - 14, 1944	: Chicago, Ill., Chicago Theatre
December 15 - 18, 1944	: Akron, Ohio, Palace Theatre
December 19 - 21, 1944	: Columbus, Ohio, Palace Theatre
December 22 - 28, 1944	: Cleveland, Ohio, Palace Theatre
Dec 29, 1944 - January 4, 1945	: Detroit, Mich., Downtown Theatre

ARTIE SHAW AND HIS ORCHESTRA

RCA-VICTOR RECORDING SESSION

band personnel same as before, except Paul Cohen and Tony Faso (Fazzo) (tp) replace Linn and Pupa; Bobby Sherwood, Ray Conniff, Buster Harding (arr)

January 9, 1945 (1:30 to 9:00 PM), New York City

D5VB 0028-6	I'LL NEVER BE THE SAME (s)	Victor 20-1638
D5VB 0029-11	CAN'T HELP LOVIN' 'DAT MAN (ILv) (/)	Victor 20-1931
D5VB 0030-2	'S WONDERFUL (s)	Victor 20-1638
D5VB 0031-10	BEDFORD DRIVE (/)	Victor 20-1696

Artie Shaw And His Gramercy Five
Roy Eldridge (tp), Artie Shaw (cl), Dodo Marmarosa (p),
Barney Kessel (g), Morris Rayman (b), Lou Fromm (d) :

(recorded from 10:00 PM to 1:00 AM)

D5VB 0032-4	THE GRABTOWN GRAPPLE (s)	Victor 20-1647
D5VB 0033-4	THE SAD SACK (s)	–

Note :

BEDFORD DRIVE was Artie Shaw's home address in Beverly Hills, Calif., where in his garden also the first band rehearsals of his 1944/1945 orchestra took place.

GRABTOWN GRAPPLE was named in honor of Ava Gardner's birthplace Grabtown in North Carolina. Gardner was Artie Shaw's fiancée at the time.

THE SAD SACK originally was titled WHAT HAPPENED TO ACE?, but then was renamed after the comic figure "The Sad Sack", a dumb soldier.

I'll NEVER BE THE SAME and S'WONDERFUL also on V-Disc 412 and BML P-282.

LP reissue:

All six titles also on Bluebird AXM2-5579.

CD reissues:

I'LL NEVER BE THE SAME, 'S WONDERFUL, BEDFORD DRIVE, THE GRABTOWN GRAPPLE, and THE SAD SACK also on RCA CD ND 89914.

THE GRABTOWN GRAPPLE and THE SAD SACK also on Living Era CD-AJS-2007.

All six titles also on Hep CD 70(3) and Classics CD 1242.

According to Vladimir Simosko in his Artie Shaw biography Shaw's band played two more theatre dates during January 1945:

mid January 1945   : Boston, Mass., RKO Theatre
mid January - January 25, 1945   : Philadelphia, Pa., Earle Theatre

For late January and February 1945 the following engagement of the Artie Shaw Orchestra was advertised in the trade papers:

January 26 - March 1, 1945   : New York City, Strand Theatre

ARTIE SHAW
AND HIS GRAMERCY FIVE

PHILCO RADIO HALL OF FAME
ABC RADIO BROADCAST

Roy Eldridge (tp), Artie Shaw (cl), Dodo Marmarosa (p), Barney Kessel (g), Morris Rayman (b), Louis Fromm (dm)

<u>March 4, 1945, New York City</u>

      THE SAD SACK (s)
      THE GRABTOWN GRAPPLE (s)

Note :

As America's leading manufacturer of radio receivers the Philco Corporation aptly acted as sponsor of a radio program series, which over the years changed its format several times. In 1945 it was headlined "The Philco Radio Hall Of Fame" and featured well known stars of radio, film and show business in episodes of one hour. Paul Whiteman's was the program's orchestra in residence during this time.

The above show was broadcast on March 4, 1945 on the ABC network, but may have been produced in advance, as the engagement of the Shaw orchestra at the Strand theatre had ended on March 1, 1945, and Shaw may have been already on a tour way back to California on the above given date.
The Artie Shaw Gramercy Five appeared as musical guests besides Jo Stafford, comedian Bert Lahr, and actor Peter Lorre. Announcer of the show was Glenn Riggs, and the Canadian comedienne Beatrice Lilly had been invited as mistress of ceremonies.

After closing at the Strand Theatre and appearing on the above mentioned radio program, Shaw went on a cross-country tour with his orchestra, which ended back in Hollywood (Simosko, Shaw biography).

ARTIE SHAW
AND HIS GRAMERCY FIVE

KRAFT MUSIC HALL
RADIO BROADCAST

Artie Shaw (cl), Dodo Marmarosa (p), Barney Kessel (g), Morris Rayman (b), Lou Fromm (d)

<u>March 15, 1945, Hollywood, Calif.</u>

dress rehearsal:

I WAS DOING ALL RIGHT (s)	BML P-305
YOU TOOK ADVANTAGE OF ME (s)	BML P-305

broadcast:

I WAS DOING ALL RIGHT (s)	AFRS Kraft Music Hall No. 119
YOU TOOK ADVANTAGE OF ME (s)	AFRS Kraft Music Hall No. 119

Note :

The "Kraft Music Hall" radio program series was sponsored by the Kraft Food Company, and from 1936 to 1946 Bing Crosby acted as its master of ceremonies. During the war years AFRS transcribed the programs and rebroadcast them over their radio net.

The Artie Shaw Gramercy Five appeared as musical guests on the above edition of the show.
The "Basic Musical Library"- releases are definitely alternate takes to the broadcast versions reissued on ASC-13 and were taken from a rehearsal prior to the show according to Kiner and Mackenzie's "Basic Musical Library"-Discography.
LP reissue:
All four takes on Artie Shaw Club ASC-13 (other sources number this LP as ASC-11 or ASG5).
CD reissue:
Broadcast takes also on Hep CD 70(3).

ARTIE SHAW AND HIS ORCHESTRA

**RCA-VICTOR
RECORDING SESSION**

Roy Eldridge, Paul Cohen, Bernie Glow, George Schwartz (tp), Gus Dixon, Harry Rodgers, Ollie Wilson, Bob Swift (tb), Artie Shaw (cl), Louis Prisby, Rudy Tanza (as), Jon Walton, Herbie Steward (ts), Chuck Gentry (bs), Dodo Marmarosa (p), Barney Kessel (g), Morris Rayman (b), Louis Fromm (dm), Ray Conniff, Buster Harding (arr)

<ins>April 5, 1945 (8:00 to 11:00 PM), Hollywood, Calif.</ins>

D5VB 1045-1	SEPTEMBER SONG (/)	Victor 20-1668
D5VB 1046-2	LITTLE JAZZ (/)	–

LP reissue:
Both titles also on Bluebird AXM2-5579.
CD reissue:
LITTLE JAZZ also on RCA CD ND 89914.
Both titles also on Hep CD 70(3) and Classics CD 1242.

For early April 1945 the following engagement of the Artie Shaw Orchestra was listed in the trade papers:

<ins>   ?   - April 8, 1945</ins>   : San Diego, Calif., Pacific Square Ballroom

ARTIE SHAW
AND HIS ORCHESTRA

FITCH BANDWAGON SHOW
NBC RADIO BROADCAST

band personnel same as before

April 8, 1945, Hollywood, Calif.

BEGIN THE BEGUINE ( )	AFRS Bandwagon No. 148
MY HEART STOOD STILL ( )	–
LITTLE JAZZ (/)	–
LIMEHOUSE BLUES (/)	–

LP reissues:

LITTLE JAZZ and LIMEHOUSE BLUES also on Joyce LP-1148.

LIMEHOUSE BLUES also on Golden Era GE-15006.

For mid April 1945 the following engagement of the Artie Shaw Orchestra was listed in the trade papers:

April 10 - 16, 1945   : Los Angeles, Calif., Orpheum Theatre

ARTIE SHAW AND HIS ORCHESTRA   RCA-VICTOR
                                                   RECORDING SESSION

band personnel as before, except Ralph Roselund (ts) replaces Herbie Steward; Dick Jones, Jimmy Mundy, Eddie Sauter (arr)

Note : After the Orpheum Theatre engagement (see above) Steward had briefly been in the army, but according to eye- and ear-witnesses he returned within a short time substituting possibly on alto or tenor or simply being added to the band on stage as well as in the recording studio without being mentioned in personnel listings...

<u>April 17, 1945 (2:00 to 11:50 PM), Hollywood, Calif.</u>

D5VB 1047-1	BUT NOT FOR ME (/)	Victor 20-1745
D5VB 1048-1	TEA FOR TWO (/)	RCA PM 42403 (LP)
D5VB 1091-1	SUMMERTIME (s)	Victor 28-0406
D5VB 1091-lA	SUMMERTIME (s)	Victor LPM 1648

Note :

TEA FOR TWO remained unissued on Victor 78rpm.

Both issues of SUMMERTIME are 12" versions due to more than four minutes of duration.

Matrix 1091-1 of SUMMERTIME also on V-Disc 731 and BML P-1113.

LP reissues:

First two titles and Matrix 1091-1 of SUMMERTIME also on Bluebird AXM2-5579.

Matrix 1091-1A of SUMMERTIME also on Bluebird AXM2-5580.

CD reissues:

Matrix 1091-1 of SUMMERTIME also on RCA CD ND 89914.

Matrix 1091-1A of SUMMERTIME also on Bluebird CD 07863 66087 2.

First two titles and Matrix 1091-1 of SUMMERTIME also on Classics CD 1242.

All four takes also on Hep CD 70(3).

For the time from the end of April until May 1945 the following engagements of the Artie Shaw Orchestra were listed in the trade papers:

<u>April 25 - May 1, 1945</u>	: San Francisco, Calif., Golden Gate Theatre
<u>May 3 - 9, 1945</u>	: Oakland, Calif., Orpheum Theatre
<u>May 11 - 13, 1945</u>	: Ocean Park, Calif., Casino Gardens

NOTE: The following is Marmarosa's first small band recording date with a studio group outside the orchestras he regularly worked in. At the time he was nineteen years old.

CORKY CORCORAN'S COLLEGIATES   KEYNOTE RECORDING SESSION

Emmett Berry (tp), Willie Smith (as), Corky Corcoran (ts), Dodo Marmarosa (p), Allan Reuss (g), Ed Mihelich (b), Nick Fatool (dm), Johnny Thompson (arr)

May 15, 1945, Hollywood, Calif.

HL 94-3	WHAT IS THIS THING CALLED LOVE (s)	Keynote K 621
HL 95-3	MINOR BLUES (s)	–
HL 96-2	YOU KNOW IT (s)	Keynote 18PJ-1051-71
HL 96-5	YOU KNOW IT (s)	Keynote K 654
HL 97-3	LULLABY OF THE LEAVES (s)	EmArcy MG 36023

LP reissues
LULLABY OF THE LEAVES also on Verve LP 840 032-1.
All takes also on Mercury 830.121 and on Keynote 18PJ-1051-71.
CD reissues:
LULLABY OF THE LEAVES also on Verve CD 840 032-1.
All takes also on Mercury CD 830.923-2.

For the next three succeeding weekends the Artie Shaw Orchestra played again at the Casino Gardens (Simosko, Shaw biography):

May 18 - 20, 1945	: Ocean Park, Calif., Casino Gardens
May 25 - 27, 1945	: Ocean Park, Calif., Casino Gardens
June 1 - 3, 1945	: Ocean Park, Calif., Casino Gardens

ARTIE SHAW AND HIS ORCHESTRA

RCA-VICTOR
RECORDING SESSION

band personnel as on April 17 session, except Stan Fishelson (tp) replaces Paul Cohen; Ray Conniff (arr)

June 5, 1945 (8:00 to 12:00 PM), Hollywood, Calif.

D5VB 1054-	KASBAH ( )	Victor rejected
D5VB 1055-	LAMENT (NOSTALGIA) ( )	–

ARTIE SHAW AND HIS ORCHESTRA

RCA-VICTOR
RECORDING SESSION

band personnel as before

June 7, 1945 (8:00 to 11:30 PM), Hollywood, Calif.

D5VB 1056-1	EASY TO LOVE (/)	Victor 20-1934
D5VB 1057-1	TIME ON MY HANDS (/)	Victor 20-1930
D5VB 1058-1	TABU (/)	Victor 20-1696

LP reissue:

All titles also on Bluebird AXM2-5579.

CD reissues:

TIME ON MY HANDS also on RCA CD ND 89914.

All titles also on Hep CD 70(3) and Classics CD 1242.

ARTIE SHAW AND HIS ORCHESTRA

RCA-VICTOR
RECORDING SESSION

band personnel as for June 7, 1945 RCA-Victor session

June 8, 1945 (2:00 to 5:30 PM), Hollywood, Calif.

D5VB 1059-1	A FOGGY DAY (/)	Victor 20-1933
D5VB 1060-1	THESE FOOLISH THINGS (/)	Victor 20-1930
D5VB 1061-1	LUCKY NUMBER (s)	Bluebird AXM2-5580

Note :

The above version of LUCKY NUMBER remained unissued on Victor 78rpm.

LP reissue:

A FOGGY DAY and THESE FOOLISH THINGS also on Bluebird AXM2-5579.

CD reissues:

A FOGGY DAY also on RCA CD ND 89914.

All three titles also on Hep CD 70(3) and on Classics CD 1277.

For the next weekend the Artie Shaw orchestra played again at the Casino Gardens (Simosko, Shaw biography):

June 8 - 10, 1945   : Ocean Park, Calif., Casino Gardens

ARTIE SHAW AND HIS ORCHESTRA

band personnel as before, except Dorothy Allen (voc) for Imogene Lynn; Ray Conniff, Harry Rodgers (arr)

June 9, 1945 (2:00 to 5:00 PM), Hollywood, Calif.

D5VB 1061-2	LUCKY NUMBER ( )	Victor rejected
D5VB 1062-1	YOU GO TO MY HEAD (DAv) (/)	Bluebird AXM2-5579

Note :

YOU GO TO MY HEAD remained unissued on Victor 78rpm.

CD reissues:

YOU GO TO MY HEAD also reissued on Hep CD 70(3) and on Classics CD 1277.

ARTIE SHAW AND HIS ORCHESTRA

band personnel as before; George Siravo (arr)

June 12, 1945 (2:00 to 5:00 PM), Hollywood, Calif.

D5VB 1067-1	THE MAN I LOVE (/)	Bluebird AXM2-5579
D5VB 1068-1	I COULD WRITE A BOOK (s)	Victor 20-1933

Note :

THE MAN I LOVE remained unissued on Victor 78rpm.

LP reissue:

I COULD WRITE A BOOK also on Bluebird AXM2-5579.

CD reissues:

Both titles also on RCA CD ND 89914, on Hep CD 70(3), and on Classics CD 1277.

ARTIE SHAW AND HIS ORCHESTRA   *RCA-VICTOR RECORDING SESSION*

band personnel as before; Ray Conniff, George Siravo (arr)

<u>June 13, 1945 (3:00 to 6:00 PM), Hollywood, Calif.</u>

| D5VB 1061-3 | LUCKY NUMBER ( ) | Victor rejected |
| D5VB 1069-1 | THRILL OF A LIFETIME (s) | Victor 20-1937 |

LP reissues:

THRILL OF A LIFETIME also on Sounds of Swing LP 101 and Bluebird AXM2-5579.

CD reissues:

THRILL OF A LIFETIME also on RCA CD ND 89914, Hep CD 70(3), and Classics CD 1277.

ARTIE SHAW AND HIS ORCHESTRA   *RCA-VICTOR RECORDING SESSION*

band personnel as before; Ray Conniff (arr)

<u>June 14, 1945 (12:30 to 3:00 PM), Hollywood, Calif.</u>

D5VB 1054-3	KASBAH (/)	Victor 20-1932
D5VB 1055-3	LAMENT (/)	Victor 20-1932
D5VB 1061-4	(MY) LUCKY NUMBER (s)	Victor 20-1937

LP reissue:

All titles also on Bluebird AXM2-5579.

CD reissues:

(MY) LUCKY NUMBER also on RCA CD ND 89914.

All titles also on Hep CD 70(3) and on Classics CD 1277.

The following engagements of the Shaw band during the period were listed in the trade papers:

June 15 - 17, 1945   : Ocean Park, Calif., Casino Gardens
June 29 - July 1, 1945 : San Diego, Calif., Pacific Square Ballroom

ARTIE SHAW AND HIS ORCHESTRA   RCA-VICTOR RECORDING SESSION

band personnel as before; George Siravo (arr)

July 3, 1945 (2:00 to 5:00 PM), Hollywood, Calif.

| D5VB 1070-1 | LOVE WALKED IN (s) | Victor 20-1745 |
| D5VB 1071-1 | SOON (/) | Victor 20-1742 |

LP reissues:
LOVE WALKED IN also on Bluebird AXM2-5579.
SOON also on Bluebird AXM2-5580 (LP).
CD reissues:
Both titles also on RCA CD ND 89914, on Hep CD 70(3), and on Classics CD 1277.

For July 1945 the following engagement of the Shaw band was listed in the trade papers:

July 4 - ? , 1945   : Balboa Beach, Calif., Rendezvous Ballroom
          (on weekends only)

ARTIE SHAW AND HIS ORCHESTRA   RCA-VICTOR
                                                   RECORDING SESSION

band personnel as before; George Siravo (arr)

<u>July 6, 1945 (2:00 to 5:30 PM), Hollywood, Calif.</u>

D5VB 1072-1	KEEPIN' MYSELF FOR YOU (/)	Victor 20-1936
D5VB 1073-1	NO ONE BUT YOU (s)	Victor LPV 582
D5VB 1074-1	NATCH (Roy Eldridge -voc) (/)	Victor LPV 582

LP reissues:
NO ONE BUT YOU also on RCA PM 42403.
KEEPIN' MYSELF FOR YOU and NATCH also on Bluebird AXM2-5580.
CD reissues:
NATCH also on RCA CD ND 89914.
All three titles also on Hep CD 70(3) and on Classics CD 1277.

ARTIE SHAW AND HIS ORCHESTRA   RCA-VICTOR
                                                   RECORDING SESSION

band personnel as before, add vocalist Hal Stevens (Derwin); George Siravo (arr)

<u>July 11, 1945 (2:00 to 5:00 PM), Hollywood, Calif.</u>

D5VB 1075-1	THAT'S FOR ME (HSv) (/)	Victor 20-1716
D5VB 1076-1	THEY CAN'T TAKE THAT AWAY FROM ME (/)	Victor rejected

LP reissue:
Both titles also on B1uebird AXM 2-5580.
CD reissues:
THEY CAN'T TAKE THAT AWAY FROM ME also on RCA CD ND 89914.
Both titles also on Hep CD 70(3) and on Classics CD 1277.

ARTIE SHAW AND HIS ORCHESTRA

band personnel as before; George Siravo (arr)

<u>July 14, 1945 (2:00 to 5:30 PM), Hollywood, Calif.</u>

D5VB 1076-2	THEY CAN'T TAKE THAT AWAY FROM ME (/)	Victor 20-1743
D5VB 1079-1	OUR LOVE IS HERE TO STAY (/)	
D5VB 1080-1	I WAS DOING ALL RIGHT (/)	Victor 20-1742

LP reissue:

All titles also on Bluebird AXM 2-5580.

CD reissues:

All titles also on Hep CD 70(3) and on Classics CD 1277.

ARTIE SHAW AND HIS ORCHESTRA

band personnel as before; Eddie Sauter, George Siravo (arr)

<u>July 17, 1945 (2:00 to 5:00 PM), Hollywood, Calif.</u>

D5VB 1081-1	SOMEONE TO WATCH OVER ME (/)	Victor 20-1744
D5VB 1082-1	THINGS ARE LOOKING UP (/)	–

LP reissue:

Both titles also on Bluebird AXM2-5580.

CD reissues:

Both titles on RCA CD ND 89914, Hep CD 70(3), and on Classics CD 1277.

ARTIE SHAW AND HIS ORCHESTRA

RCA-VICTOR
RECORDING SESSION

band personnel as before; Eddie Sauter (arr)

<u>July 19, 1945 (3:00 to 6:00 PM), Hollywood, Calif.</u>

D5VC 1101-1   THE MAID WITH THE FLACCID AIR (/)   Victor 28-0406 (12")

Note :
This title also on V-Disc 650 and on BML P-1113.
LP reissue:
This title also on Bluebird AXM2-5580.
CD reissues:
This title also on RCA CD ND 89914, on Hep CD 70(3), and on Classics CD 1277.

ARTIE SHAW AND HIS ORCHESTRA

RCA-VICTOR
RECORDING SESSION

band personnel as before; George Siravo (arr)

<u>July 20, 1945 (9:00 PM to 0:30 AM), Hollywood, Calif.</u>

D5VB 1073-2   NO ONE BUT YOU (s)   Victor 20-1935

LP reissue:
This title also on Bluebird AXM2-5580.
CD reissue:
This title also on RCA CD ND 89914, Hep CD 70(3), and on Classics CD 1330.

ARTIE SHAW AND HIS ORCHESTRA

RCA-VICTOR
RECORDING SESSION

band personnel as before; Eddie Sauter (arr)

<u>July 21, 1945 (8:45 to 11:45 PM), Hollywood, Calif.</u>

D5VB 1089-1　　THEY DIDN'T BELIEVE ME (s)　　　　　　　　Victor 20-1931

LP reissue:

This title also on Bluebird AXM2-5580.

CD reissue:

This title also on Hep CD 70(3) and on Classics CD 1330.

ARTIE SHAW AND HIS ORCHESTRA

RCA-VICTOR
RECORDING SESSION

band personnel as before; George Siravo, Harry Rodgers (arr)

<u>July 24, 1945 (2:00 to 5:00 PM), Hollywood, Calif.</u>

D5VB 1090-1　　DANCING ON THE CEILING (s)　　　　　　Victor 947-0216
D5VB 1091-1　　I CAN'T GET STARTED WITH YOU (/)　　　　Victor 20-1934

LP reissue:

Both titles also on Bluebird AXM2-5580.

CD reissues:

Both titles also on RCA CD ND 89914, Hep CD 70(3), and on Classics CD 1330.

ARTIE SHAW AND HIS ORCHESTRA

RCA-VICTOR
RECORDING SESSION

band personnel same as before; George Siravo (arr)

July 26, 1945 (3:00 to 6:00 PM), Hollywood, Calif.

D5VB 1096-1   JUST FLOATIN' ALONG (s)   Victor 20-1935

LP reissue:
This title also on Bluebird AXM2-5580.
CD reissues:
This title also on RCA CD ND 89914, Hep CD 70(3), and on Classics CD 1330.

ARTIE SHAW AND HIS ORCHESTRA

RCA-VICTOR
RECORDING SESSION

band personnel same as before, add vocalist Hal Stevens (Derwin); George Siravo (arr)

July 28, 1945 (2:00 to 5:00 PM), Hollywood, Calif.

D5VB 1097-1A   DON'T BLAME ME (s)   Victor unissued
D5VB 1098-1   YOLANDA (HSv) (/)   Victor 20-1716

LP reissue:
Both titles also on Bluebird AXM2-5580.
CD reissue:
Both titles also on Hep CD 70(3) and on Classics CD 1330.

ARTIE SHAW AND HIS ORCHESTRA

band personnel same as before; Dick Jones, George Siravo (arr)

<u>July 30, 1945 (1:00 to 4:00 PM), Hollywood, Calif.</u>

D5VB 1047-2	BUT NOT FOR ME (/)	Victor unissued
D5VB 1099-1	I CAN'T ESCAPE FROM YOU (/)	Victor 20-1936

Note :

BUT NOT FOR ME on RCA PM 42403 (LP), although indicated as from this session, in fact is the version recorded on April 17, 1945.

LP reissue:

I CAN'T ESCAPE FROM YOU also on Bluebird AXM2-5580.

CD reissues:

I CAN'T ESCAPE FROM YOU also on RCA CD ND 89914.

Both titles also on Hep CD 70(3) although the above take of BUT NOT FOR ME is not indicated on the track-lists of this reissue! It is nevertheless included in the box as track 7 on CD No.3.

Both titles also on Classics CD 1330.

ARTIE SHAW AND HIS GRAMERCY FIVE

Roy Eldridge (tp), Artie Shaw (cl), Dodo Marmarosa (p), Barney Kessel (g), Morris Rayman (b), Louis Fromm (dm)

<u>July 31, 1945 (1:00 to 7:10 PM), Hollywood, Calif.</u>

D5VB 1102-1	SCUTTLEBUTT (s)	Victor 20-1929

LP reissue:

This title also on Bluebird AXM2-5580.

CD reissues:

This title also on RCA CD ND 89914, Hep CD 70(3), Classics CD 1330, and on Living Era CD-AJS-2007.

ARTIE SHAW AND HIS GRAMERCY FIVE

RCA-VICTOR
RECORDING SESSION

Roy Eldridge (tp), Artie Shaw (cl), Dodo Marmarosa (p), Barney Kessel (g), Morris Rayman (b), Louis Fromm (dm)

<u>August 2, 1945 (2:00 to 5:00 PM), Hollywood, Calif.</u>

D5VB 1103-1	THE GENTLE GRIFTER (s)	Victor 20-1929
D5VB 1104-1	MYSTERIOSO (/)	Victor 20-1800
D5VB 1104-2	MYSTERIOSO (/)	Victor LPV 582
D5VB 1105-1	HOP, SKIP, AND JUMP (s)	Victor 20-1800

Note :

MYSTERIOSO is not the composition of the same title written by Thelonious Monk.

LP reissue:

All titles also on Bluebird AXM2-5580.

CD reissues:

THE GENTLE GRIFTER, MYSTERIOSO (1104-2), and HOP, SKIP, AND JUMP also on RCA CD ND 89914, Classics CD 1330, and on Living Era CD-AJS-2007.

All takes also on Hep CD 70(3).

In August 1945 Artie Shaw took a month off and went to visit New York together with Ava Gardner. The band resumed its performing in September.

ARTIE SHAW   *VICTORY PARADE OF SPOTLIGHT BANDS NO. 894*
AND HIS ORCHESTRA   *RADIO BROADCAST*

Roy Eldridge, Stan Fishelson, Bernie Glow, George Schwartz (tp), Gus Dixon, Harry Rodgers, Ollie Wilson, Bob Swift (tb), Artie Shaw (cl), Louis Prisby, Rudy Tanza (as), Jon Walton, Herbie Steward (ts), Chuck Gentry (bs), Dodo Marmarosa (p), Barney Kessel (g), Morris Rayman (b), Louis Fromm (dm), Imogene Lynn, (voc); Artie Shaw, Buster Harding, Harry Rodgers, Jerry Gray, Ray Conniff (arr)

<u>September 12, 1945, San Diego, Calif., Naval Hospital</u>

THEME (Spotlight Bands signature tune) (/)	AFRS Spotlight Bands No. 741
THEME (NIGHTMARE) (/)	AFRS Spotlight Bands No. 741
TABU (/)	AFRS Spotlight Bands No. 741
IF I LOVED YOU (ILv) (/)	
LITTLE JAZZ (/)	AFRS Spotlight Bands No. 741
OUT OF THIS WORLD (ILv) (/)	
BEGIN THE BEGUINE (/)	AFRS Spotlight Bands No. 741

Artie Shaw And His Gramercy Five
Roy Eldridge (tp), Artie Shaw (cl), Dodo Marmarosa (p),
Barney Kessel (g), Morris Rayman (b), Lou Fromm (d) :

SUMMIT RIDGE DRIVE (s)	AFRS Spotlight Bands No. 741

full orchestra again :

TOGETHER (ILv) (/)	
LUCKY NUMBER (s)	AFRS Spotlight Bands No. 741
THEME (NIGHTMARE) (/) (faded)	

Note :
Titles as indicated used on AFRS Spotlight Bands No. 741 (15 minutes duration) in partly reversed order. The AFRS release has part of BEGIN THE BEGUINE only.
LP reissues:
TABU and LUCKY NUMBER also on BBG 092.
All AFRS releases, except first THEME (Spotlight Bands Signature tune), also on Joyce LP-1003.
CD reissue:
All AFRS releases, except BEGIN THE BEGUINE, also on Soundcraft CD SC-50117-50118.
All AFRS releases, except first THEME (Spotlight Bands Signature tune), also on Joyce CD 1016.

All AFRS releases, also on Storyville CD Jazz Unlimited 201 2088.

All titles, except first THEME (Spotlight Bands signature tune), on Hep CD 84/85 (2CD set).

For September 1945 Vladimir Simosko (Shaw biography) mentions the following engagement of the Shaw band:

September 15/16 - October 6/7,1945 : Culver City, Calif., Casa Mañana
(on weekends only)

ARTIE SHAW   **VICTORY PARADE OF SPOTLIGHT BANDS NO. 897**
AND HIS ORCHESTRA   **RADIO BROADCAST**

---

band personnel as before; Jerry Gray, Lennie Hayton, Harry Rodgers, George Siravo (arr)

September 19, 1945, Fort Ord, Calif.

THEME (Spotlight Bands signature tune) (/)	AFRS Spotlight Bands No. 744
THEME (NIGHTMARE) (/)	AFRS Spotlight Bands No. 744
MY HEART STOOD STILL (/)	AFRS Spotlight Bands No. 744
STARDUST (/)	
ON THE ATCHISON, TOPEKA AND THE SANTA FE (ILv) (/)	
	AFRS Spotlight Bands No. 744
I COVER THE WATERFRONT (/)	

Artie Shaw And His Gramercy Five
Roy Eldridge (tp), Artie Shaw (cl), Dodo Marmarosa (p),
Barney Kessel (g), Morris Rayman (b), Lou Fromm (d) :

SCUTTLEBUTT (s)	AFRS Spotlight Bands No. 744

full orchestra again :

GOTTA BE THIS OR THAT (ILv) (/)	AFRS Spotlight Bands No. 744
JUST FLOATIN' ALONG (/)	AFRS Spotlight Bands No. 744
THEME (NIGHTMARE) (/) (faded)	

Note:

Titles as indicated used on AFRS Spotlight Bands No. 744 (15 minutes duration). The AFRS release of JUST FLOATIN' ALONG is faded out.

LP reissues:

MY HEART STOOD STILL also on BBG 092.

All AFRS releases, except first THEME (Spotlight Bands Signature tune), also on Joyce LP-1003.

CD reissues:

All AFRS releases, except first THEME (Spotlight Bands Signature tune), also on Joyce CD 1016.

All AFRS releases, also on Storyville CD Jazz Unlimited 201 2088.

All titles, except first THEME (Spotlight Bands signature tune), on Hep CD 84/85 (2CD set).

ARTIE SHAW   VICTORY PARADE OF SPOTLIGHT BANDS NO. 900
AND HIS ORCHESTRA   RADIO BROADCAST

band personnel as before, except Ray Linn (tp) replaces Roy Eldridge; Dave Rose, George Siravo, George Schwartz, Eddie Sauter, Ray Conniff (arr)

September 26, 1945, Camp San Louis Obispo, Calif.

THEME (Spotlight Bands signature tune) (/)   AFRS Spotlight Bands No. 747
THEME (NIGHTMARE) (/)   AFRS Spotlight Bands No. 747
BLUE SKIES (s)   AFRS Spotlight Bands No. 747
I'M GONNA LOVE THAT GUY (ILv) (/)
ON THE SUNNY SIDE OF THE STREET (s)   AFRS Spotlight Bands No. 747
SUMMERTIME (s)

Artie Shaw And His Gramercy Five
Artie Shaw (cl), Dodo Marmarosa (p), Barney Kessel (g),
Morris Rayman (b), Lou Fromm (d) :

HOP, SKIP, AND JUMP (s)   AFRS Spotlight Bands No. 747

full orchestra again :

IT HAD TO BE YOU (ILv) (/)
JUMPIN' ON THE MERRY-GO-ROUND (s)   AFRS Spotlight Bands No. 747
THEME (NIGHTMARE) (/) (faded)

Note :

Titles as indicated used on AFRS Spotlight Bands No. 747 (15 minutes duration).

LP reissues:

BLUE SKIES, ON THE SUNNY SIDE OF THE STREET, and JUMPIN' ON THE MERRY-GO-ROUND also on BBG 092.

All AFRS releases, except first THEME (Spotlight Bands Signature tune), also on Joyce LP-1003.

CD reissues:

All AFRS releases, except first THEME (Spotlight Bands Signature tune), also on Joyce CD 1016.

All AFRS releases also on Storyville CD Jazz Unlimited 201 2088.

All titles, except first THEME (Spotlight Bands signature tune), on Hep CD 84/85 (2CD set).

ARTIE SHAW AND HIS ORCHESTRA   VICTORY PARADE OF SPOTLIGHT BANDS NO. 903   RADIO BROADCAST

band personnel same as before; Buster Harding, Lennie Hayton, Dick Jones, Jerry Gray, Harry Rodgers, Ray Conniff (arr)

<u>October 3, 1945, Santa Ana, Calif. (Army Air Force Base)</u>

THEME (NIGHTMARE) (/)	AFRS Spotlight Bands No. 750
BEDFORD DRIVE (/)	AFRS Spotlight Bands No. 750
DANCING IN THE DARK (/)	
ALONG THE NAVAJO TRAIL (ILv) (/)	AFRS Spotlight Bands No. 750
SOFTLY AS IN A MORNING SUNRISE (/)	

Artie Shaw And His Gramercy Five
Artie Shaw (cl), Dodo Marmarosa (p), Barney Kessel (g),
Morris Rayman (b), Lou Fromm (d) :

THE SAD SACK (s)	AFRS Spotlight Bands No. 750

full orchestra again :

OUT OF THIS WORLD (ILv) (/)	
'S WONDERFUL (s)	AFRS Spotlight Bands No. 750
THEME (NIGHTMARE) (/) (faded)	

Note :
Titles as indicated used on AFRS Spotlight Bands No. 750 (15 minutes duration).
LP reissue:
All AFRS releases also on Joyce LP-1010.
CD reissues:
All AFRS releases also on Joyce CD 1016 and on Storyville CD Jazz Unlimited 201 2088.
All titles on Hep CD 84/85 (2CD set).

ARTIE SHAW   VICTORY PARADE OF SPOTLIGHT BANDS NO. 906
AND HIS ORCHESTRA   RADIO BROADCAST

band personnel same as before; Paul Jordan, Harry Rodgers, Dick Jones, George Siravo, Lennie Hayton, Buster Harding (arr)

<u>October 10, 1945, Santa Barbara, Calif., Hoff General Hospital</u>

THEME (NIGHTMARE) (/)	AFRS Spotlight Bands No. 753
HINDUSTAN (s)	AFRS Spotlight Bands No. 753
CAN'T YOU READ BETWEEN THE LINES (ILv) (/)	AFRS Spotl. Bands No. 753
LOVE WALKED IN (s)	AFRS Spotlight Bands No. 753
I CAN'T GET STARTED WITH YOU (/)	

Artie Shaw And His Gramercy Five
Artie Shaw (cl), Dodo Marmarosa (p), Barney Kessel (g),
Morris Rayman (b), Lou Fromm (d) :

THE GRABTOWN GRAPPLE (s)

full orchestra again :
IT MIGHT AS WELL BE SPRING (ILv) (/)
THE GLIDER (/)   AFRS Spotlight Bands No. 753
THEME (NIGHTMARE) (/) (faded)

Note :
Titles as indicated used on AFRS Spotlight Bands No. 753 (15 minutes duration) in partly reversed order. The AFRS release of THE GLIDER is faded out.
LP reissues:
CAN'T YOU READ BETWEEN THE LINES also on BBG 092.
All AFRS releases also on Joyce LP-1010.
CD reissues:
All AFRS releases also on Joyce CD 1016 and on Storyville CD Jazz Unlimited 201 2088.
All titles on Hep CD 84/85 (2CD set).

D uring October and November 1945 the Artie Shaw Orchestra played an engagement at the newly decorated Meadowbrook Gardens, previously known as the Casa Mañana on Washington Boulevard in Culver City, Calif.:

October ? - November 18, 1945:   Culver City, Calif., Meadowbrook Gardens
(four nights weekly)

LEM DAVIS SEXTET   SUNSET RECORDING SESSION

Emmett Berry (tp), Vic Dickenson (tb), Lem Davis (as), Dodo Marmarosa (p), John Simmons (b), Henry "Tucker" Green (dm), Ernie Sheppard (voc)

October 20, 1945, Hollywood, Calif.

SRC-122-3	NOTHIN' FROM NOTHIN' (ESv) (/)	Sunset 7558
SRC-122-5	NOTHIN' FROM NOTHIN' (ESv) (/)	Sunset unissued
SRC-123-5	BLUES IN MY HEART (s)	Sunset unissued
SRC-124-4	IT WAS MEANT TO BE (s)	Sunset unissued
SRC-125-6	MY BLUE HEAVEN (s)	Sunset 7558

Note :

LP reissue:

All titles, except matrix 122-3 of NOTHIN' FROM NOTHIN', also on Black Lion 28 404-2Z.

CD reissue:

All titles, except matrix 122-3 of NOTHIN' FROM NOTHIN', also on Black Lion BLCD 760171.

ARTIE SHAW
AND HIS ORCHESTRA

FITCH BANDWAGON SHOW
NBC RADIO BROADCAST

band personnel same as on October 10, 1945; Ray Conniff, David Rose, George Siravo (arr)

<u>November 7, 1945, Santa Barbara, Calif., Hoff General Hospital</u>

'S WONDERFUL (s)	AFRS Bandwagon No. ? [poss. No. 178]
NIGHT AND DAY (/)	–
LET'S WALK (/)	–
NO ONE BUT YOU ( )	–

Note :

As already the Victory Parade of Spotlight Bands program No. 906 of October 10, 1945 the above Fitch Bandwagon Show was recorded at Hoff General Hospital in Santa Barbara, California.

According to Vladimir Simosko (Shaw biography) there was also a title (MY MAN) performed by Betty Hutton on this broadcast, accompanied, however, by a different group.

Marmarosa's usual brief solo on Ray Conniff's arrangement of 'S WONDERFUL is barely audible due to heavy underamplifying.

LP reissues:

NIGHT AND DAY and LET'S WALK also on BBG 092 and on Golden Era GE-15078.

CD reissue:

'S WONDERFUL, NIGHT AND DAY, and LET'S WALK on Hep CD 84/85 (2CD set).

ARTIE SHAW AND HIS ORCHESTRA   (MUSICRAFT)
RECORDING SESSION

band personnel as before, except Paul Cohen (tp) and Ralph Roselund (ts) replace Bernie Glow and Jon Walton; George Siravo, Artie Shaw, Harry Rodgers, Buster Harding (arr)

<u>November 13, 1945, Hollywood, Calif., Radio Recorders Studio</u>

5408	LET'S WALK ( )	test pressing
5408	LET'S WALK (/)	Musicraft 357
5416	LOVE OF MY LIFE (/)	Musicraft 378
5417	GHOST OF A CHANCE (HSv) (/)	Musicraft 357
5418	HOW DEEP IS THE OCEAN (HSv) (/)	Musicraft 409
5419	THE GLIDER (/)	Musicraft 378
5420	THE HORNET (/)	Musicraft 409

Note :

At the time of the above recording session Shaw was still tied to RCA-Victor by an exclusive contract, which did not allow him to make recordings for any other company. When shortly after his break with RCA-Victor he signed with Musicraft and handed over for later release the above recordings to his new company in December 1945, RCA claimed that he had violated his contract. Shaw replied to have made the above recordings at his own expense and in view of a recording label of his own he was planning to form (John Harding, liner notes to Hep CD70). As the METRONOME magazine issue of December 1945, however, in a short note on Shaw's departure from RCA unambiguously states, that he has "already recorded for Musicraft", Shaw's excuse to RCA may after all have been a feint and his move to Musicraft an agreed upon matter at the above date.

Usually in discographies the above recording session is given the two recording dates of November 13 (LET'S WALK) and November 14 or 16, 1945 (all other titles). There is no evidence for this splitting of dates, however. Especially the Musicraft matrix-numbers, which have been brought in as an argument causing speculation that the session might have taken place from before midnight on November 13 and having continued into the early hours of November 14, seem not to bear any relevance for the discussion of the above date, for they had not been assigned before March or April 1946 (most certainly when the recordings were being mastered for release). In another note on Shaw the above cited issue of METRONOME magazine clearly states, that he "cut wax for the Musicraft label on November 13. Following this information there is no reason to assume, that the titles had been recorded on more than one day.

Vladimir Simosko cites Artie Shaw in his Shaw biography, that the above titles had been recorded before the departure of Roy Eldridge, who left the band in the second half of September 1945. Trumpet solos on LET'S WALK, GHOST OF A CHANCE, THE GLIDER, and THE HORNET, however, to our ears seem not to be by Eldridge but by Ray Linn, who had replaced Eldridge after his leave. Also Shaw's recollections on this point are clearly contradicted by the above recording date.

The above sequence of titles follows the Musicraft matrix-numbers. Being assigned belated, however (see above), they do not necessarily reveal the original recording chronology of the date.

According to Vladimir Simosko (Shaw biography) a test pressing of the title LET'S WALK is circulating among collectors.

CD reissues:

The issued version of LET'S WALK and THE GLIDER also on Musicraft MVSCD-50.

LOVE OF MY LIFE, GHOST OF A CHANCE, HOW DEEP IS THE OCEAN, and THE HORNET also on Musicraft MVSCD-51.

All titles, except test pressing of LET'S WALK, also on Hep CD 70(3) and on Classics CD 1330.

When the Artie Shaw Orchestra closed at the Meadowbrook Gardens in Culver City, Calif., on November 18, 1945, Shaw immediately disbanded.

Marmarosa soon had new offers...

GLADYS HAMPTON QUARTET   HAMP-TONE RECORDING SESSION

Herbie Fields (cl), Dodo Marmarosa (p), Charlie Harris (b), unknown [George Jenkins ?] (d)

<u>late 1945, Hollywood, Calif.</u>

BRH 0004 A 2968	FOUR SQUARES ONLY (s)	Hamp-Tone 105
BRH 0005 A 2969	STAR TIME (s)	–

Note :

Although the label of Hamp-Tone 105 - and consequently all discographies - indicate Billy Mackel on guitar as participating in this session, there is no guitar audible on both titles. "Gladys Hampton's quartet" instead is completed by an unknown drummer, who may possibly be George Jenkins, then playing drums with Lionel Hampton's orchestra.

The Lionel Hampton Orchestra, including Fields, and Harris was playing the Orpheum Theatre, Los Angeles, Calif., from October 23-29, and the Trianon Ballroom in Southgate, Calif., from November 6 - December 9, 1945. Subsequently the orchestra returned to New York City.

The above recording session must have taken place most likely in November or early December 1945, which is also confirmed by the matrix numbers. The recordings were made at Lionel Hampton's Hollywood home.

The label of Hamp-Tone 105 spells „Gladys Hampton's Quartet" and „Dodo Momorosa".

$\mathbf{F}$rom October 1945 into the first months of 1946, Slim Gaillard was a featured attraction at Billy Berg's Supper Club in Hollywood. It is not reported that Marmarosa worked with Gaillard at the club, but Gaillard did use him on several recording sessions...

SLIM GAILLARD QUARTET　　　　BEE-BEE RECORDING SESSION

Dodo Marmarosa (p), Slim Gaillard (g, p, voc), Bam Brown (b, voc), Zutty Singleton (dm)

<u>ca. early December 1945, Hollywood, Calif.</u>

BB 101-3	LAGUNA (SG & BBv) (s)	Bee-Bee 101
BB 102-5	DUNKIN' BAGEL (SG & BBv) (s)	Bee-Bee 102
BB 103-5	BOOGIN' AT BERG'S (/)	Bee-Bee 101
BB 104-5	DON'T BLAME ME (SGv) (s)	Bee-Bee 102

Note :

Bee-Bee (which stands for the monogram "B.B.") was Billy Berg's own label.

Take numbers for DUNKIN' BAGEL, BOOGIN' AT BERG'S, and DON'T BLAME ME vary from source to source due to vague markings on the original Bee-Bee 78rpm releases. The above numbering follows the label indication of early 78rpm reissues of the three titles on Melodisc M 1012 (BOOGIN' AT BERG'S) and M 1013 (DUNKIN' BAGEL, DON'T BLAME ME), but may be incorrect for the same reason.

LP reissues:

LAGUNA, DUNKIN' BAGEL, and BOOGIN' AT BERG'S also on Savoy SJL 2215.

DON'T BLAME ME also on Swingtime LP ST 1018.

CD reissue:

Complete session on Classics CD 864.

SLIM GAILLARD QUARTET   BEE-BEE RECORDING SESSION

Dodo Marmarosa (p) ?, Slim Gaillard (g, p, voc), Bam Brown (b, voc), Zutty Singleton (dm)

<u>ca. early December 1945, Hollywood, Calif.</u>

BB 117	CHILI AND BEANS (SG & BBv) ( )	Melodisc 1001
BB	MILLIONAIRES DON'T WHISTLE (voc ?) ( )	Melodisc 1013

Note :

As we were only able to check two titles of this session (BB 118 LAGUNA, issued on Classics CD 864, and BB 119 FROGLEGS AND BOURBON, issued on Classics 24) , which are either without piano (LAGUNA) or with Slim Gaillard on piano (FROGLEGS...), we are not sure of Marmarosa's presence on the remaining two titles, although it is claimed by several sources.

BARNEY KESSEL'S ALL STARS   ATOMIC RECORDING SESSION

Herbie Steward (ts), Johnny White (vib), Dodo Marmarosa (p), Barney Kessel (g), Morris Rayman (b), Louis Fromm (dm)

December 5, 1945 (2:30 to 5:30 PM), Hollywood, Calif., Sound Workshop studio

A-209-A	ATOM BUSTER (s)	Atomic 209
A-209-B	WHAT IS THIS THING CALLED LOVE (s)	–
A-210-A	SLICK CHICK (s)	Atomic 210
A-210-B	THE MAN I LOVE (s)	–

Note :

The above recording session is by all sources dated on June 7, 1945. However, the original recording contract between Atomic Records and Barney Kessel as leader, signed on November 27, 1945 and preserved in copy at the archive of Los Angeles' Professional Musicians Local 47, gives the above recording date and location.

Other sources give matrix nos. 135 A and 135 B for Atomic 209 and 136 A and 136 B for Atomic 210.

Labels and engravings on the original Atomic releases bear no indications of take numbers for the above recordings.

LP reissue:

All titles also on Onyx ORI 215.

CD reissues:

ATOM BUSTER also on ABM ABMCD 1065.

ATOM BUSTER, WHAT IS THIS THING CALLED LOVE, and SLICK CHICK also on EPM 152382.

All titles also on Classics CD 1165.

In the meantime Marmarosa received an offer to join the **Boyd Raeburn** Orchestra, which was more or less a rehearsal band at the period.

BOYD RAEBURN
AND HIS ORCHESTRA

AFRS "JUBILEE"
RADIO SHOW

Ray Linn, Dale Pearce, Nelson Shelladay, Zeke Zarchey (tp), Britt Woodman, Ollie Wilson, Fred Zito (tb), Wilbur Schwartz (cl,as), Harry Klee (fl,as), Ralph Lee, Lucky Thompson (ts), Hy Mandel (bs), Boyd Raeburn (bass-sax), Dodo Marmarosa (p), Joe Mondragon (b), Jackie Mills (dm,arr), Ginny Powell, David Allyn (voc), Ed Finckel, George Handy, Johnny Mandel, Milt Kleeb, Dizzy Gillespie (arr), Dizzy Gillespie (tp) appears as guest soloist

between December 10 - 17, 1945, Hollywood, Calif., NBC studios

THEME (ONE O'CLOCK JUMP) (/)	AFRS Jubilee Program No. 163
TONSILLECTOMY (s)	–
PICNIC IN THE WINTERTIME (DAv) (/)	–
A NIGHT IN TUNISIA (Dizzy Gillespie -tp) (/)	–
RIP VAN WINKLE (GPv) (s)	–
YERXA (p-intro)	–
THE EAGLE FLIES (s)	–
THEME (ONE O'CLOCK JUMP) (/)	–

Note :

The AFRS "Jubilee" program series originally had been created by AFRS as an entertainment platform for mostly black performers, although during the later war years also many white artists were featured. The actual "Jubilee" shows had a duration of one hour and were initially staged on Monday nights at the studios of the large radio stations in Hollywood like NBC or CBS in front of 'live' audiences. After the war also performances from other sites were transcribed and released within the series. The transcription of one show provided AFRS with recorded material for edition and release of at least one "Jubilee" program of 30 minutes with the left over titles often being used as fills or additions to later program issues. Broadcast time for the AFRS "Jubilee" transcriptions usually was Friday evening.

Included in AFRS "Jubilee" program release No. 163 was also one title by the Gillespie-Parker sextet as it appeared at Billy Berg's Supper Club at the time. As the Dizzy Gillespie-Charlie Parker combo opened at Billy Berg's on December 10, 1945, and the recordings from the "Jubilee" 'live'-show had been mastered by AFRS for release on December 17, the actual concert must have taken place between both these dates...

YERXA is announced as "ELEGY MOVEMENT FROM JITTERBUG SUITE", but arranger George Handy declared in a 1966 interview that there had been no such work as a JITTERBUG SUITE in Raeburn's band book. Complete program also used for AFRS Jubilee program No. 209.

TONSILLECTOMY, YERXA, and THE EAGLE FLIES also used for AFRS Jubilee program No. 189.

LP reissue:
All titles, except THEME, also on Hep 1.
CD reissues:
TONSILLECTOMY and THE EAGLE FLIES also on Storyville STCD 8313.
All titles, except THEME, also on Hep CD 1.
All titles also on RST JUBCD 1011.

RAY LINN AND HIS ORCHESTRA   ENCORE RECORDING SESSION

Ray Linn (tp), Joe Howard (tb), Mahlon Clark (cl, as), Harry Klee (as), Deacon Dunn (ts), Tommy Todd (p), Al Hendrickson (g), Phil Stephens (b), Jacky Mills (dm), Dodo Marmarosa (arr)

December 14, 1945, Hollywood, Calif., Radio Recorders studio

114 (668)   ESCAPE   Encore 512, Signature 28122

Note :
ESCAPE composed and arranged by Marmarosa.
There were three more titles recorded at the above session, in which Marmarosa was not involved (TEA TIME and SERENADE IN SEVENTHS, arranged by Tommy Todd, CARAVAN, arranged by Sonny Burke).
The above recording session and Marmarosa's arranging were reviewed in the March 1946 issue of METRONOME magazine (p. 21).
Matrix No. in parentheses assigned by Signature Records.

SLIM GAILLARD QUARTET   ATOMIC RECORDING SESSION

Dodo Marmarosa (p), Slim Gaillard (g, p, voc), Bam Brown (b, voc), Zutty Singleton (dm)

<u>December 15, 1945, Hollywood, Calif.</u>

A-215-A-1	ATOMIC COCKTAIL (SG & BBv) (s)	Atomic 215
A-215-B-1	YEP-ROC HERESAY (SG & BBv) (s)	–
A-216-A-1	PENICILLIN BOOGIE (s)	Atomic 216
A-216-B-2	JUMPIN' AT THE RECORD SHOP (SGv) (s)	–

LP reissues:

ATOMIC COCKTAIL and YEP-ROC HERESAY also on Official LP 3050 and Solid Sender SOL 514.

PENICILLIN BOOGIE and JUMPIN' AT THE RECORD SHOP also on Swingtime LP ST 1018.

CD reissue:

Complete session also on Classics CD 911.

SLIM GAILLARD QUARTET   *ATOMIC RECORDING SESSION*

Dodo Marmarosa (p), Slim Gaillard (g, p, voc), Bam Brown (b, voc), Zutty Singleton (dm)

<u>December 1945, Hollywood, Calif.</u>

A-230-A-	DREI SIX CENTS (SG & BBv) (s)	Atomic 230
A-230-B-	MINUET IN VOUT (s)	–
A-231-A-	TEE SAY MALEE (SG & BBv) (/)	Atomic 231

Note :

There was one more title recorded at the above session (A-231-B-: NOVACHORD BOOGIE), on which Marmarosa did not participate. Gaillard simultaneously played novachord (right hand) and piano (left hand). Some sources claim "December 15" too as recording date for these titles.

Labels and engravings on the original Atomic releases bear no indications of take numbers for the above recordings.

LP reissues:

DREI SIX CENTS also on Folklyric LP 9038.

TEE SAY MALEE also on Solid Sender SOL 514.

MINUET IN VOUT and TEE SAY MALEE also on Official LP 3050.

CD reissue:

Complete session also on Classics CD 911.

SLIM GAILLARD QUARTET   CADET RECORDING SESSION

Dodo Marmarosa (p), Slim Gaillard (g, p, voc), Bam Brown (b, voc), Zutty Singleton (dm)

<u>December 20, 1945, Hollywood, Calif.</u>

5	BABY WON'T YOU PLEASE COME HOME (SGv) (s)	Cadet 202
6	GROOVE JUICE JIVE (SGv) (s)	Cadet 204
7	THE HOP (s)	Cadet 202
8	THREE HANDED BOOGIE (/)	Cadet 204

Note :

Other sources claim matrix 8 for CUBAN RHUMBARINI and unknown matrix for THREE HANDED BOOGIE.
CUBAN RHUMBARINI is done in trio setting without participation of Marmarosa. Therefore this title most likely
belongs to Gaillard's recording session for Cadet of December 1, 1945, which besides CUBAN RHUMBARINI
also produced the trio titles SCOTCHIN' WITH SODA, AS LONG AS I HAVE YOUR LOVE, and the famous
CEMENT MIXER.

LP reissue:

GROOVE JUICE JIVE and THREE HANDED BOOGIE also on Folklyric LP 9038.

CD reissues:

BABY WON'T YOU PLEASE COME HOME and THE HOP also on Jazz Anthology CD 550282.
Complete session on Classics CD 911.

LESTER YOUNG QUINTET   PHILO RECORDING SESSION

Vic Dickenson (tb), Lester Young (ts), Dodo Marmarosa (p), Red Callender (b), Henry "Tucker" Green (dm)

<u>second half of December 1945, Hollywood, Calif.</u>

P 123 A	D.B. BLUES (s)	Philo 123
P 123 B	LESTER BLOWS AGAIN (s)	–
P 124 A-2	THESE FOOLISH THINGS (omit Dickenson) (p-intro)	Philo 124
P 124 B-2	JUMPIN' AT MESNER'S (s)	–

Note :

Usually this is given as a sextet session with guitarist Freddie Green. We could not trace any guitar on the above titles. Green is neither given in the personnel on the original Philo- nor Aladdin-labels ("Lester Young And His Band").

The session must have taken place shortly after December 15th, when Lester Young was discharged from the Army. The recording was supervised by Norman Granz.

All four titles also issued on Aladdin 78rpm records with release nos. 123 and 124 and matrix nos. A 123 and A 124.

LP reissue:

All titles also on Blue Note BST 84483/84.

CD reissues:

All titles also on Blue Moon BMCD-1003, Blue Note CDP 7243 8 32787 2 5, and on Classics CD 932.

BOYD RAEBURN AND HIS ORCHESTRA   STANDARD RECORDINGS

personnel similar as on "Jubilee" No. 163, possibly Harry Babasin (b) for Joe Mondragon

Note :   Some sources also give Tony Rizzi (g) for these recordings. If Rizzi was still present here, he was replaced by Al Hendrickson at the latest in early 1946.

<u>mid - late December 1945, Hollywood, Calif.</u>

YTH-1576-	TONSILLECTOMY (s)	Standard X 200
	RIP VAN WINKLE (GPv) (s)	–
	FORGETFUL (DAv) (/)	–
	MEMPHIS IN JUNE (GP & DAv) (s)	–
YTH-1577-	I DON'T CARE WHO KNOWS IT (DAv) (/)	–
	IF I LOVED YOU (DAv) (/)	–
	HOW DEEP IS THE OCEAN? (/)	–
	YERXA (p-intro)	–
YTH-1597-1A	BOYD'S NEST (/)	Standard X 202
	BLUE PRELUDE (/)	–
	PICNIC IN THE WINTERTIME (DAv) (celesta-s)	–
	HIGH TIDE (/)	–
	ARE YOU LIVIN' OLD MAN (GP & DAv) (s)	–
YTH-1598-1	TUSH (brief-s)	–
	CONCERTO FOR DUKE : MOOD INDIGO (/)	–
	(Medley) C-JAM BLUES (/)	
	SOPHISTICATED LADY (/)	
	IT DON'T MEAN A THING (/)	
	WHERE YOU AT? (GP & DAv) (/)	–
	OUT OF THIS WORLD (DAv) (/)	–
YTH-1713-	BOYD MEETS STRAVINSKY (s)	Standard X 207
	PERSONALITY (GPv) (/)	–
	DALVATORE SALLY (s)	–
	BLUE ECHOES (DAv) (s)	–
	I ONLY HAVE EYES FOR YOU (DAv) (/)	–

Note :

These Electrical Transcriptions ("ETs") were made by Standard Radio Library Service for broadcasting purposes only. Standard served 400 radio stations in the USA.

LP reissues:

TONSILLECTOMY, MEMPHIS IN JUNE, I DON'T CARE WHO KNOWS IT, and HOW DEEP IS THE OCEAN also on Hep 22.

FORGETFUL, MEMPHIS IN JUNE, HOW DEEP IS THE OCEAN, and OUT OF THIS WORLD also on Sounds of Swing LP-115.

BOYD'S NEST also on First Heard FHR-8.

HIGH TIDE, TUSH, and CONCERTO FO DUKE also on First Time FTR1515.

ARE YOU LIVIN' OLD MAN and WHERE YOU AT? also on Golden Era GE-15014.

BOYD MEETS STRAVINSKY and WHERE YOU AT? also on Hep 3.

CD reissues:

TONSILLECTOMY, RIP VAN WINKLE, FORGETFUL, MEMPHIS IN JUNE, I DON'T CARE WHO KNOWS IT, YERXA, BOYD'S NEST, BLUE PRELUDE, PICNIC IN THE WINTERTIME, ARE YOU LIVIN' OLD MAN, OUT OF THIS WORLD, BOYD MEETS STRAVINSKY, PERSONALITY, DALVATORE SALLY, and BLUE ECHOES also on Echo Jazz EJCD 13.

MEMPHIS IN JUNE, I DON'T CARE WHO KNOWS IT, and HOW DEEP IS THE OCEAN also on Hep CD 1.

TONSILLECTOMY, RIP VAN WINKLE, FORGETFUL, IF I LOVED YOU, and YERXA also on Hep CD 22.

Complete Standard X 202 and X 207 also on Hep CD 42

Complete recording session also on Audiophonic ABR060812.

SLIM GAILLARD AND HIS ORCHESTRA   *BEL-TONE RECORDING SESSION*

Dizzy Gillespie (tp), Charlie Parker (as), Jack McVea (ts), Dodo Marmarosa (p), Slim Gaillard (g, p, voc), Bam Brown (b, voc), Zutty Singleton (dm)

December 29 (?), 1945, Hollywood, Calif.

BTJ 38-2 (T 821-5M)	DIZZY BOOGIE (/)	Bel-Tone 753, Majestic 9002
BTJ 38-	DIZZY BOOGIE (alternate take) (/)	Polydor Special 545 107
BTJ 39-3 (T 822-4)	FLAT FOOT FLOOGIE (SG & BBv) (/)	Bel-Tone 758, Majestic 9002
BTJ 39-	FLAT FOOT FLOOGIE (alternate take) (SG & BBv) (/)	
		Allegro Elite 4050
BTJ 40-2 (T 823-)	POPITY POP (SG & BBv) (s)	Bel-Tone 753, Majestic 9001
BTJ 41-RE (T 824-)	SLIM'S JAM (SGv) (s)	Bel-Tone 761, Majestic 9001

Note :

The recording date of December 29 is agreed upon by all sources but not finally verified.

Marmarosa is present on DIZZY BOOGIE, but the piano solo is by Gaillard.

In early summer 1946 the Bel-Tone Recording Corporation sold their masters to Majestic Records. Majestic soon reissued the above titles with own matrix numbers. Geoffrey Wheeler in an article for the discographical magazine NAMES & NUMBERS (October 2007, p.15-17) claims the take of DIZZY BOOGIE released on Majestic 9002 to be an alternate take 5 according to its Majestic matrix indication of "T-821-5M". The version offered on Majestic 9002, however, is identical to Bel-Tone release 753 and thus take 2.

The alternate take of DIZZY BOOGIE may possibly have been released earlier than on Polydor Special 545 107 (1969), but certainly not on Halo 50723, as claimed by several sources. The Halo version is the same as on Bel-Tone 753 and thus take 2.

Most sources claim take 2 (or 4) for the Bel-Tone release of FLAT FOOT FLOOGIE. The markings, according to verification on several original copies of Bel-Tone 758, however, clearly denote take 3.

Matrix numbers in brackets for Majestic releases.

LP reissues:

DIZZY BOOGIE (BTJ 38-2), FLAT FOOT FLOOGIE (alternate take), POPITY POP, and SLIM'S JAM on Allegro Elite 4050, Halo 50273, and on Alamac QSR 2441.

All titles including the two alternate takes on Polydor Special 545 107, Spotlite SPJ-150 D and on Savoy SJL 1177.

CD reissues:

All titles including the two alternate takes on Savoy ZDS 1177.

Bel-Tone releases also on Blue Moon BMCD-1008 and on Classics CD 911.

At the end of 1945 Marmarosa was no unknown anymore. In early 1946 he was listed in the popularity polls by the US trade papers...
In *Down Beat* magazine he was voted 6th popular pianist with a total of 187 votes.
In *Esquire* magazine he got votes for the "New Star"-category by Mal Braveman (Head of New Jazz Foundation) in the "Board of Experts"-section, and by Anita O'Day, Milt Hinton, and Remo Palmieri in the "Musicians' Point Tabulation".

DODO MARMAROSA TRIO/QUARTET   ATOMIC RECORDING SESSION

Lucky Thompson (ts), Dodo Marmarosa (p), Ray Brown (b), Jackie Mills (dm)

<u>January 11, 1946 (3:00 to 6:00 PM), Hollywood, Calif., Radio Recorders studio</u>

A 225 A	MELLOW MOOD (trio) (s)	Atomic 225
A 225 B	HOW HIGH THE MOON (quartet) (s)	–
A 226 A	DODO'S BLUES (trio) (s)	Atomic 226
A 226 B	I SURRENDER DEAR (quartet) (s)	–

Note :

This was Marmarosa's debut as bandleader in a recording studio.

LP reissues:

All titles also on Onyx ORI 212 and on Raretone 5020 FC.

CD reissues:

HOW HIGH THE MOON and I SURRENDER DEAR also on ABM ABMCD 1065.

MELLOW MOOD and DODO'S BLUES also on Lone Hill Jazz LJH10119.

All titles also on EPM/Xanadu CD FDC 5174, Classics CD 1165, and on Proper INTRO CD 2055.

SLIM GAILLARD AND HIS ORCHESTRA   *BEL-TONE RECORDING SESSION*

Howard McGhee (tp), Marshall Royal (cl), Lucky Thompson (ts), Dodo Marmarosa (p), Slim Gaillard (g, voc), Bam Brown (b, voc), Zutty Singleton (dm)

<u>ca. January 1946, Hollywood, Calif.</u>

BTJ 58-3	CHICKEN RHYTHM (SG & BBv) (s)	Bel-Tone 762
BTJ 59-1	SANTA MONICA JUMP (s)	Bel-Tone 761
BTJ 60-1	MEAN PRETTY MAMA (SGv) (/)	Bel-Tone 762
BTJ 61-2	SCHOOL KIDS HOP (SG & BBv) (s)	Bel-Tone 758

Note :

Some sources claim "March 1946" as recording date for this session.

LP reissue:

All titles also on Alamac LP QSR 2441.

CD reissue:

All titles also on Classics CD 962.

BOYD RAEBURN AND HIS ORCHESTRA

AFRS "JUBILEE" RADIO SHOW

band personnel as on Standard recordings, definitely Al Hendrickson (g), Harry Babasin (b), add Gail Laughton or Loretta Thompson (harp)

<u>January / early February 1946, Hollywood, Calif., NBC studios</u>

THEME (ONE O'CLOCK JUMP) (/)	AFRS Jubilee Program No. 169
BOYD MEETS STRAVINSKY (s)	–
TEMPTATION (GPv) (/)	–

only Dodo Marmarosa (p-solo) :

DEEP PURPLE	–
TEA FOR TWO	–

full orchestra again :

THERE'S NO YOU (DAv) (/)	–

<u>Ray Linn Jazz Octet:</u>
Ray Linn (tp), Wilbur Schwartz (cl), Harry Klee (fl), Lucky Thompson (ts), Dodo Marmarosa (p), Al Hendrickson (g), Harry Babasin (b), Jackie Mills (dm)

CARAVAN (/)	–

full orchestra again :

MEMPHIS IN JUNE (GP & DAv) (/)	–
TWO SPOOS IN AN IGLOO (s)	–
THEME (ONE O'CLOCK JUMP) (/)	–

Note :
The above version of TWO SPOOS IN AN IGLOO also used on AFRS Jubilee program No. 189.
LP reissues:
TEMPTATION also on Joyce LP-5010.
THERE'S NO YOU, CARAVAN, MEMPHIS IN JUNE, and TWO SPOOS IN AN IGLOO also on Joyce LP-5011.
BOYD MEETS STRAVINSKY, TEA FOR TWO, and CARAVAN also on Hep 3.
DEEP PURPLE and TEA FOR TWO also on Spotlite SPJ-128 (numbered "Spotlite 108" as US release).

CD reissues:

BOYD MEETS STRAVINSKY, TEMPTATION, CARAVAN, and TWO SPOOS IN AN IGLOO also on Hep CD 1.

BOYD MEETS STRAVINSKY, TEMPTATION, CARAVAN, and MEMPHIS IN JUNE also on Storyville STCD 8313.

DEEP PURPLE and TEA FOR TWO also on Fresh Sound FSCD-1019, Spotlite SPJ-(CD) 128, Jazz Classics CD-JZCL-6008, and on Proper INTRO CD 2055.

DEEP PURPLE also on Sounds Of Yesteryear DSOY 610.

Complete "Jubilee" program No. 169 also on RST JUBCD 1007 2 with original announcement for DEEP PURPLE and TEA FOR TWO.

In an Interview, given in 1995 to Robert E. Sunenblick, Marmarosa mentioned, that he worked for some three days or more with Lester Young's band, probably in San Diego. This may have been the engagement that prevented Young from being on the first recording session of the label DIAL, as is told by Ross Russell in his comments on the preparations for the session. Originally scheduled for January 22, 1946 and teaming Young with the Gillespie/Parker Quintet from Billy Berg's, the date was postponed because Young had gone to San Diego for a gig the same week. As there is no reference to such an engagement to be found in contemporary periodicals nor in the relevant literature on Lester Young, it remains open, if this actually was the engagement that Marmarosa referred to in his interview.

BOYD RAEBURN AND HIS ORCHESTRA   STANDARD RECORDINGS

Ray Linn, Dale Pearce, Nelson Shelladay, Carl Groen (tp), Ollie Wilson, Britt Woodman, Hal Smith (tb), Wilbur Schwartz (cl,as), Harry Klee (fl,as), Ralph Lee, Guy Reynolds (Guy McReynolds) (ts), Hy Mandel (bs), Boyd Raeburn (bass-sax), Dodo Marmarosa (p), Dave Barbour (g), Harry Babasin (b), Jackie Mills (dm), Ginny Powell, David Allyn (voc), Ed Finckel, George Handy (arr)

early February 1946, Hollywood, Calif.

YTH-1714-	TWO SPOOS IN AN IGLOO (s)	Standard X 207
	TEMPTATION (GPv) (/)	–
	I CAN'T BELIEVE THAT YOU'RE IN LOVE WITH ME (GPv) (s)	–
YTH-1928-1	I DON'T KNOW WHY (DAv) (s)	Standard X 220
	THAT LITTLE DREAM GOT NOWHERE (DAv) (/)	–
	MORE THAN YOU KNOW (GPv) (/)	–
	AMNESIA (s)	–
YTH-1929-1A	CARTAPHILIUS (THE WANDERING JEW) (/)	–
	A NIGHT IN TUNISIA (/)	–
	I COVER THE WATERFRONT (GPv) (s)	–
	FOOLISH LITTLE BOY (s)	–

Note :

AMNESIA is a composition and arrangement by Marmarosa.

These titles concluded the series of recordings for Standard Radio Library Service by the Raeburn orchestra.

LP reissue:

I CAN'T BELIEVE THAT YOU'RE IN LOVE, AMNESIA, CARTAPHILIUS, and FOOLISH LITTLE BOY also on Onward To Yesterday OTY-1515.

CD reissue:

TWO SPOOS IN AN IGLOO, TEMPTATION, I CAN'T BELIEVE THAT YOU'RE IN LOVE, I DON'T KNOW WHY, MORE THAN YOU KNOW, AMNESIA, CARTAPHILIUS, A NIGHT IN TUNISIA, I COVER THE WATERFRONT, and FOOLISH LITLLE BOY also on Hep CD 42.

All titles also on Audiophonic ABR060812.

BOYD RAEBURN AND HIS ORCHESTRA JEWELL RECORDING SESSION

band personnel as before

<u>February 5, 1946, Hollywood, Calif.</u>

JRC-131-2	TEMPTATION (GPv) (/)	Jewell D 1-5
JRC-132-2	DALVATORE SALLY (/)	Jewell D 1-1
JRC-133-2	BOYD MEETS STRAVINSKY (s)	Jewell GN 10002
JRC-134-2	I ONLY HAVE EYES FOR YOU (DAv) (/)	–

Note :

Jack McKinney in his liner notes to Savoy SJL 2250 reissue denotes Lucky Thompson to play the tenor saxophone solo on BOYD MEETS STRAVINSKY as guest star for this title only. This seems doubtful, however, the solo clearly sounding as being played by Ralph Lee.

LP reissue:

All titles also on Savoy SJL 2250.

CD reissue:

All titles also on Savoy SV-0185.

On February 7, 1946, Ginny Powell (Mrs. Raeburn) left her husband's band to replace Kitty Kallen with the Harry James Orchestra at the Meadowbrook Gardens in Culver City, California.

The February 11, 1946 issue of *Down Beat* magazine reported that Lucky Thompson (*"recently with Dizzy Gillespie at Billy Berg's"*) would join Boyd Raeburn. Thompson however had already been with Raeburn's band from December 1945 until January 1946. In fact he had already left Raeburn around this time.

In February 1946 the Boyd Raeburn Orchestra played several one-nighters in the Los Angeles area.

SLIM GAILLARD QUARTET   FOUR STAR RECORDING SESSIONS

Dodo Marmarosa (p), Slim Gaillard (g, vib, voc), Bam Brown (b, voc), Zutty Singleton (dm)

March 23, 1946, Hollywood, Calif.

4F-366-ME	YA HA HA (SG & BBv) (s)	4 Star 1078

March 26, 1946, Hollywood, Calif.

4F-367-ME	CARNE (SG & BBv) (s)	4 Star 1079
4F-368-ME	DING DONG OREENEY (s)	4 Star 1078
4F-369-ME	BUCK DANCE RHYTHM (SG & BBv) (s)	4 Star 1079

LP reissue:
All titles also on Onyx ORI 215.
CD reissues:
All titles also on Jazz Anthology CD 550282 and Classics CD 864.

During February - March 1946 Charlie Parker led a quintet at the Finale Club in Los Angeles, Calif., which included Miles Davis (tp), who officially worked with the Benny Carter Orchestra at the time, Addison Farmer (b), Chuck Thompson (dm), and Joe Albany (p). Shortly before the following recording session Albany left Parker due to a quarrel over musical questions and Marmarosa was chosen to replace him for the recording date.

CHARLIE PARKER SEPTET   DIAL RECORDING SESSION

Miles Davis (tp), Charlie Parker (as), Lucky Thompson (ts), Dodo Marmarosa (p), Arv Garrison (g), Vic McMillan (b), Roy Porter (dm)

<u>March 28, 1946 (1:00 to 6:00 PM), Hollywood, Calif., Radio Recorders studio</u>

D 1010-1	MOOSE THE MOOCHE (s) (omit guitar)	Dial LP 201
D 1010-2	MOOSE THE MOOCHE (s) (omit guitar)	Dial 1003, 1004
D 1010-3	MOOSE THE MOOCHE (s) (omit guitar)	Spotlite SPJ-101
D 1011-1	YARDBIRD SUITE (s)	Dial LP 201
D 1011-2	YARDBIRD SUITE ( )	Dial unissued
D 1011-3	YARDBIRD SUITE ( )	Dial unissued
D 1011-4	YARDBIRD SUITE (s)	Dial 1003
D 1012-1	ORNITHOLOGY (s)	Dial LP 208
D 1012-2	ORNITHOLOGY ( )	Dial unissued
D 1012-3	ORNITHOLOGY (/) (orig. released as BIRD LORE)	Dial 1006
D 1012-4	ORNITHOLOGY (/)	Dial 1002
D 1013-1	FAMOUS ALTO BREAK (/)	Dial LP 905
D 1013-2	A NIGHT IN TUNISIA ( )	Dial unissued
D 1013-3	A NIGHT IN TUNISIA ( )	Dial unissued
D 1013-4	A NIGHT IN TUNISIA (/)	Dial LP 201
D 1013-5	A NIGHT IN TUNISIA (/)	Dial 1002

Note :

The above session lasted about five to six hours! It was supervised by the owner of Dial Records, Ross Russell. The original recording contract between Dial Records (Ross Russell) and Charlie Parker, dated March 25, 1946, lists Jackie Mills as drummer among the musicians selected for the above session. Obviously Roy Porter was a short-term replacement.

Although, as it seems, not scheduled, Marmarosa plays a solo in Charlie Parker's place on take-1 of ORNITHOLOGY. For this reason take-1 was first issued on Dial LP 208 as by the "Dodo Marmarosa Sextet". FAMOUS ALTO BREAK actually is the beginning of the first take of A NIGHT IN TUNISIA, which breaks off after a breathtaking introductory solo-break by Parker and part of the theme.

MOOSE THE MOOCHE was the nickname of Emry Byrd, jazz aficionado, shoe shine- and jazz record-stand owner on Central Avenue, L.A. He was crippled and sold narcotics to musicians, due to which he passed several years in San Quentin prison in later times.

LP reissue:

All issued titles also on Spotlite SPJ-101.

CD reissues:

All issued titles also on Spotlite SPJ-CD 4-101.

Matrix D 1012-1 of ORNITHOLOGY also on Spotlite SPJ-(CD) 128 and Jazz Classics CD-JZCL-6008.

D 1010-2, D 1011-4, D 1012-4, and D 1013-5 (master takes) also on Classics CD 980.

For the below mentioned tour of concerts by the Boyd Raeburn Orchestra there were some minor changes in the personnel. Ray Linn (tp) left and Fred Zito (tb) definitely replaced Britt Woodman, Jean Louise came in as vocalist and there were possibly no french horns and harp.

Dodo Marmarosa's participation in the tour is confirmed by two sources. In a letter to the authors Dr. Jack McKinney mentions a personal conversation between him and arranger George Handy, in the course of which Handy remembered Marmarosa having nearly been killed one day of the tour, when he walked towards the running propeller of a transport airplane. Second, the biography of arranger Tom Talbert, written by Bruce Talbot, conveys a further Marmarosan anecdote from this tour: According to trumpeter Billy Morris, who was a member of the band then, the pianist almost overslept the start of their transport plane sunbathing on the rooftop of a Wichitan airport building.

early to mid April 1946   : military camp tour from Texas to Colorado

In mid-April 1946 Marmarosa appeared at the following jazz concert in L.A.:

April 12, 1946   : Los Angeles, Calif., University of California (UCLA)

Metronome magazine of June 1946 reported that "*...the Carver Club of the Los Angeles campus sponsored this concert to raise funds for its scholarship program and its support of inter-racial good will. The concert was held on the anniversary of Franklin Roosevelt's death...*".

At the concert Marmarosa appeared with a group consisting of:

Miles Davis (tp), Britt Woodman (tb), Charlie Parker (as), Lucky Thompson (ts), Arv Garrison (g), Red Callender (b), Perc White (dm)

Other participators at the concert were Joe Graves (tp), Sonny Criss, Benny Carter (as), Lester Young, Hubert "Bumps" Meyers (ts), Ray Bauduc (dm), the Eddie Beal Quintet, the Delta Rhythm Boys, Kay Starr, and Herb Jeffries (voc).

Marmarosa was back with Boyd Raeburn at latest in May 1946 (see following entry).

BOYD RAEBURN
AND HIS ORCHESTRA

AFRS "JUBILEE"
"CONCERT OF MODERN JAZZ"

Ray Linn, Dale Pearce, Nelson Shelladay, Frank Beach (tp), Fred Zito, Ollie Wilson, Hal Smith (tb), Lloyd Otto, Evan Vail (frh), Wilbur Schwartz (cl,as), Harry Klee (fl,as), Jules Jacobs (ts,oboe,englh.), Ralph Lee (ts,bassoon), Guy McReynolds (ts,reeds), Hy Mandel (bs), Boyd Raeburn (bass-sax), Dodo Marmarosa (p), Tony Rizzi (g), Harry Babasin (b), Jackie Mills (dm), Ginny Powell, David Allyn (voc), George Handy, Ed Finckel (arr), Mel Tormé and The Mel-Tones (voc) appear as guest stars

Note :   The Mel-Tones at that time consisted of Ginny O'Connor, Betty Beveridge, Bernie Parke, and Les Baxter.

<u>ca. early May 1946, Hollywood, Calif., NBC studios</u>

THEME (HEP BOYDS) (/)	AFRS Jubilee Program No. 188
BOYD MEETS STRAVINSKY (s)	AFRS Jubilee Program No. 188
BODY AND SOUL (GPv) (/)	AFRS Jubilee Program No. 189
OL' MAN RIVER (/) (Mel Tormé & The Mel-Tones -voc)	
	AFRS Jubilee Program No. 188
TONE POEM Part 1&2: DALVATORE SALLY (s)	AFRS Jubilee Program No. 188
HEY LOOK, I'M DANCING (/)	AFRS Jubilee Program No. 188
THAT'S WHERE I CAME IN (s) (Mel Tormé & The Mel-Tones -voc)	
	AFRS Jubilee Program No. 188
TONE POEM Part 3&4: GREY SUEDE, SPECIAL MADE (/)	
	AFRS Jubilee Program No. 188
KEY F (/)	AFRS Jubilee Program No. 188
I CAN'T BELIEVE THAT YOU'RE IN LOVE WITH ME (GPv) (s)	
	AFRS Jubilee Program No. 189
A NIGHT IN TUNISIA (/)	AFRS Jubilee Program No. 188
THEME (HEP BOYDS) (/)	AFRS Jubilee Program No. 188

Note :

The above "Jubilee" show was announced by master of ceremonies Ernie "Bubbles" Whitman as a "Concert of Modern Jazz". The sequence of Raeburn titles from this concert is a reconstruction from the music and 'live'-announcements preserved on AFRS "Jubilee" programs No. 188 and 189. Other participators at this concert were Tommy Todd (p) with Al Hendrickson, Bob Bain (g), and Artie Shapiro (b) forming "Tommy Todd and his Trio". The four movements of TONE POEM together form a Suite (or "Jazz Symphony", as it was also billed).

Metronome magazine of June 1946 reported in its "news of the month" column about George Handy's TONE POEM:

"Handy recently introduced his new Jazz Symphony on a program for Armed Forces Radio Service." This note would suggest a date for the above concert in May 1946 rather than mid-April or late March, as has been supposed by Richard S. Sears in his V-Disc Discography.

All four parts of TONE POEM also used for AFRS BML P-651 and V-Disc 677, with the V-Disc release bearing spoken introductions to all four movements by Handy, which were recorded at a later date in New York City, and have been patched in for the V-Disc release exclusively.

According to Richard S. Sears in the supplement (1986) to his V-Disc Discography, George Handy supposed the V-Disc release of his TONE POEM to have been recorded in the studio and not from an AFRS "Jubilee" show. This statement seems corroborated by a note in Metronome magazine of July 1946. It is said that, while being on tour on the West Coast in May/June 1946, Sgt. Tony Janak recorded several ensembles for "V-Disc", among them Boyd Raeburn's orchestra with "George Handy's four-part suite". Regarding that all existing versions of TONE POEM on V-Disc, BML, and on AFRS "Jubilee" are identical, we nevertheless believe, that Janak gained his recordings from the above "Jubilee" transcriptions and that they remained the only recorded version of TONE POEM.

To complete AFRS Jubilee program No. 189, for which also parts of the above concert were used, Raeburn titles from late 1945 to early 1946 were filled in, which already had been released on AFRS Jubilee programs No. 163 and 169.

LP reissues:

BODY AND SOUL and I CAN'T BELIEVE THAT YOU'RE IN LOVE WITH ME also on Joyce LP-5011.

OL' MAN RIVER, THAT'S WHERE I CAME IN, and I CAN'T BELIEVE also on First Heard FHR-8.

TONE POEM as AFRS BML P-651 release also on Savoy ZNLY 33313 and on Sounds of Swing SoS-115 (TONE POEM here is titled "SUITE FOR SWING").

CD reissues:

BOYD MEETS STRAVINSKY, TONE POEM, THAT'S WHERE I CAME IN, A NIGHT IN TUNISIA, and THEME also on Hep CD 1.

OL' MAN RIVER, DALVATORE SALLY, HEY, LOOK, I'M DANCING, and THAT'S WHERE I CAME IN also on Storyville STCD 8313.

<u>**NOTE**</u>:   For June 1946 there are rumors that Marmarosa, together with Dale Pearce and Wilbur Schwartz of the Raeburn personnel, played with the Bob Crosby Orchestra. Nevertheless the AFRS "One Night Stand" program No. 1025 (June 1, 1946, Meadowbrook Gardens, Culver City, L.A.), listed with Marmarosa as piano player in Erik Raben's "Jazz Records 1942-1980", definitely shows Tommy Todd at the piano (also confirmed by the announcement).

At the end of June 1946 Marmarosa appeared at another Los Angeles jazz-concert:

June 24, 1946   : Los Angeles, Calif., Embassy Theatre

The concert was held under the heading "Swingposium" and was sponsored by Fran Kelley (of Fran-Tone Records). Other participators were Howard McGhee (tp), Vido Musso (ts), Erroll Garner (p), Allen Reuss (g), the Tommy Todd Trio, and the Red Callender Trio.

Also at the end of June 1946 the Boyd Raeburn Orchestra started a lengthy engagement at Hollywood's Club Morocco, located on North Vine Street about midway between Sunset and Hollywood boulevards. *Down Beat* magazine of July 1, 1946 reported that the club had to be almost completely remodelled to accommodate Raeburn's 19-piece orchestra.
Seemingly Marmarosa stayed with the orchestra only for the first half of the engagement, which lasted almost two months and procured Raeburn regular radio broadcasts over the CBS-network:

June 27 - August 25, 1946   : Club Morocco, Hollywood, Calif.

BOYD RAEBURN
AND HIS ORCHESTRA

AFRS "ONE NIGHT STAND"
RADIO BROADCAST

band personnel similar as before

<u>July 1, 1946, Hollywood, Calif., Club Morocco</u>

TEMPTATION (GPv) (/)	AFRS One Night Stand No. 1138
BLUE ECHOES (DAv) (/)	–
YERXA (p-intro)	–
BOYD MEETS STRAVINSKY (s)	–
I DON'T KNOW WHY (DAv) (s)	–
MEMPHIS IN JUNE (GP & DAv) (s)	–
TONSILLECTOMY (s)	–
FULL MOON AND EMPTY ARMS (DAv) (/)	–
A NIGHT IN TUNISIA (/)	–
THEME (DALVATORE SALLY) (/)	–

BOYD RAEBURN
AND HIS ORCHESTRA

AFRS "MAGIC CARPET"
RADIO BROADCAST

band personnel similar as before

<u>ca. early July 1946, Hollywood, Calif., Club Morocco</u>

THEME (DALVATORE SALLY) (/)	AFRS Magic Carpet No. 402
BLUE ECHOES (DAv) (/)	–
YERXA (p-intro)	–
TEMPTATION (GPv) (/)	–
TWO SPOOS IN AN IGLOO (/)	–
DALVATORE SALLY (part only) (/)	–
THEME (TWO SPOOS IN AN IGLOO) (faded) (/)	–

Note :

Besides their "One Night Stand" programs the Armed Forces Radio Service also transcribed portions of Raeburn's radio broadcasts from the Club Morocco for their "Magic Carpet" program series. These programs had 15 minutes duration and were released usually a few weeks after the actual recording date of the used materials. The release date for the above program was July 23, 1946, indicating recording probably in early July.

Instead of the usual piano solo on TWO SPOOS IN AN IGLOO there is a solo by the guitar player on the above version of the title.

LP reissue:
All titles also on Joyce LP-4012.

BOYD RAEBURN
AND HIS ORCHESTRA

AFRS "MAGIC CARPET"
RADIO BROADCAST

band personnel similar as before

<u>ca. early July 1946, Hollywood, Calif., Club Morocco</u>

THEME ( )	AFRS Magic Carpet No. 408
MORE THAN YOU KNOW (GPv) (/)	–
TONSILLECTOMY (s)	–
I DON'T KNOW WHY (DAv) ( )	–
[unknown title ?]	–
THEME ( )	–

Note :

Unfortunately we could not check this program completely. Considering issue number and two reissued titles, which possibly stem from this program (see below), we believe that Marmarosa was present on this broadcast, which was released by AFRS at the end of July 1946.

LP reissue:

MORE THAN YOU KNOW and TONSILLECTOMY most certainly as the above versions on First Heard FHR-8.

BOYD RAEBURN
AND HIS ORCHESTRA

AFRS "MAGIC CARPET"
RADIO BROADCAST

band personnel similar as before

<u>ca. mid July 1946, Hollywood, Calif., Club Morocco</u>

THEME (DALVATORE SALLY) (/)	AFRS Magic Carpet No. 416
MEMPHIS IN JUNE (GP & DAv) (s)	–
A NIGHT IN TUNISIA (/)	–
I DON'T KNOW WHY (DAv) (s)	–
MARCH OF THE BOYDS (faded) (s)	–

Note :

Other sources give the above program release no. as "415".

Release date of AFRS "Magic Carpet" No. 416 was August 5, 1946.

CD reissue:

The complete program has been reissued on Hep CD 22.

BOYD RAEBURN
AND HIS ORCHESTRA

AFRS "MAGIC CARPET"
RADIO BROADCAST

band personnel similar as before

<u>ca. mid July 1946, Hollywood, Calif., Club Morocco</u>

THEME ( )	AFRS Magic Carpet No. 423
THAT LITTLE DREAM GOT NOWHERE (DAv) ( )	–
A NIGHT IN TUNISIA ( )	–
I COVER THE WATERFRONT (GPv) ( )	–
MARCH OF THE BOYDS ( )	–
THEME ( )	–

Note :

Unfortunately we could not check this program, which was released by AFRS on August 13, 1946. Considering this date, we believe that Marmarosa, who left Raeburn in early August, was still present on this broadcast.

BOYD RAEBURN
AND HIS ORCHESTRA

SPOTLIGHT BANDS
RADIO BROADCAST

band personnel similar as before

<u>July 20, 1946, Hollywood, Calif., Club Morocco</u>

THEME (DALVATORE SALLY) (/)	AFRS Spotlight Bands No. 874
BLUE PRELUDE (/)	–
RIP VAN WINKLE (GPv) (s)	–
WHERE OR WHEN (s)	–
DALVATORE SALLY (faded for closing announcement) (/)	–
THEME (MARCH OF THE BOYDS) (faded) (/)	–

Note :

In April 1946 the Coca Cola company once more changed the format of its "Victory Parade of Spotlight Bands" program series. The title of the show was shortened to "Spotlight Bands" again, and on three remaining days a week three bands were broadcast in a rotating system: Guy Lombardo (Mondays), Xavier Cugat (Wednesdays), and Harry James (Fridays).

The above performance was broadcast as a replacement program for Guy Lombardo's orchestra, whose band was on summer vacation at the period.

BOYD RAEBURN AND HIS ORCHESTRA

AFRS "ONE NIGHT STAND" RADIO BROADCAST

band personnel similar as before

<u>July 22, 1946, Hollywood, Calif., Club Morocco</u>

THEME (DALVATORE SALLY) (/)	AFRS One Night Stand No. 1051
TONSILLECTOMY (s)	–
TEMPTATION (GPv) (/)	–
YERXA (p-intro)	–
BLUE ECHOES (DAv) (/)	–
I COVER THE WATERFRONT (GPv) (s)	–
BOYD'S NEST (s)	–
I ONLY HAVE EYES FOR YOU (DAv) (/)	–
TWO SPOOS IN AN IGLOO (s)	–
I DON'T KNOW WHY (DAv) (s)	–
THEME (BOYD'S NEST) (/)	–

LP reissues:
I COVER THE WATERFRONT and I ONLY HAVE EYES FOR YOU also on I.A.J.R.C. 48.
BOYD'S NEST and TWO SPOOS IN AN IGLOO also on First Heard FH-8.
CD reissue:
BOYD'S NEST also on Storyville STCD 8313.

*D*own Beat magazine of August 12, 1946 reported about the following concert, which was a benefit for an interracial hospital to be erected. It was sponsored by Al Jarvis' "Make Believe Ballroom" radio show, by the Daily News and by radio station KLAC:

<u>July 22, 1946</u>   : Hollywood, Calif., Hollywood Bowl

Besides the Boyd Raeburn Orchestra other participators were the orchestras of Al Sack, Tommy Dorsey, and Stan Kenton, the Lecuona Cuban Boys, the Slim Gaillard Trio, Eddie Heywood, Art Tatum, Larry Adler, and Bob Hope.

BOYD RAEBURN
AND HIS ORCHESTRA

AFRS "MAGIC CARPET"
RADIO BROADCAST

band personnel similar as before

<u>ca. late July 1946, Hollywood, Calif., Club Morocco</u>

THEME ( )	AFRS Magic Carpet No. 428
I ONLY HAVE EYES FOR YOU (DAv) ( )	–
A NIGHT IN TUNISIA ( )	–
I COVER THE WATERFRONT (GPv) ( )	–
MARCH OF THE BOYDS ( )	–
THEME ( )	–

Note :

Unfortunately we could not check this program, which was released by AFRS on August 17, 1946. Considering this date, we believe that Marmarosa, who left Raeburn in early August, was still present on this broadcast.

BOYD RAEBURN
AND HIS ORCHESTRA

AFRS "ONE NIGHT STAND"
RADIO BROADCAST

band personnel similar as before

<u>July 29, 1946, Hollywood, Calif., Club Morocco</u>

TONSILLECTOMY (s)	AFRS One Night Stand No. 1087
I DON'T KNOW WHY (DAv) (s)	–
I CAN'T BELIEVE THAT YOU'RE IN LOVE WITH ME (GPv) (s)	–
HOW DEEP IS THE OCEAN (/)	–
BLUE ECHOES (DAv) (/)	–
MEMPHIS IN JUNE (GP & DAv) (s)	–
BOYD MEETS STRAVINSKY (s)	–
I ONLY HAVE EYES FOR YOU (DAv) (/)	–
BLUE PRELUDE (/)	–

Note :

The above program in its entirety has also been used for AFRS One Night Stand program No. 1046.

BOYD RAEBURN
AND HIS ORCHESTRA

AFRS "MAGIC CARPET"
RADIO BROADCAST

band personnel similar as before

<u>late July/early August 1946, Hollywood, Calif., Club Morocco</u>

THEME (DALVATORE SALLY) (/)	AFRS Magic Carpet No. 436
I ONLY HAVE EYES FOR YOU (DAv) (/)	–
MARCH OF THE BOYDS (s)	–
MORE THAN YOU KNOW (GPv) (/)	–
DUCK WADDLE (part only) (/)	–
THEME (MARCH OF THE BOYDS) (faded) (/)	–

Note :
Release date of the above program was August 26, 1946.

BOYD RAEBURN
AND HIS ORCHESTRA

AFRS "MAGIC CARPET"
RADIO BROADCAST

band personnel similar as before

<u>late July/early August 1946, Hollywood, Calif., Club Morocco</u>

THEME (DALVATORE SALLY) (/)	AFRS Magic Carpet No. 444
I COVER THE WATERFRONT (GPv) (s)	–
TONSILLECTOMY (s)	–
THERE'S NO YOU (DAv) (/)	–
TWO SPOOS IN AN IGLOO (s)	–
THEME (MARCH OF THE BOYDS) (faded) (/)	–

Note :
Release date of the above program was September 3, 1946.

NOTE: Although it is not possible to make any definitive statements regarding
the date of Marmarosa's departure from Raeburn and the Club Morocco,
AFRS Magic Carpet No. 444 from ca. early August 1946 was possibly the
last transcribed program on which Marmarosa could have played. A
program from August 5, 1946 (AFRS One Night Stand No. 1205) already
has Hal Schaefer playing piano in Marmarosa's place.

Down Beat magazine of August 26, 1946 reported about this change and
others in the Raeburn band personnel:
*"Not rumor but fact this time is the departure of George Handy. Also out are
Ray Linn, Jackie Mills, Dodo Marmarosa, Harry Babasin, and singer David
Allyn."* In spite of the loss of most of his stars, *"...Raeburn denied reports
that the band was on notice at the Morocco"* (*Down Beat*).
Of these 'stars' Marmarosa was obviously one of the first to leave Raeburn.
Allyn is heard on three more programs from the Club Morocco (One
Night Stand No. 1205, Magic Carpet No. 463, and Magic Carpet No.
502), before he was replaced by Jackie Searle.

Transcriptions for AFRS "Magic Carpet" programs featuring the Raeburn
Orchestra from the Morocco (program Nos. 449, 456, 463, 488, 496, and
502) continued until late August 1946.
On all of these remaining Raeburn programs as well as on AFRS One Night
Stand programs No. 1205, 1235, and AFRS "Popular Music Replacement"
No. 45 - all three also transcribed from the Morocco -, the piano playing
is by Hal Schaefer with one exception. The pianist on AFRS Magic Carpet
program No. 502 may be George Handy.

ELLA MAE MORSE   CAPITOL RECORDING SESSION
ACC. BY RAY LINN ORCHESTRA

Ray Linn (tp), Ollie Wilson (tb), Skeets Herfurt (cl, as, ts), Herbie Steward (cl, ts), Chuck Gentry (bs), Dodo Marmarosa (p), Barney Kessel (g), Harry Babasin (b), Jackie Mills (dm), Ella Mae Morse (voc)

<u>August 14, 1946, Hollywood, Calif., Radio Recorders studio</u>

1352-3	THAT'S MY HOME (EMMv) (/)	Capitol 301
1353-5	THE MERRY HA-HA (EMMv) (p-intro)	–

Note :

Jackie Mills in an interview with Burt Korall for his publication "Drummin' Men: The Bebop Years" remembered a recording session he did with Marmarosa and Babasin as members of a studio band for Capitol Records around the time they were playing with Boyd Raeburn. Also he remembered the date to have been one of singer Jo Stafford's vocal sessions for Capitol. Mills' point of interest was the conservatism of Capitol's musical director Paul Weston and his discontent with their modern style of playing. As we could not find any indication of Dodo Marmarosa's playing on Stafford's recordings from 1946 and 1947 nor the mention of his name on recording contracts for these productions, we believe Mills' anecdote to refer to the above recording session and that he mistook the name of the day's vocal star.

CD reissue:

Both titles also on Bear Family Records BCD 16117 (4 CD-set).

<u>NOTE</u>:   Two days later Marmarosa was back with his old boss Artie Shaw for the following studio recording session:

ARTIE SHAW AND HIS ORCHESTRA   MUSICRAFT RECORDING SESSION

Clyde Hurley, Mannie Klein, Zeke Zarchy, Ray Linn (tp), Ed Kusby, Elmer Smithers, Ollie Wilson (tb), Artie Shaw (cl), Harry Klee, Les Robinson (as), Don Raffell, Babe Russin (ts), Chuck Gentry (bs), Dodo Marmarosa (p), Al Hendrickson (g), Phil Stephens (b), Louis Singer (dm), Harry Bluestone, Sam Cytron, Sam Freed, David Frisina, Howard Halbert, George Kast, Nick Pisani, Mischa Russell, Marshall Sosson (vl), Paul Robyn, Stanley Spiegelmann, David Sterkin (viola), Fred Goerner, Arthur Krafton, Nicolas Ochi-Albi (cello), Mel Tormé, The Mel-Tones (voc), Sonny Burke, Mel Tormé (arr)

<u>August 16, 1946 (8:15 PM to 0:15 AM), Hollywood, Calif., Radio Recorders studio</u>

5629-2	FOR YOU, FOR ME, FOR EVERMORE (MTv) (/)	Musicraft 412
5635-4	CHANGING MY TUNE (MT&Mel-Tones -vcl) (/)	–
5636	LOVE FOR SALE ( )	Musicraft unissued

CD reissue:
FOR YOU, FOR ME, FOR EVERMORE and CHANGING MY TUNE also on Musicraft MVSCD-50 and on Classics CD 1368.

During August and September 1946, Dodo Marmarosa played in a rehearsal big band, led by Lucky Thompson in Los Angeles. *Down Beat* magazine of December 16, 1946 reported about this group as a *"...mixed unit which was formed primarily as a musical experiment and which was dissolved when its purpose had been accomplished."* According to Jackie Kelso, who played alto saxophone in the band, the brass section was made up of mostly white players. He also remembered Buddy DeFranco to have done some of the writings and one public appearance by the band at Elks Hall located on Los Angeles' Central Avenue (interview in Bryant et al.: "Central Avenue Sounds").

The October 1946 issue of Capitol Records' monthly newsletter *Capitol News from Hollywood* besides Marmarosa mentioned trumpeter Frank Beach, trombonist Ollie Wilson, and Jackie Mills on drums as better known members of this band. Mills himself named Britt Woodman, Herbie Steward, and Marshall Royal as others. According to his words, they "performed only in black areas", the band being "too wild for Hollywood" (chapter "Jackie Mills" in B. Korall: "Drummin' Men: The Bebop Years").

Charles Mingus played bass with the band and also contributed compositions and arrangements to its repertoire.

Miles Davis in his autobiography remembers the band to have lasted three to four weeks and to have played three nights a week for dancers at Elks Hall.

To Miles Davis, who also participated in the project, Marmarosa dedicated a composition called MILES' INFLUENCE, which was discussed in *DOWN BEAT* magazine of December 16, 1946 (p. 12) as an example for the pianist's advanced piano stylings. This composition was recorded by Marmarosa about a year later as a piano-solo under the title "TONE PAINTINGS II (medium)".

DODO MARMAROSA TRIO   ATOMIC RECORDING SESSION

Dodo Marmarosa (p), Barney Kessel (g), Gene Englund (b)

September 23, 1946, Hollywood, Calif.

V 2070	RAINDROPS	Atomic 227
RL 90163	I'VE GOT NEWS FOR YOU (Dodo Marmarosa -voc)	–

Note :

I'VE GOT NEWS FOR YOU is the only title ever where Marmarosa appears as vocalist. According to Marmarosa's own words (conveyed by Danny Conn) a neighbourhood friend in Los Angeles, Harvey Eastman, sang the melody to him and gave him the lyrics to it. Marmarosa wrote both down on paper and recorded it.

LP reissues:

Both titles also on Onyx ORI 212 and Raretone FC 5020.

CD reissues:

RAINDROPS also on Proper INTRO CD 2055.

Both titles also on EPM/Xanadu CD FDC 5175, on Classics CD 1165, and on Lone Hill Jazz LJH10119.

ORCHESTRA DIRECTED
BY RALPH BURNS / GEORGE HANDY

RECORDING SESSION

<u>Ralph Burns And His Orchestra</u> :

Sonny Berman, Conrad Gozzo (tp), Bill Harris, Ollie Wilson (tb), Vincent De Rosa (frh), Hal McKusick, Harry Klee (fl,cl,as), Herbie Steward, Lucky Thompson (ts), Chuck Gentry (bs), Dodo Marmarosa (p), Arvin Garrison (g), Red Callender (b), Don Lamond (dm), Ralph Burns (comp, arr)

<u>October 15, 1946, Hollywood, Calif., Radio Recorders studio</u>

5003-1	INTROSPECTION (/)	Jazz Scene (unnumbered)
5003-2	INTROSPECTION (/)	Verve 314 521 661-2

<u>George Handy And His Orchestra</u> :

above personnel plus : Pete Candoli, Al Killian, Dale Pearce (tp), Ed Kusby (tb), Evan Vail (frh), Julius Jacobs (oboe), Robert Swanson (bassoon), Arthur Flemming (contra bassoon), Harry Bluestone, Robert Jamison, Carl Walker (vl), Arthur Krafton (cello), Jackie Mills, Jimmy Pratt (percussion), George Handy (comp, arr)

<u>probably same date</u>

5004-2	THE BLOOS (/)	Verve 314 521 661-2
5004-3	THE BLOOS (/)	Jazz Scene (unnumbered)

Note :

"The Jazz Scene" was a six record album (78rpm) produced by Norman Granz and originally released in late 1949. It was intended to cover the contemporary jazz scene in recordings, photographs and comments. Granz asked both, Burns and Handy, for the above contributions to this project.

Other sources give matrix nos. C 2075-1, C 2075-2 for INTROSPECTION and C 2076-2, C 2076-7 for THE BLOOS.

LP reissue:

Matrix 5003-1 and 5004-3 also on Verve MGV-8060.

CD reissue:

All four takes also on Verve 314 521 661-2.

ARTIE SHAW AND HIS ORCHESTRA   MUSICRAFT RECORDING SESSION

Frank Beach, Mannie Klein, Zeke Zarchy, Ray Linn (tp), Ed Kusby, Elmer Smithers, Bill Schaefer, Joe Howard (tb), Artie Shaw (cl), Harry Klee, Skeets Herfurt (as), Harold Lawson, Babe Russin (ts), Bob Lawson (bs), Dodo Marmarosa (p, celesta), Allen Reuss (g), Phil Stephens (b), Nick Fatool (dm), Alex Law, Sam Cytron, Sam Freed, Lewis Elias, Olcott Vail, George Kast, Nick Pisani, Mischa Russell, Edgar Bergman, Walter Edelstein (vl), Maurice Perlmutter, Harry Weiss, David Sterkin (viola), Fred Goerner, Cy Bernard, Jack Sewell (cello), Mel Tormé, Ralph Blane, Lilian Lane, The Mel-Tones (voc), Sonny Burke (arr)

October 17, 1946 (7 to 10:30 PM), Hollywood, Calif., Radio Recorders studio

5650-2	AND SO TO BED (MT&Mel-Tones -vcl) (s)	Musicraft 441-L
5651-2	CONNECTICUT (RBv) (/)	Musicraft 445
5701-1	DON'T YOU BELIEVE IT, DEAR (MT&Mel-Tones -vcl) (/)	–
5702	IT'S THE SAME OLD DREAM (MTv) ( )	Musicraft unissued
5703	I BELIEVE (MTv) ( )	–
5704	WHEN YOU'RE AROUND (LLv) ( )	–

Note :

The Musicraft worksheets for the above recording session give October 18 as date of recording (personal information by George Hulme). Recording contracts preserved in the archive of the Los Angeles local musicians union, however, indicate October 17 as recording date (L. C. do Nascimento Silva, I.A.J.R.C.-Journal, Winter 1998). As the session was a lengthy one (see above) and Marmarosa participated in two more recording sessions on October 18, we believe it to be unlikely, that all three sessions took place on the same day. Thus October 17 possibly may be the correct date for this session.

CD reissue:

First three titles also on Musicraft MVSCD-50 and on Classics CD 1368.

MEL TORMÉ   *MUSICRAFT*
WITH RAY LINN AND HIS ORCHESTRA   *RECORDING SESSION*

Ray Linn (tp), poss. Si Zentner (tb), five unknown reeds, Dodo Marmarosa (p), unknown (g), unknown (b), unknown (d), Mel Tormé, The Mel-Tones (voc), Hal Mooney, Ray Conniff (arr)

<u>October 18, 1946, Hollywood, Calif., Radio Recorders studio</u>

5800-2A	ONE FOR MY BABY (MTv) (/)	Musicraft 15107
5801-113	A LITTLE KISS EACH MORNING (MTv) (/)	–
5802-4	DREAM AWHILE (MT&Mel-Tones -vcl) (/)	Musicraft 15099
5803-6-B	THERE'S NO BUSINESS LIKE SHOW BUSINESS (MT&Mel-Tones -vcl) (/)	–

Note :

According to the Musicraft worksheets for the above session the vocals of Mel Tormé were to be dubbed over the recordings of the instrumental backings at a later date. George Hulme suggests November 27, 1946 as the date for this overdubbing, which would also explain the unfittingly high matrix-numbers assigned to these titles.

LP reissues:

ONE FOR MY BABY also on Sutton SU 281.

THERE'S NO BUSINESS LIKE SHOWBUSINESS and DREAM AWHILE also on Musicraft MVS-510.

CD reissues:

A LITTLE KISS EACH MORNING also on Musicraft MVSCD-60 and on Living Era CD AJA 5346.

THERE'S NO BUSINESS LIKE SHOWBUSINESS also on Musicraft MVSCD-54.

HOWARD MCGHEE SEXTET   DIAL RECORDING SESSION

Howard McGhee (tp), Teddy Edwards (ts), Dodo Marmarosa (p), Arvin Garrison (g), Bob Kesterson (b), Roy Porter (dm)

October 18, 1946 (1:00 to 4:00 PM), Hollywood, Calif., Universal Recorders studio

D 1041-1	DIAL-ATED PUPILS [MAX MAKING WAX] ( )	Dial unissued
D 1041-2	DIAL-ATED PUPILS [MAX MAKING WAX] ( )	Dial unissued
D 1041-3	DIAL-ATED PUPILS [MAX MAKING WAX] ( )	Dial unissued
D 1041-4	DIAL-ATED PUPILS [MAX MAKING WAX] (s)	Dial 1011
D 1041-5	DIAL-ATED PUPILS [MAX MAKING WAX] (s)	Dial 1011
D 1042-1	MIDNIGHT AT MINTON'S ( )	Dial unissued
D 1042-2	MIDNIGHT AT MINTON'S ( )	Dial unissued
D 1042-3	MIDNIGHT AT MINTON'S ( )	Dial unissued
D 1042-4	MIDNIGHT AT MINTON'S (s)	Dial 1011
D 1043-1	UP IN DODO'S ROOM (s)	Dial 1010
D 1043-2	UP IN DODO'S ROOM (s)	Dial 1010, 1050
D 1044-1	HIGH WIND IN HOLLYWOOD [52nd STREET THEME] ( )	Dial unissued
D 1044-2	HIGH WIND IN HOLLYWOOD [52nd STREET THEME] (s)	Dial 1010

Note :

This session was supervised by the owner of Dial Records, Ross Russell.

Some sources give "D 1044-C" for matrix D 1044-2.

Obviously both issued takes of matrix 1041 have been used for the pressing of Dial 1011, as well as both takes of matrix 1043 for Dial 1010.

D 1043-2 issued on Dial 1050 as by the "Dodo Marmarosa Sextet".

LP reissues:

All titles also on Spotlite SPJ-131.

D 1041-4, D 1042-4, and D 1043-2 also on Cicala BLJ 8022.

CD reissues:

D 1041-4, D 1042-4, D 1043-2, and D 1044-2 also on Cool & Blue CD 115.

D 1041-4 and D 1043-1 also on Jazz Classics CD-JZCL-6008.

D 1042-4 and D 1044-2 also on ABM ABMCD 1065.

D 1041-5, D 1042-4, D 1043-2, and D 1044-2 also on Classics CD 1089.

All issued titles also on Spotlite SPJ-(CD) 128 and Spotlite SPJ-(CD) 131.

LYLE GRIFFIN AND HIS ORCHESTRA   ATOMIC / IRRA
RECORDING SESSION

Al Killian, Ray Linn, Ronnie Rochat (tp), Ray Sims, Ollie Wilson, Gene Roland (tb), Hal McKusick (cl,as), Ethmer Roten (as), Lucky Thompson, Ralph Lee (ts), Larry Patton (bs), Dodo Marmarosa (p), Mike Bryan (g), Paul Morsey (b), Lou Fromm (dm), David Allyn (voc), Lyle Griffin (arr), Thomas Talbert, Frank Davenport (arr) add Cee Pee Johnson (tom-tom) on matrix 271-2.

<u>November 4, 1946 (2:00 to 5:00 PM), Hollywood, Calif., Radio Recorders studio</u>

270-1	FLIGHT OF THE VOUT BUG (TTarr) (s)	Atomic 270
270-2	DEEP IN THE BLUES (DAv) (FDarr) (solo-break)	–
271-1	IT SHOULDN'T HAPPEN (DAv) (FDarr) (/)	Atomic 271
271-2	BIG CHIEF ALBUQUERQUE (Lyle Griffin -voc) (LGarr) ( )	–
	LOVE EYES (TTarr)	Atomic unissued

Note :

Thomas Talbert in his biography (written by Bruce Talbot) remembers to have also composed and arranged the title LOVE EYES for the above session. It was recorded on the date, but not issued, because Lyle Griffin did not like it enough.

Both Atomic issues also on IRRA with the same numbers.

IRRA (Independent Record Releasing Association) was affiliated with the Atomic label. Proprietor of both labels was Lyle Griffin.

FLIGHT OF THE VOUT BUG reissued in 1956 as FLIGHT OF THE SAUCER Pts. 1 & 2. This version has a vocal by Richard "Lord" Buckley dubbed over the original recording and was produced and issued by Lyle Griffin's HIP label on two sides of a single record with issue no. HI-270-1/-2.

CD reissues:

FLIGHT OF THE VOUT BUG and IT SHOULDN'T HAPPEN also on I.A.J.R.C. CD-1001.

FLIGHT OF THE VOUT BUG also on Sea Breeze SB-2069 (CD).

ARTIE SHAW AND HIS ORCHESTRA   *MUSICRAFT*
RECORDING SESSION

Frank Beach, Mannie Klein, Zeke Zarchy, Ray Linn (tp), Ed Kusby, Si Zentner, Bill Schaefer, Joe Howard (tb), Artie Shaw (cl), Harry Klee, Skeets Herfurt (as), Herbie Haymer, Babe Russin (ts), Bob Lawson (bs), Dodo Marmarosa (p), Dave Barbour (g), Artie Shapiro (b), Nick Fatool (dm), Marshall Sosson, Sam Cytron, Sam Freed, Felix Slatkin, Olcott Vail, George Kast, Nick Pisani, Mischa Russell, Harry Bluestone, Howard Halbert, Morris King, Peter Ellis (vl), David Sterkin, Stanley Spiegelmann, Maurice Perlmutter (viola), Fred Goerner, Cy Bernard, Jack Sewell (cello), Mel Tormé, Lilian Lane, The Mel-Tones (voc), Sonny Burke (arr)

November 9, 1946 (12:30 to 4:15 PM), Hollywood, Calif., Radio Recorders studio

5702-1	IT'S THE SAME OLD DREAM (MTv) (/)	Musicraft 492
5703-3	I BELIEVE (MTv) (/)	–
5704-1	WHEN YOU'RE AROUND (LLv) (/)	Musicraft 512

CD reissue:

All three titles also on Musicraft MVSCD-51 and on Classics CD 1368.

WARDELL GRAY QUARTET   SUNSET RECORDING SESSION

Wardell Gray (ts), Dodo Marmarosa (p), Red Callender (b), Harold „Doc" West (dm)

<u>November 23, 1946, Hollywood, Calif.</u>

162-1	DELL'S BELLS (s)	Sunset unissued
162-2	DELL'S BELLS (incomplete) (/)	–
162-3	DELL'S BELLS (s)	–
162-4	DELL'S BELLS (s)	Jazz Selection 797
162-5	DELL'S BELLS (s)	Sunset unissued
163-1	ONE FOR PREZ (s)	Sunset unissued
163-2	ONE FOR PREZ (s)	–
163-3	ONE FOR PREZ (s)	–
163-4	ONE FOR PREZ (s)	Fontana 683907 JCL
163-5	ONE FOR PREZ (s)	Jazz Selection 803
164-1	THE MAN I LOVE (s)	Sunset unissued
164-2	THE MAN I LOVE (s)	Fontana 683907 JCL
164-3	THE MAN I LOVE (s)	Jazz Selection 803
165-1	EASY SWING (s)	Fontana 683907 JCL
165-2	EASY SWING (s)	Jazz Selection 797
	Chuck Thompson (dm) replaces West :	
166-1	THE GREAT LIE (Part I) (s)	Jazz Selection 805
166-1	THE GREAT LIE (Part II) (ts/p-chase)	–

Note :

This session was produced by Eddie Laguna for his own Sunset label, but was never issued on Sunset. First issue of the master takes was on Jazz Selection 78rpm-records in 1950.

ONE FOR PREZ is based on the chords of HOW HIGH THE MOON.

EASY SWING also known as STEEPLECHASE.

LP reissue:

Complete session reissued on Black Lion BLP 60106.

CD reissue:

Complete session reissued on Black Lion BLCD 760106.

MEL TORMÉ   MUSICRAFT
WITH SONNY BURKE A. H. ORCHESTRA   RECORDING SESSION

Ray Linn (tp), Si Zentner (tb), Harry Klee, Skeets Herfurt (as), Don Raffell, Babe Russin (ts), Bob Lawson (bs), Dodo Marmarosa (p, celesta), Dave Barbour (g), Lewis Popp (b), Nick Fatool (dm), Felix Slatkin, Olcott Vail, Walter Edelstein, Jacques Gasselin, Edward Bergman, Harry Bluestone, Nick Pisani, Anthony Olson (vl), Gail Laughton (harp), Mel Tormé (voc), Hal Mooney (arr), Sonny Burke (ld, arr)

<u>November 29, 1946, Hollywood, Calif., Radio Recorders studio</u>

5805-3	IT'S DREAMTIME (MTv) (/)	Musicraft 15102
5806-5	YOU'RE DRIVING ME CRAZY (MTv) (/)	–
5807-3	WHO CARES WHAT PEOPLE SAY (MTv) (/)	Musicraft 15104
5808-1	I'M YOURS (MTv) (/)	–

CD reissues:

All titles also on Musicraft MVSCD-54.

IT'S DREAMTIME and YOU'RE DRIVING ME CRAZY also on Living Era CD AJA 5346.

*D*own *Beat* magazine from December 16, 1946 reported about a benefit concert for Charlie Parker held at Los Angeles' Club Royale the same month. Presented by *Down Beat*, Ross Russell of Dial Records, and Eddie Laguna of Keynote was an all star line up including among others Erroll Garner, Red Callender, Howard McGhee, Al Killian, Barney Kessel, Lucky Thompson, Teddy Edwards, Wardell Gray, Chuck Thompson, and Dodo Marmarosa.

SLIM GAILLARD QUARTET   RECORDING SESSION

Dodo Marmarosa (p), Slim Gaillard (g, voc), Bam Brown (b, voc), poss. Oscar Bradley (dm)

<u>1946 or 1947, Hollywood, Calif.</u>

THE JAM MAN (SG&BBv) (s)	Savoy SJL 2242
SLIM'S RIFF (s)	–
I'M CONFESSIN' (SG&BBv) (s)	–

Note :

These titles, possibly stemming from one recording session, had been found undated in the files when they were first issued by Savoy Records on LP in 1980. Their recording year is most likely 1946 (1947 ?).

THE JAM MAN had already been recorded by Gaillard in April 1946 with Bill Early on piano. The above is a new and different version.

SLIM'S RIFF had remained on the Savoy shelves as an untitled original. It was named SLIM'S RIFF by Savoy for its first release in 1980.

A fourth title (OXYDOL HIGHBALL) issued with the above titles is without Dodo Marmarosa. Slim Gaillard plays piano.

CD reissues:

All titles also on Savoy SV-0274 and Classics CD 962.

When the trade papers printed their popularity polls in early 1947, Marmarosa again was ranked considerably high:
Metronome magazine readers voted him as 5th popular pianist, *Down Beat* magazine readers as 6th. *Esquire's* "Board of Experts" voted him as winner of their "New Star" category, just ahead of Bud Powell. Winner of the previous year had been Erroll Garner.

<u>NOTE</u>:   The titles of the following entry were originally issued on AFRS Jubilee Programs No. 228 and 229, which had obviously been compiled from transcriptions of two different performances in both of which Woody Herman was involved as master of ceremonies. One part of the music was possibly derived from a kind of pilot "Just Jazz"-concert, produced and introduced by Gene Norman, dated by some sources on January 10, 1947, and held probably at an open-air stage ("*right from the middle of a*

school yard", as Woody Herman announces on "Jubilee" No. 228). The sound quality of the other part differs from the first. These latter titles were possibly recorded at the NBC studios on Vine Street in Hollywood, and therefore are likely to stem from a different date. All titles involving Dodo Marmarosa's playing belong to this second performance.

WOODY HERMAN **& THE JUST JAZZ ALL STARS**	**AFRS "JUBILEE" [?]** **JAZZ CONCERT [?]**

personnel in various groupings incl.:

unknown (tp), unknown (tb), Woody Herman (cl, voc), Herbie Steward (cl, ts), Dodo Marmarosa (p), Arnold Fishkin (b), Jackie Mills (dm)

Note :   Some sources give Chuck Peterson (tp) and Vic Dickenson (tb).

<u>January 10 (?), 1947, Hollywood, Calif., NBC Studios (?)</u>

unknown (tp), unknown (tb), Steward (ts), Marmarosa (p),
Fishkin (b), Mills (dm) :
THE GREAT LIE (s)   AFRS Jubilee Program No. 229

Steward (cl), Marmarosa (p), Fishkin (b), Mills (dm) :
SOMEBODY LOVES ME (WHv) (/)   AFRS Jubilee Programs No. 229 and 228

unknown (tp), unknown (tb), Herman (cl), Steward (ts), Marmarosa (p),
Fishkin (b), Mills (dm) :
ROSE ROOM (s)   into...   AFRS Jubilee Program No. 229
IN A MELLOTONE (s)   –

Note:

In the original announcement to AFRS Jubilee program No. 229, which is not an announcement from the actual concert from which these titles were taken, the above groupings are billed as the "Dodo Marmarosa All Stars". There are four other titles on this program by a Jesse Price group with an unknown pianist. Some sources have guessed this group to be identical with the accompanying quartet on SOMEBODY LOVES ME (see above). The clarinetist on these titles, however, seems not to be Steward and the pianist most certainly is not Marmarosa (the four titles are KANSAS CITY BOOGIE, 4 MONTHS-THREE WEEKS-TWO DAYS-ONE HOUR BLUES, and I AIN'T MAD AT YOU, all issued on Swing House SWH-8 (LP), and BOOGIE BLUES issued on "Jubilee" No. 229 only). The closing theme ONE O'CLOCK JUMP of the program also seems to be accompanied by this unknown pianist.

SOMEBODY LOVES ME and ROSE ROOM / IN A MELLOTONE also used for AFRS Jubilee program No. 291.

LP reissues:

THE GREAT LIE and ROSE ROOM/IN A MELLOTONE also on Jazz Showcase 5005 and Swing House SWH-10.

CD reissues:

THE GREAT LIE and ROSE ROOM/IN A MELLOTONE also on Sounds Of Yesteryear DSOY 610.

SOMEBODY LOVES ME and ROSE ROOM/IN A MELLOTONE also on RST JUBCD 1005 2.

NOTE: Older discographies and *Verve*-reissues mention Dodo Marmarosa as pianist of Slim Gaillards M-G-M recording session of February 11, 1947, a session which produced the four titles BOIP! BOIP!, THE BARTENDER'S JUST LIKE A MOTHER TO ME, ARABIAN BOOGIE, and TIP LIGHT. To our ears, however, Marmarosa is definitely not the pianist on these recordings. The session can be found on Verve CD 521 651-2 or on Classics CD 1221, the latter rightly leaving out Marmarosa's name.

In early 1947 Marmarosa joined the newly formed orchestra of trombonist **Tommy Pederson**, with whom he had already played together in the bands of Gene Krupa, Charlie Barnet, and Tommy Dorsey. According to a brief feature in the August 1947 issue of *Metronome* magazine Pederson's was a kind of 'part-time' orchestra with only one consistent engagement as the Monday night dance band at the Hollywood Palladium and rehearsals once a week. *"All the guy's in Pederson's band"*, is said, *"have other job's too."* There is no information how long Marmarosa stayed with the band, but with possible interruptions he may well have played with Pederson until fall of the year.

TOMMY PEDERSON	***AFRS "JUBILEE"***
AND HIS ORCHESTRA	***RADIO SHOW***

Billie Rogers (tp,voc), Vernon Arslan, Mickey Mangano, George Seaberg, Joe Triscari (tp), Tommy Pederson (tb,arr), Tex Satterwhite, Charlie LaRue, Ollie Wilson (tb), Wilbur Schwartz (cl,as), Jimmy Rudge (as), Charlie Brosen, Corky Corcoran (ts), Herb Stowe (bs), Dodo Marmarosa (p), Ed Mihelich (b), Max Albright (dm), Hugh Brown (arr), comedian Jack Parr [Paar] and Margaret Whiting (voc) appeared as guest stars

<u>ca. mid February 1947, Van Nuys, Calif., Birmingham General Hospital</u>

THEME (ONE O'CLOCK JUMP) (/)   AFRS Jubilee Program No. 236
TONE BONE (s)   –
FANFARE (two bars only) (/)   –

    short orchestral introduction and ending, piano playing probably
    Jack Parr's own:
Comedy act (Jack Parr)   –

    Margaret Whiting accompanied by Marmarosa, Mihelich, and
    Albright only (plus full orchestra on final chord):
THIS CAN'T BE LOVE (Margaret Whiting -voc) (/)   –

    full orchestra again :
SUMMERTIME (/)   –

    Margaret Whiting accompanied by Marmarosa, Mihelich, and
    Albright only (plus full orchestra on final chord):
THE MAN I LOVE (Margaret Whiting -voc) (/)   –

    full orchestra again :
ANNIVERSARY SONG (BRv) (/)   –
MISTER JUMP (s)   –
THEME (ONE O'CLOCK JUMP) (faded) (/)   –

Note :

Richard S. Sears in his "V-Disc" discography states that the newly formed Tommy Pederson Orchestra appeared on a "Jubilee" show prior to its opening at the Hollywood Palladium on February 24, 1947. Thus the above transcription most certainly was made in the second half of February 1947.

Gene Norman and M-G-M musical star Marie McDonald acted as masters of ceremonies on this show.

The above version of TONE BONE also on V-Disc 811 (with Marmarosa's piano introduction edited out).

Beginning with February 24, 1947 the following engagement of the Tommy Pederson Orchestra was listed in the trade papers:

February 24, 1947 - ca. August/September 1947   :   Los Angeles, Calif.,
                                                         Hollywood Palladium (as "Monday night attraction" only)

At the period the Hollywood Palladium was allowed to feature its main attractions on a 'six nights a week only' schedule. On Mondays, which was the regular 'off night', local bands were hired to entertain the dancers. Pederson's held the post of the 'Monday night band' for at least six months and was transcribed playing at the Palladium on several Mondays by the AFRS for their "One Night Stand" program series. According to *Metronome* magazine of August 1947 the engagement also offered airing time twice every Monday, first on a local radio station and then on the West Coast radio network *Capitol News from Hollywood* in their April 1947 issue additionally mentioned a San Diego engagement of Tommy Pederson as "*his first job with new band. He's playing the Palladium Mondays, too*":

probably late February 1947 : San Diego, Calif., unknown location

NOTE: The dating of Tommy Pederson's six AFRS "One Night Stand" broadcast programs from the Hollywood Palladium is open to some speculation, as only their mastering dates are known. *Down Beat* magazine's regular listing of band routes in its column "Where the Bands are Playing" gives no indication of Pederson at the Palladium before the April 23, 1947 issue. Oddly enough from then on until July 16 his band is listed under the "Combos" section, although it was introduced as a large orchestra with detailed personnel information already in the same magazine's February 26 issue. The July 30, 1947 issue then for the first time lists an engagement of the large orchestra, from whereon listings in the column document dates of the larger band until at least early October 1947. Thus it seems possible (although not very likely), that Pederson temporarily reduced the size of his band for the Palladium 'Monday nights' between mid April and late July 1947.

This would mean, that all AFRS transcriptions of the large orchestra were made between the opening night at the Palladium on February 24 and mid April of the year. As all six of Pederson's "One Night Stand" programs were mastered in (almost) weekly distance and as the AFRS even provided every seventh issue number of the series for Pederson's appearances, there may nevertheless have been some planned chronology with the release of these transcriptions, although we have no final evidence for this assumption.

Left open is also the question, when the Pederson transcription series actually started. This may have been on opening night at the Palladium or possibly on one of the two subsequent Mondays. The series seems to have ended, when Pederson, at least for the Palladium engagement, may have reduced the size of his band to a combo in April 1947.

TOMMY PEDERSON
AND HIS ORCHESTRA

AFRS "ONE NIGHT STAND"
RADIO BROADCAST

band personnel probably similar as before

<u>poss. February 24, 1947, Hollywood, Calif., Hollywood Palladium</u>

THEME (MY LITTLE NEST OF HEAVENLY BLUE (/)

AFRS One Night-Stand No. 1371

ONE FOR THE BOYS (s)	–
IT'S THE TALK OF THE TOWN (/)	–
IF YOU WERE THE ONLY GIRL IN THE WORLD (s)	–
THAT'S WHERE I CAME IN (BRv) (I)	–
TONE BONE (s)	–
ON THE SUNNY SIDE OF THE STREET (BRv) (/)	–
LOVE JUMPED OUT (s)	–
MAYBE YOU'LL BE THERE (BRv) (/)	–
ONE FOR THE BOYS (partial repeat of above) (s)	–

Note :

AFRS transcribed six of Tommy Pederson's Monday night appearances at the Hollywood Palladium for their "One Night Stand" program series. Mastering of these transcriptions began in June 1947 with AFRS "One Night Stand" program No. 1371 being edited for release on June 14, 1947 (information kindly conveyed by the Library of Congress). For discussion of recording dates of Pederson's "One Night Stand" broadcasts see preceding "note".

Pederson's theme song is 'Armand's serenade' from the second act of Franz Lehar's operetta "Frasquita", also known by the first line of its lyrics "When the moon is shining white".

CHARLIE PARKER'S NEW STARS   DIAL RECORDING SESSION

Howard McGhee (tp), Charlie Parker (as), Wardell Gray (ts), Dodo Marmarosa (p), Barney Kessel (g), Red Callender (b), Don Lamond (dm)

February 26, 1947, Hollywood, Calif., C.P. MacGregor Studios

D 1071-A	RELAXIN' AT CAMARILLO (s)	Dial 1030
D 1071-B	RELAXIN' AT CAMARILLO ( )	Dial unissued
D 1071-C	RELAXIN' AT CAMARILLO (s)	Dial 1012
D 1071-D	RELAXIN' AT CAMARILLO (s)	Dial LP 901
D 1071-E	RELAXIN' AT CAMARILLO (s)	Dial LP 202
D 1072-A	CHEERS (s)	Dial LP 202
D 1072-B	CHEERS (s)	Spotlite SPJ-103
D 1072-C	CHEERS (s)	Spotlite SPJ-103
D 1072-D	CHEERS (s)	Dial 1013
D 1073-A	CARVIN' THE BIRD (s)	Dial 1013
D 1073-B	CARVIN' THE BIRD (s)	Dial 1013
D 1074-A	STUPENDOUS (s)	Dial 1022, 1030
D 1074-B	STUPENDOUS (s)	Dial LP 202

Note :

This session was supervised by the owner of Dial Records, Ross Russell.

Obviously both takes of matrix D 1073 have been used for the pressing of Dial 1013.

LP reissues:

Matrix D 1074-B also issued on Blue Star LP 6811 as SURPRISING.

All issued titles also on Spotlite SPJ-103.

CD reissues:

All issued titles also on Spotlite SPJ CD 4-101.

D 1071-D, D 1072-C, D 1073-B, and D 1074-A (master takes) also on Classics CD 980.

| **TOMMY PEDERSON** | **AFRS "ONE NIGHT STAND"** |
| **AND HIS ORCHESTRA** | **RADIO BROADCAST** |

band personnel probably similar as before

<u>poss. March 3, 1947, Hollywood, Calif., Hollywood Palladium</u>

THEME (MY LITTLE NEST OF HEAVENLY BLUE ( )

AFRS One Night-Stand No. 1378

IF YOU WERE THE ONLY GIRL IN THE WORLD ( )   –

GUILTY (BRv) ( )   –

TONE BONE ( )   –

GOTTA GET ME SOMEBODY TO LOVE (BRv) ( )   –

IT'S THE TALK OF THE TOWN ( )   –

THE ANNIVERSARY SONG (BRv) ( )   –

ON THE SUNNY SIDE OF THE STREET (BRv) ( )   –

Note :

AFRS transcribed six of Tommy Pederson's Monday night appearances at the Hollywood Palladium for their "One Night Stand" program series, with AFRS One Night Stand program No. 1378 being mastered for release as second on June 21, 1947 (information kindly conveyed by the Library of Congress).

For discussion of recording dates of Pederson's "One Night Stand" broadcasts see "note" preceding the February 24, 1947 entry.

During the rest of the week, when the Tommy Pederson Orchestra did not appear at the Palladium (see "note" for February 24, 1947), Pederson and some fellow musicians played in a sextet under the direction of his female trumpet star Billie Rogers (George Hoefer: "The recorded flights of Dodo", in *Down Beat* of December 29, 1966):

Billie Rogers Sextet
Billie Rogers (tp, voc), Tommy Pederson (tb), Charlie Brosen (Bruce Branson) (cl), Dodo Marmarosa (p), Joe Mondragon (b), Keith Williams (dm) :

<u>ca. March 1947</u>   : Palm Springs, Calif., Desert Inn Hotel

TOMMY PEDERSON
AND HIS ORCHESTRA

AFRS "ONE NIGHT STAND"
RADIO BROADCAST

band personnel probably similar as before

<u>poss. March 10, 1947, Hollywood, Calif., Hollywood Palladium</u>

THEME (MY LITTLE NEST OF HEAVENLY BLUE ( )

AFRS One Night-Stand No. 1385

LOVE JUMPED OUT ( )   –
MAYBE YOU'LL BE THERE (BRv) ( )   –
TONE BONE ( )   –
THAT'S WHERE I CAME IN (BRv) ( )   –
IF YOU WERE THE ONLY GIRL IN THE WORLD ( )   –
ONE FOR THE BOYS ( )   –
VALSE TRISTE ( )   –
THAT'S THE BEGINNING OF THE END (BRv) ( )   –

Note :

AFRS transcribed six of Tommy Pederson's Monday night appearances at the Hollywood Palladium for their "One Night Stand" program series, with AFRS One Night Stand program No. 1385 being mastered for release as third on June 30, 1947 (information kindly conveyed by the Library of Congress). Garrod in his discography of "AFRS One Night Stands 1001 Thru 2000" gives June 28, 1947 as mastering date.

For discussion of recording dates of Pederson's "One Night Stand" broadcasts see "note" preceding the February 24, 1947 entry.

TOMMY PEDERSON   AFRS "ONE NIGHT STAND"
AND HIS ORCHESTRA   RADIO BROADCAST

band personnel probably similar as before

<u>poss. March 17, 1947, Hollywood, Calif., Hollywood Palladium</u>

THEME (MY LITTLE NEST OF HEAVENLY BLUE (/)

AFRS One Night-Stand No. 1392

TONE BONE (s)   –
WOULD YOU BELIEVE ME (BRv) (/)   –
IT DON'T MEAN A THING IF IT AIN'T GOT THAT SWING (/)   –
DREAMS ARE A DIME A DOZEN (BRv) (/)   –
IT HAD TO BE YOU (s)   –
MAMMA, DO I GOTTA... (BRv) (/)   –
WILD MAN'S BLOOD (/)   –
GOTTA GET ME SOMEBODY TO LOVE (BRv) (/)   –
IT'S THE TALK OF THE TOWN (/)   –
IF YOU WERE THE ONLY GIRL IN THE WORLD (s)   –
THEME (MY LITTLE NEST OF HEAVENLY BLUE) (s) (faded during p-solo)   –

Note :

AFRS transcribed six of Tommy Pederson's Monday night appearances at the Hollywood Palladium for their "One Night Stand" program series, with AFRS One Night Stand program No. 1392 being mastered for release as fourth on July 4, 1947 (information kindly conveyed by the Library of Congress). Garrod in his discography of "AFRS One Night Stands 1001 Thru 2000" gives July 5, 1947 as mastering date.

For discussion of recording dates of Pederson's "One Night Stand" broadcasts see "note" preceding the February 24, 1947 entry.

| TOMMY PEDERSON | AFRS "ONE NIGHT STAND" |
| AND HIS ORCHESTRA | RADIO BROADCAST |

band personnel probably similar as before

<u>poss. March 24, 1947, Hollywood, Calif., Hollywood Palladium</u>

THEME (MY LITTLE NEST OF HEAVENLY BLUE ( )

AFRS One Night-Stand No. 1399

ROADSIDE REST ( )	–
ASK ANYONE WHO KNOWS (BRv) ( )	–
TONE BONE ( )	–
THE MAN I LOVE (BRv) ( )	–
VALSE TRISTE ( )	–
ON THE SUNNY SIDE OF THE STREET (BRv) ( )	–
ONE FOR THE BOYS ( )	–

Note :

AFRS transcribed six of Tommy Pederson's Monday night appearances at the Hollywood Palladium for their "One Night Stand" program series, with AFRS One Night Stand program No. 1399 being mastered for release as fifth on July 12, 1947 (information kindly conveyed by the Library of Congress).

For discussion of recording dates of Pederson's "One Night Stand" broadcasts see "note" preceding the February 24, 1947 entry.

There is no reason to doubt that Marmarosa continued to play with Pederson's orchestra through March and April 1947, but as we could not check this program, we were not able to definitely verify his presence on the above titles.

TOMMY PEDERSON
AND HIS ORCHESTRA

AFRS "ONE NIGHT STAND"
RADIO BROADCAST

band personnel probably similar as before

<u>poss. March 31, 1947, Hollywood, Calif., Hollywood Palladium</u>

THEME (MY LITTLE NEST OF HEAVENLY BLUE ( )

                                             AFRS One Night-Stand No. 1406

MRS. JUMP ( )   –

ASK ANYONE WHO KNOWS (BRv) ( )   –

TONE BONE ( )   –

THE MAN I LOVE (BRv) ( )   –

LOVE JUMPED OUT ( )   –

THAT'S WHERE I CAME IN (BRv) ( )   –

EMBRACEABLE YOU ( )   –

MISTER JUMP ( )   –

Note :

AFRS transcribed six of Tommy Pederson's Monday night appearances at the Hollywood Palladium for their "One Night Stand" program series, with AFRS One Night Stand" program No. 1406 being mastered for release as last of the six on July 20, 1947 (information kindly conveyed by the Library of Congress).

For discussion of recording dates of Pederson's "One Night Stand" broadcasts see "note" preceding the February 24, 1947 entry.

There is no reason to doubt that Marmarosa continued to play with Pederson's orchestra through March and April 1947, but as we could not check this program, we were not able to definitely verify his presence on the above titles.

LUCKY THOMPSON AND HIS LUCKY SEVEN   RCA-VICTOR RECORDING SESSION

Neal Hefti (tp), Benny Carter (as,arr), Lucky Thompson (ts), Bob Lawson (bs), Dodo Marmarosa (p), Barney Kessel (g), Red Callender (b), Jackie Mills (dm), Leonard Feather (arr)

Note : Jorgen Grunnet Jepsen (Jazz Records, 1965) and Berger/Berger/Patrick (Benny Carter discography, 1982) give Lee Young (dm) instead of Mills. All other sources, including Tony Williams' Lucky Thompson discography (1967), Leonard Feather's liner notes to RCA Victor LPV-544 (1967), booklet informations to RCA Bluebird ND 82177 CD (1990), and even RCA Victor 78rpm labels give Jackie Mills.

<u>April 22, 1947, Hollywood, Calif.</u>

D7VB 510-1	JUST ONE MORE CHANCE (/)	Victor 20-2504
D7VB 511-2	FROM DIXIELAND TO BE-BOP (LFarr) (s)	Victor 20-3142
D7VB 511-J	FROM DIXIELAND TO BE-BOP (LFarr) ( )	Victor unissued
D7VB 511-K	FROM DIXIELAND TO BE-BOP (LFarr) ( )	–
D7VB 512-1	BOULEVARD BOUNCE (BCarr) (omit guitar) (s)	Victor 20-3142
D7VB 512-B	BOULEVARD BOUNCE (BCarr) (omit guitar) ( )	Victor unissued
D7VB 512-D	BOULEVARD BOUNCE (BCarr) (omit guitar) ( )	–
D7VB 513-2	BOPPIN' THE BLUES (s)	Victor 20-2504

Note:

The above recording session featured a sort of Esquire "All Star" line up with Benny Carter having won the magazine Esquire's gold award on alto sax for 1947, Barney Kessel having won silver on guitar, and Lucky Thompson and Dodo Marmarosa as winners of their categories in the "New Star" competition. Red Callender and Neal Hefti had been voted as close competitors for the "New Star" award on bass and trumpet.

FROM DIXIELAND TO BE-BOP is subtitled "CONDON MEETS GILLESPIE".

LP reissue:

All four issued takes also on RCA NL 86757.

CD reissues:

BOPPIN' THE BLUES also on RCA CD ND 82177.

All four issued takes also on Classics CD 1113 and on Ocium CD OCM 0038.

NOTE: The following entry was the first official "Just Jazz" concert presented by Gene Norman and sponsored by Norman and Eddie Laguna. The 2978 seats of the Pasadena Civic Auditorium were sold out.

Besides the recorded groups given below other participators at the concert were Erroll Garner and the Benny Goodman Sextet consisting of Goodman, Red Norvo, Jimmy Rowles, Al Hendrickson, Harry Babasin, and Don Lamond.

Gene Norman remembers the bassist with the Howard McGhee All Stars (see below) to have been Red Callender, who indeed is listed for some (or all) of their titles in the standard discographies and on many of the LP- or CD-reissues. Nevertheless Norman himself, when concluding AFRS Jubilee Program No. 261 with his sign off, mentions Charlie Drayton as bassist on BE-BOP. On the same occasion he wrongly announces this title as GROOVIN' HIGH. As Gene Norman seems to be no reliable source, it remains uncertain who actually played bass on these titles.

Elaine Cohen in her discography to Red Callender's autobiography *Unfinished Dream* does not include these titles.

GENE NORMAN'S "JUST JAZZ" ALL STARS   "JUST JAZZ" CONCERT

<u>April 29, 1947, Pasadena, Calif., Civic Auditorium</u>

<u>Benny Carter All Stars</u>

Chuck Peterson (tp), Vic Dickenson (tb), Benny Carter (as), Charlie Barnet (ts), Dodo Marmarosa (p), Irving Ashby (g), Red Callender (b), Jackie Mills (dm) :

MM 1000	PERDIDO Part I (s)	AFRS Jubilee Program No. 261
MM 1001	PERDIDO Part II (/)	AFRS Jubilee Program No. 261
	HOW HIGH THE MOON (s)	AFRS Jubilee Program No. 262
	JUST YOU, JUST ME (s)	Vogue VJT 3003

<u>Howard McGhee All Stars</u>

Howard McGhee (tp), Sonny Criss (as), Wardell Gray (ts), Dodo Marmarosa (p), prob. Charlie Drayton (b), Jackie Mills (dm) :

MM 908	BE-BOP Part I (/)	AFRS Jubilee Program No. 261
MM 909	BE-BOP Part II (/)	AFRS Jubilee Program No. 261
MM 910	GROOVIN' HIGH Part I (/)	Modern 20-639
MM 911	GROOVIN' HIGH Part II (/)	Modern 20-639
MM 1003	HOT HOUSE Part I (/)	Modern 20-694
MM 1119	HOT HOUSE Part II (s)	Modern 20-694

Lee Young (dm) replaces Mills :
I SURRENDER DEAR ( )   unissued

<u>Peggy Lee (voc)</u>

accompanied by Dodo Marmarosa (p), Irving Ashby (g), Charlie Drayton (b) :

THE BLUES (p-intro)   AFRS Jubilee Program No. 261
HAPPINESS IS JUST A THING CALLED JOE (omit Ashby) (p-intro)
                                        AFRS Jubilee Program No. 262
THEM THERE EYES (p-intro)   AFRS Jubilee Program No. 262

Note:

Some sources also claim a recorded live performance of DONNA LEE to be from this concert and by the same group as on GROOVIN' HIGH etc. The horn line-up for DONNA LEE, however, includes tenor saxophonist Teddy Edwards, who is mentioned nowhere in contemporary reviews or comments on the above concert. The title most certainly was recorded at the "Just Jazz" concert of mid- (11?) April 1949 with Art Farmer and Art Pepper sharing the horn frontline with Edwards, and Hampton Hawes doing the comping on piano. As all issued versions of this title are incomplete and seem to break off immediately before the piano solo, no final statement to the pianist's identity can be made.

DONNA LEE (see above note) issued as "SCRATCH" on Crown CLP 5008 and as "STOMPIN'" on Crown CLP 5009. DONNA LEE also on Cicala BLJ 8022.

BE-BOP is wrongly announced as GROOVIN' HIGH on AFRS Jubilee No. 261.

PERDIDO (matrix numbers MM 1000 & MM 1001) also on Modern 20-660 (78rpm). This issue has trombone solo omitted and tenor-sax chorus cut down from five to three choruses. The release of PERDIDO on AFRS Jubilee program No. 261 is uncut.

LP reissues:

PERDIDO and BE-BOP also on Swing House SWH-10.

HOW HIGH THE MOON also on Swing Treasury LP ST-109.

PERDIDO, GROOVIN' HIGH, and HOT HOUSE also on Vogue VJT 3003 .

BE-BOP, GROOVIN' HIGH, and HOT HOUSE also on Spotlite SPJ-134.

CD reissues:

PERDIDO, JUST YOU, JUST ME, BE-BOP, GROOVIN' HIGH, and HOT HOUSE also on Vogue CD 600 126.

PERDIDO, JUST YOU, JUST ME, GROOVIN' HIGH, and HOT HOUSE also on Giants of Jazz CD 53097.

BE-BOP and PERDIDO also on Sounds Of Yesteryear DSOY 610.

BE-BOP, GROOVIN' HIGH, and HOT HOUSE also on Fresh Sound FSCD-156, and Masters of Jazz MJCD 171.

F or the end of May 1947 *Capitol News from Hollywood* in their June 1947 issue mentioned the following two engagements of *"Tommy Pederson's young band"* as accompaniment for singer Margaret Whiting:

May 30, 1947   : Sacramento, Calif., unknown location
May 31, 1947   : Stockton, Calif., unknown location

It is not clear, how long Dodo Marmarosa remained with the band, but he may possibly still have played with Pederson's orchestra at the above two engagements.

From early July on he will have been definitely out, when he started to play with Benny Carter's new ensemble at Billy Berg's in Hollywood (see "note" for July 2, 1947). He may have returned to Pederson thereafter, however.

At the end of June 1947 Marmarosa once more appeared in the line-up of the second "Just Jazz" concert promoted by Gene Norman and Eddie Laguna. The seats of the Pasadena Civic Auditorium were again sold out.

June 23, 1947   : Pasadena, Calif., Civic Auditorium

This time the All Star line-up featured Anita O'Day and the Nat 'King' Cole Trio as top attractions, as well as Charlie Shavers, Willie Smith, Stan Getz, Red Norvo, Andre Previn, Dodo Marmarosa, Barney Kessel, Red Callender, Don Lamond and Jackie Mills. Although parts of the concert have been preserved on record, Marmarosa's appearance seems to have passed unrecorded. While the surviving transcriptions either feature Nat 'King' Cole or Andre Previn on piano, the context of Marmarosa's performance at the event remains unknown.

During July and August 1947 Marmarosa was a member of Benny Carter's orchestra and participated in the following engagement:

Benny Carter And His Orchestra
Harry "Parr" Jones (tp), Henry Coker (tb), Benny Carter (tp,cl,as,ts,p,arr), Lucky Thompson (ts), Dodo Marmarosa (p), Thomas Moultrie (b), Henry "Tucker" Green (dm), Dave Cavanaugh (arr) :

July 2, 1947 - early August 1947   : Hollywood, Calif., Billy Berg's

LUCKY THOMPSON QUARTET   *DOWN BEAT RECORDING SESSION*

Lucky Thompson (ts), Dodo Marmarosa (p), Red Callender (b), Jackie Mills (dm)

poss. July 16, 1947, Hollywood, Calif.

DB 100 A	DODO'S BOUNCE (s)	Downbeat 100
DB 100 B	DODO'S LAMENT (s)	–
DB 105 A	SLAM'S MISHAP (s)	Downbeat 105
DB 105 B	SCUFFLE THAT RUFF (SHUFFLE THAT RIFF) (s)	–
DB 107 A	SMOOTH SAILING (s)	Downbeat 107
DB 107 B	COMMERCIAL EYES (s)	–

Note :

The above recording session is by all discographies and reissues dated on September 13, 1946. The archive of the Professional Musicians Local 47 in Los Angeles, however, preserves a document, which makes the above given date seem more likely. It is a letter from the financial secretary of AFM Local 767 documenting payment for Dodo Marmarosa and Jackie Mills for, as is said, "services on recording session held July 16th [1947], Downbeat Recording Co.". As the leader of the recorded group had obviously been a member of Local 767, this letter most certainly refers to the above recording session led by Lucky Thompson. This assumption is also corroborated by comparing issue numbers of original Downbeat 78rpm releases, with nos. 100, 105, and 107 being more likely to belong into the year 1947 than into 1946.

LP reissue:

All titles also on Phoenix LP-20.

CD reissues:

All titles also on Fresh Sound FSCD-1019, Indigo IGO CD 2104, Classics CD 1113, Ocium CD OCM 0038, and on Proper INTRO CD 2055.

From Billy Berg's (see preceding note) the Benny Carter Orchestra went to the Million Dollar Theatre for its next engagement:

Benny Carter And His Orchestra
Harry "Parr" Jones (tp), Henry Coker (tb), Benny Carter (tp,cl,as,ts,p,arr), Wardell Gray (ts), Dodo Marmarosa (p), Thomas Moultrie (b), Henry "Tucker" Green (dm), Dave Cavanaugh (arr) :

early August 1947   : Los Angeles, Calif., Million Dollar Theatre (for one week)

SLIM GAILLARD QUARTET   MGM RECORDING SESSION

Dodo Marmarosa (p), Slim Gaillard (g, voc), Bam Brown (b, voc), unknown (dm)

October 1, 1947 (19:00 to 22:00 PM), Hollywood, Calif., Radio Recorders studio

47-S-3163-3	MOMMA'S IN THE KITCHEN (BUT WE'VE GOT "POP" ON ICE) (SGv) (s)	
		MGM 10231
47-S-3164-3	(I DON'T STAND) A GHOST OF A CHANCE (SGv) (/)	MGM 10309
47-S-3165-3	LITTLE RED RIDING WOOD (SG & BBv) (/)	MGM 10599
47-S-3166-3	PUERTO VOOTIE (SGv) (s)	MGM 10231

Note :

Folklyric LP-reissue gives Cyril Haynes (p) and 1949 as recording year. Verve LP-reissue gives "possibly Dodo Marmarosa" and 1947 as recording year. Stylistical comparisons make undoubtfully clear that Marmarosa actually is the pianist on these recordings.

LP reissues:

MOMMA'S IN THE KITCHEN, A GHOST OF A CHANCE, and PUERTO VOOTIE also on Verve 2304 554. LITTLE RED RIDING WOOD also on Folklyric LP 9038.

CD reissues:

MOMMA'S IN THE KITCHEN also on Verve PCD-1401. All four titles also on Classics CD 1221.

DODO MARMAROSA   ATOMIC RECORDING SESSION

Dodo Marmarosa (p-solo)

November 1, 1947, Hollywood, Calif., Radio Recorders Studio

| Test A | TONE PAINTINGS (I) (slow) | Atomic unissued |
| Test B | TONE PAINTINGS (II) (medium) | Atomic unissued |

Note :

First issue of the above recordings was in 1975 on British Spotlite LP SPJ-128 together with trio titles recorded for the label Dial. In the liner notes to this LP Ross Russell, former owner of Dial records, states that the above had been privately made studio recordings originally not intended for release. The archive of Los Angeles' Professional Musicians Local 47, however, preserves a recording contract between Marmarosa and the Atomic Record Company for a solo recording session held on the above given date. As there is no other solo recording session by Marmarosa known, it seems plausible to refer this contract to the above recordings.

TONE PAINTINGS (II) (medium) actually is Marmarosa's composition MILES' INFLUENCE.

LP reissue:

Both titles on Spotlite SPJ-128 (numbered "Spotlite 108" as US release).

CD reissues:

Both titles on Spotlite SPJ-(CD) 128, Fresh Sound FSCD-1019, Jazz Classics CD-JZCD-6008, and on Proper INTRO CD 2055.

DODO MARMAROSA TRIO   DIAL RECORDING SESSION

Dodo Marmarosa (p), Harry Babasin (b and (*) cello), Jackie Mills (dm)

<u>November 12, 1947 (2:00 to 5:30 PM), Hollywood, Calif., C.P. MacGregor Studios</u>

D 1131-A	BOPMATISM (*)	Dial unissued
D 1131-B	BOPMATISM (*)	Dial unissued
D 1131-C	BOPMATISM (*)	Dial LP 208
D 1131-D	BOPMATISM (*)	Dial unissued
D 1131-E	BOPMATISM (*)	Dial unissued
D 1131-F	BOPMATISM (*)	Dial 752
D 1131-G	BOPMATISM (*)	Dial unissued
D 1132-A	DODO'S DANCE	Dial LP 208
D 1132-B	DODO'S DANCE	Dial unissued
D 1132-C	DODO'S DANCE	Dial 1050
D 1132-D	DODO'S DANCE	Dial unissued
D 1132-E	DODO'S DANCE	Dial unissued
D 1132-F	DODO'S DANCE	Dial unissued
D 1132-G	DODO'S DANCE	Dial unissued
D 1133-A	TRADE WINDS (YOU GO TO MY HEAD) (*)	Dial 1025, 752
D 1133-B	TRADE WINDS (YOU GO TO MY HEAD) (*)	Dial unissued
D 1133-C	TRADE WINDS (YOU GO TO MY HEAD) (*)	Dial LP 208
D 1133-D	TRADE WINDS (YOU GO TO MY HEAD) (*)	Dial unissued
D 1134-A	DARY DEPARTS	Dial unissued
D 1134-B	DARY DEPARTS	Dial unissued
D 1134-C	DARY DEPARTS	Dial unissued
D 1134-D	DARY DEPARTS	Dial unissued
D 1134-E	DARY DEPARTS	Dial 1025
D 1134-F	DARY DEPARTS	Dial LP 208
D 1134-G	DARY DEPARTS	Dial 1025
D 1135-A	LOVER (*)	Dial unissued
D 1135-B	LOVER (*)	Dial unissued
D 1135-C	LOVER (*)	Dial unissued
D 1135-D	COSMO STREET (LOVER) (*)	Dial LP 208
D 1135-E	LOVER (*)	Dial 1025

Note :

This session was supervised by Eddie Laguna, and it seems that a total of 31 tracks have been recorded on the date. According to Geoffrey Wheeler ("Jazz by mail", p.44) this is the most ever recorded on any Dial session. All reissues and discographies give December 3, 1947 as recording date for the above session. Only Wheeler follows the original recording contract (preserved in copy at the archive of Los Angeles' AFM Local 47) with the correct date of November 12.

Dial 1025 gives matrix number 1033-A instead of 1133-A. TRADE WINDS here is issued as YOU GO TO MY HEAD.

Dial 752 incorrectly gives matrix numbers 1031-F and 1033-A respectively, instead of 1131-F and 1133-A. Obviously matrix numbers 1134-E and 1134-G both have been used for the pressing of Dial 1025.

LP reissues:

D 1131-C, D 1132-A, D 1133-C, D 1134-F, D 1135-D were issued in 1951 on a 10" Dial LP 208 called "Piano Moods", combined with Charlie Parker's ORNITHOLOGY-take D 1012-1, indicated here as by the "Dodo Marmarosa Sextet" (see March 28, 1946). The titles issued on this LP represent Marmarosa's final choice of all recorded versions.

D 1131-F, D 1132-C, D 1133-A, D 1134-G, D 1135-E also were issued on Jazztone J 1001 (10" LP "Piano Contrasts"). The sound quality of this LP is much superior to all later issues, including CD-release!

D 1131-C, D 1132-A, D 1133-A, D 1134-F also on Cicala BLJ 8032, D 1131-F and D 1133-C also on Cicala BLJ 8017.

All issued takes also on Spotlite SPJ-128 (numbered "Spotlite 108" as US release).

CD reissues:

All issued takes, except D 1134-G, also on Fresh Sound FSCD-1019.

D 1131-C, D 1132-A, D 1133-C, D 1134-F, and D 1135-D also on Classics CD 1165 and Proper INTRO CD 2055.

All issued takes on Spotlite SPJ-(CD) 128, Jazz Classics CD-JZCCL-6008, Toshiba EMI TOCJ-6206, and Lone Hill Jazz LHJ10119.

LIONEL HAMPTON SEXTET   DECCA RECORDING SESSION

Benny Bailey (tp), Morris Lane (ts), Dodo Marmarosa (p), Billy Mackel (g), Charles Mingus (b), Earl Walker, Curley Hamner (dm), Lionel Hampton (vib)

<u>November 14, 1947 (2:15 to 5:15 PM), Hollywood, Calif., Decca recording studios</u>

DLA-4560-A	CHEROKEE (Lionel Hampton -voc) (s)	Decca 24430
DLA-4561-A	RE-BOP AND BE-BOP No. 2 (s)	–
DLA-4562-A	ZOO-BABA-DA-OO-EE (Lionel Hampton & Ens -voc) (s)	Decca 24431

Note :

The original recording contract for the above session also lists a musician named Bill Castagino, whom we could not identify any further.

On one more title from this session (REBOP'S TURNING BLUE) Milt Buckner plays piano.

Some sources give Charles Mingus (voc) for CHEROKEE.

LP reissues:

All titles also on MCA Coral 6.22181 and MCA 510.181.

CD reissues:

All titles also on Classics CD 994.

WILLIE SMITH QUINTET   *RECORDING SESSION*

Willie Smith (as), Dodo Marmarosa (p), Barney Kessel (g), Red Callender (b), Jo Jones (dm)

<u>November 1947, Hollywood, Calif., Radio Recorders studio</u>

5008-	SOPHISTICATED LADY (/)	Jazz Scene (unnumbered)
5016-2	NOT SO BOP BLUES (s)	unissued
5016-3	NOT SO BOP BLUES (s)	Mercury/Clef 8901
5017-1	TEA FOR TWO (/)	unissued
5017-3	TEA FOR TWO (/)	Mercury/Clef 8901

Note :

These titles had been recorded by Norman Granz for his six record album "The Jazz Scene", but only the title SOPHISTICATED LADY found entrance into the final album release.

Mercury matrix numbers were : 1898 NOT SO BOP BLUES, 1899 TEA FOR TWO, and 1900 SOPHISTICATED LADY.

CD reissue:

Matrix Nos. 5008-, 5016-3, and 5017-3 also on Ocium CD OCM 0013.

All five takes also on Verve 314 521 661-2 (2CD Box).

RED NORVO AND HIS BAND   CAPITOL RECORDING SESSION

Ray Linn (tp), Jimmy Giuffre, Dexter Gordon (ts), Red Norvo (vib), Dodo Marmarosa (p), Barney Kessel (g), Red Callender (b), Jackie Mills (dm)

November 28, 1947, Hollywood, Calif.

2644-4   BOP (s)   Capitol 15253

Note :

The recording date of November 28 is given for the latest reissue of this session by Mosaic Records. All other sources claim this title to be recorded on November 30.

There were three other titles recorded at this session, on which Marmarosa did not play.

LP reissue:

This title also on EMI (Capitol) 1C 056-85 609 and Capitol T 20579.

CD reissues:

This title also on Capitol ECJ-50077 and Capitol TOCJ-5621-28 (8 CD Box).

This title also on Mosaic MD 12-170 (12 CD Box) and on Blue Moon BMCD 1046.

MISS DANNA
WITH THE DODO MARMAROSA TRIO

IRRA RECORDING SESSION

Dodo Marmarosa (p), Barney Kessel (g), Gene Englund (b), Miss Danna (voc)

Note : Miss Danna was a discovery by Slim Gaillard and was billed as "The Female Frankie Laine".

December 1, 1947 (2:00 to 5:00 PM), Hollywood, Calif., Radio Recorders studio

M-291-(1)	BLACK AND BLUE (Miss Danna -voc) (s)	IRRA M 291
M-291-(2)	REMEMBER I KNEW YOU WHEN (Miss Danna -voc) (/)	–

Note :

According to George Hoefer in his article "The recorded flights of Dodo", written for DOWN BEAT magazine in December 1966, there had been recorded two more titles at the above session, which remained unissued. Discographies and reissues give no exact date for the above recording session. However, the archive of Los Angeles' Professional Musicians Local 47 preserves a recording contract between Marmarosa as leader of the above accompanying trio and the Mirror Recordings company, signed on November 29 and dated December 1, 1947. As Mirror actually was the manufacturer for several recording firms including IRRA, this contract most certainly refers to the above session. Miss Danna, who as vocalist was not a member of the Musicians Union, consequently is not mentioned in the contract.

LP reissue:

Both titles also on Solid Sender SOL 514.

CD reissue:

Both titles also on Classics CD 1165.

SLIM GAILLARD QUARTET   MGM RECORDING SESSION

Slim Gaillard (g, voc), Dodo Marmarosa (p), Bam Brown (b, voc), unknown (dm)

<u>December 22, 1947 (19:00 to 22:00 PM), Hollywood, Calif., Radio Recorders studio</u>

47-S-3371-3	DOWN BY THE STATION (SG & Ens -voc) (/)	MGM 10309
47-S-3372-2	COMMUNICATIONS (SG & Ens -voc) (s)	MGM 10442
47-S-3373-	THREE LITTLE WORDS (voc ?) ( )	MGM unissued
47-S-3374-	SOLITUDE (voc ?) ( )	–

Note :

Although discographies list the pianist for this recording session as "unknown", stylistical comparisons make clear that this is Marmarosa. The vocal to DOWN BY THE STATION also includes a text line-up of the musician's hometowns, and the mentioning of Pittsburgh further confirms Marmarosa's presence on these recordings.

LP reissues:

DOWN BY THE STATION and COMMUNICATIONS also on Verve 2304 554.

CD reissues:

DOWN BY THE STATION and COMMUNICATIONS also on Verve PCD-1401 and on Classics CD 1221.

DODO MARMAROSA TRIO   ATOMIC RECORDING SESSION

Dodo Marmarosa (p), Barney Kessel (g), Gene Englund (b)

prob. December 24, 1947 (16:00 to 19:00 PM), Hollywood, Calif.,
International Recorders Studio

MMO 1096	OPUS # 5	MacGregor Transcription 518
	YOU THRILL ME SO	–
	COMPADOO	–
	I'M IN LOVE	–
	COSMO STREET [BOPMATISM]	–
MMO 1097	LOVER COME BACK TO ME	MacGregor Transcription 598
	RAINDROPS	–
	SMOKE GETS IN YOUR EYES	–
	DODO'S BOUNCE	–
	ESCAPE	–

Note :

According to George Hoefer in his article "The recorded flights of Dodo", written for DOWN BEAT magazine in December 1966, the above titles had originally been intended for release on an album called "Tone Paintings" by Atomic Records. This statement seems corroborated by a recording contract between Marmarosa and the Atomic Record Company preserved in the Archive of Professional Musicians Local 47 in Los Angeles. This contract mentions the above recording location, date, and personnel. It was signed on December 22, 1947. From the very same date a set of agreements between Marmarosa and the MacGregor Music Library Service has survived, granting MacGregor all rights concerning the release for broadcasting of some of the above recorded compositions by Marmarosa. It seems that Atomic sold the titles to or possibly recorded them for the MacGregor recording company, who released them within their transcription series in two portions in spring and summer 1948.

The above order of titles represents their release and not necessarily the sequence of recording.

YOU THRILL ME SO obviously is a reworking of Fritz Kreisler's I'M IN LOVE through a change of key and thematic variation.

Some sources spell CAMPADOO instead of COMPADOO.

The above COSMO STREET on an earlier Dial recording session is called BOPMATISM (see November 12, 1947).

LP reissues:

All titles also on Phoenix LP-20 and Raretone FC 5020.

CD reissue:

All titles also on Fresh Sound FSCD-1019, Lone Hill Jazz LJH10119, and on Proper INTRO CD 2055.

The popularity polls for 1947 (printed in early 1948) again reveal that Dodo Marmarosa's piano playing was well appreciated by the public in those days. He was placed as 4th popular pianist by the readers of *Down Beat* and as sixth popular pianist by the readers of *Metronome* magazine.

Probably referring to the turn of the year the January 1948 issue of Capitol Records' monthly newsletter *Capitol News from Hollywood* reported in its "Vine Street Gab" column of Marmarosa's piano playing at The Club Manchester in South Los Angeles. He was member of a quartet led by saxophonist Red Dorris and joined in the rhythm by Joe Mondragon on bass and Jimmy Landreth on drums.

THE INTERNATIONAL ALL STARS   AFRS "JUBILEE" RADIO SHOW

Stan Hasselgard (cl), Wardell Gray (ts), Dodo Marmarosa (p), Al Hendrickson (g), poss. Harry Babasin (b), Frank Bode (Uffe Baadh) (dm)

<u>February 9 (?) 1948, Pasadena, Calif., McCormack General Hospital</u>

THEME (ONE O'CLOCK JUMP, part only) (/)	AFRS Jubilee Program No. 278
C-JAM BLUES (s)	–
I NEVER LOVED ANYONE (Frances Wayne -voc) (/)	–
WHAT IS THIS THING CALLED LOVE (incomplete) (s)	AFRS Jubilee unissued
HOW HIGH THE MOON (s)	AFRS Jubilee Program No. 278
WHO'S SORRY NOW (Frances Wayne -voc) (/)	–
THEME (ONE O'CLOCK JUMP, part only) (with signoff) (/)	–

Note :

The above performance was not a "Just Jazz" concert as claimed by some sources due to the presence of Gene Norman as master of ceremonies.

Lotz and Neuert (AFRS "Jubilee" discography) suggest March 1948 as possible recording date. The program was broadcast for the first time on June 18, 1948.

All musicians of the above personnel are named by Norman on the show, except for the bass player.

Other participators on "Jubilee" program No. 278 were the Bill Doggett Trio and Pete Dailey And His Chicagoans.

HOW HIGH THE MOON is named "JAM SESSION AT JUBILEE" on the original AFRS Jubilee program release as well as on Nostalgia cassette reissue.

The announcement by Woody Herman to C-JAM BLUES on Swing House SWH-10 release does not derive from the above "Jubilee" Show, but from AFRS Jubilee program No. 229 and has obviously been dubbed in by the editor.

The announcement of Gene Norman to WHAT IS THIS THING CALLED LOVE on Dragon DRLP 29 issue points at the placing of this title before HOW HIGH THE MOON in the original "Jubilee" concert show. The title was dropped by the sound engineers for the release of AFRS Jubilee program No. 278.

LP reissues:

C-JAM BLUES and HOW HIGH THE MOON also on Spotlite SPJ-134 and Swing House SWH-10.

Contrary to cover and label information, Spotlite SPJ-134 has reversed order of C JAM BLUES and HOW HIGH THE MOON.

C-JAM BLUES, HOW HIGH THE MOON, and WHAT IS THIS THING CALLED LOVE also on Dragon DRLP 29.

MC reissue:

All titles, except WHAT IS THIS THING CALLED LOVE, on Nostalgia 0026.

CD reissue:

C-JAM BLUES and HOW HIGH THE MOON also on Sounds Of Yesteryear DSOY 610.

Due to growing illness Marmarosa left Los Angeles in early 1948 and returned to his hometown Pittsburgh, Pa.

Back in Pittsburgh Marmarosa was presented at the Midway Lounge as leader of a trio with Tony Fenarro (g) and Marty Shor (b). He also participated in several horn trios, a Pittsburgh tradition of combining a horn with piano and drums. Among the horn players he accompanied in these trios in 1948/49 were trumpeter Sal La Perche, whom Marmarosa had already met in Tommy Dorsey's orchestra, and saxophonist Vic Powell.

From April until June/July 1949 Marmarosa played with a small group led by **Johnny "Scat" Davis**, for whom he already had worked for several months in 1942.
According to *Down Beat* magazine of May 6, 1949 the group performed at the Melody Lounge in Pittsburgh, Pa., until April 28, then went on tour. While in Chicago, Ill., with Davis, Marmarosa again had to leave due to illness and once more returned to Pittsburgh.

NOTE: Most discographies (including Raben and Lord) mention Dodo Marmarosa as probable member of a Benny Carter group accompanying tenor saxophonist Ben Webster on a recording session for the label MODERN from reputedly May 1949 (four recorded titles: COTTON TAIL, TIME OUT FOR THE BLUES, SURF BOARD, and YOU ARE TOO BEAUTIFUL, reissued on Classics CD 1297). Not only was Marmarosa on tour in the East with Johnny "Scat" Davis at the time (see above), but the personnel usually given for this date seems to be an unverified and rather implausible transfer from Carter's group of the April 29, 1947 "Just Jazz" concert (see entry for this date) with mostly the same participating musicians, except for Ben Webster. The piano-playing on these recordings does not sound like Marmarosa's and the only secure data on the session seem to be Carter's leadership and Webster's participation.

In September 1949 **Artie Shaw** put together a new orchestra, which was scheduled to go on a two months' tour of one-nighters starting in mid September 1949.

Down Beat magazine of Sept. 23, 1949 - which was available on newsstands already on the 9th of September (!) - mentions pianist Gene DiNovi as tentative member of this band. He was replaced, however, by Marmarosa before the tour started on September 14 with a concert at the Symphony Hall in Boston, Mass.:

Artie Shaw And His Orchestra
Don Fagerquist, Don Paladino, Vic Ford, Dale Pearce (tp), Angie Callea (tb,arr), Porky Cohen, Sonny Russo, Freddie Zito (tb), Artie Shaw (cl), Tony Ragusa, Frank Socolow (as), Al Cohn, Herbie Steward (ts), Danny Bank (bs), Dodo Marmarosa (p), Jimmy Raney (g), Dick Niveson (b), Irv Kluger (dm), Pat Lockwood (voc), Gene Roland, Al Cohn, Johnny Mandel, Tadd Dameron, John Bartee, Roger Segure, Paul Jordan, Ray Conniff, Eddie Sauter, John La Porta (arr) :

The following are the stages of the tour, as advertised in *Down Beat* magazine from September 23, 1949:

September 14, 1949	: Boston, Mass., Symphony Hall
September 15, 1949	: Providence, Rhode Island, place unknown
September 16-18, 1949	: Hartford, Conn., State Theatre
September 21-24, 1949	: One-nighters in Canada, towns unknown*
October 1, 1949	: Kansas City, Mo., Pla-Mor Ballroom
October 4, 1949	: Sioux Falls, South D., Arkota Ballroom
October 5, 1949	: Sioux City, Iowa, Tomba Ballroom
October 6, 1949	: Marion, Iowa, Armar Ballroom
October 8, 1949	: St. Joseph, Mo., Frog Hop Ballroom
October 9, 1949	: Des Moines, Iowa, Tromar Ballroom
October 12, 1949	: Mankato, Minn., Kato Ballroom
October 15, 1949	: Iowa City, Iowa, State University
October 16, 1949	: Milwaukee, Wisc., Sagle's Ballroom
October 18, 1949	: Kaukauna, Wisc., Nightingale Ballroom
October 21-22, 1949	: Purdue, Ind., Purdue University
October 23, 1949	: Peoria, Ill., Inglaterra Ballroom
October 29, 1949	: Minneapolis, Minn., University of Minnesota
October 30, 1949	: Waterloo, Iowa, Electric Park
November 5, 1949	: Flint, Mich., I. M. A. Auditorium

* Marmarosa in a 1995 interview remembered *"a couple of one-nighters in Maine and Canada"* and Montreal as one of the Canadian stages.

At the end of the tour the Artie Shaw Orchestra started a two weeks' engagement in Chicago, Ill., during which Marmarosa is said to have left, presumably after the first week:

November 7 - 20, 1949   : Chicago, Ill., Blue Note

NOTE: The stories about the circumstances and time of Marmarosa's break with Shaw differ considerably. While most sources and seemingly also Artie Shaw have spread the story of Marmarosa leaving on stage one night at the Blue Note in Chicago, Ill. because of his discontent with the public's repeated requests for Shaw's old hit tunes, the pianist himself in a 1995 interview with Robert E. Sunenblick (Uptown Records) remembered to have joined Shaw in New York and to have played with him only *"a couple of one-nighters in Maine and Canada"*. Asked how long he had stayed with Shaw, Marmarosa answered *"about a couple of weeks"*. As reason for his departure he told Sunenblick, that he had gotten drunk one evening, had broken some windows and finally got fired because of his untenable behaviour.

The front page of *Down Beat* from December 2, 1949 shows a photograph of Marmarosa together with Shaw and singer Pat Lockwood in the studio of a South Dakotan radio station (KSOO). According to the plan of the tour this photograph must have been taken around October 4, 1949.
The same issue, however, also mentions that at the time of printing Marmarosa's place with Shaw had been taken over by Gil Barrios.

From March until May 1950 Marmarosa appeared as soloist at the Playhouse Grill in Pittsburgh, Pa.

DODO MARMAROSA TRIO   SAVOY RECORDING SESSION

Dodo Marmarosa (p), Thomas Mandrus (b), Joe "Jazz" Wallace (dm)

<u>July 21, 1950, Pittsburgh, Pa.</u>

PIT 8600	MY FOOLISH HEART	Savoy 756
PIT 8601	BLUE ROOM	Savoy SJL 2247
PIT 8602	WHY WAS I BORN	Savoy 756
PIT 8603	THE NIGHT IS YOUNG	Savoy SJL 2247

Note :

The above session was supervised by Ralph Bass.

LP reissue:

All titles also on Savoy SJL 2247 and Savoy WL 70510.

CD reissues:

All titles also on Savoy ZDS 4425, Savoy SV-0272, on Classics CD 1165, and on Lone Hill Jazz LHJ10119.

<u>early 1950's:</u>   In 1950 Marmarosa got married in Pittsburgh, Pa., and eventually became father of two daughters.

He tried to organize his musical activities around his new family and in 1952 went back to Los Angeles with his wife and daughters. The marriage failed, however, and Marmarosa returned to Pittsburgh in the fall of 1952, his wife having told him that she wanted a divorce. Before Marmarosa left Los Angeles, he was caught sitting in with the Lighthouse All Stars by Los Angeles-jazz devotee Bob Andrews with a portable Pentron recorder in August 1952:

LIGHTHOUSE ALL STARS   LIVE RECORDINGS

Shorty Rogers (tp), Milt Bernhart (tb), Bob Cooper (ts), Jimmy Giuffre (ts), Dodo
Marmarosa (p), Howard Rumsey (b), Shelly Manne (dm)

<u>August 17, 1952, Los Angeles, Calif., The Lighthouse, Hermosa Beach</u>

JUST YOU, JUST ME (omit trombone) (s)	Norma Vantage NLP 5011
HOW HIGH THE MOON (s)	–
GOOD BAIT (s)	–

CD reissue:

All titles also on Vantage BA 006.

mid 1950's: In 1953 the pianist joined the trio of
saxophonist Vic Powell for an engagement at
the Alhambra Club in Butler, Pa. (on the north
side of Pittsburgh).

Subsequently Marmarosa went on the road for a
few months with the orchestra of **Charlie Spivak**
through a recommendation by Vic Powell.

In 1954 he was reclassified and drafted in the
army, where he stayed for three unpleasant
months. Eventually he was discharged in a
seriously bad psychological disposition and
withdrew from public appearances completely.
It was possibly during this period that the
pianist turned down an offer from Artie Shaw
to travel to Europe with the clarinetist's trio.
Marmarosa's temporary retirement came to
an end, when he finally followed a call from
trumpeter Danny Conn to join him for a
concert in March 1956...

DODO MARMAROSA TRIO   *UNIVERSITY OF PITTSBURGH STUDENT UNION CONCERT*

Dodo Marmarosa (p), Johnny Vance (b), Chuck Spatafore (dm)

<u>March, 1956, Oakland, Pa., Stephen Foster Memorial Hall</u>

I'VE NEVER BEEN IN LOVE BEFORE   Uptown UPCD 27.44

Note :

The above performance has a spoken introduction by trumpeter Danny Conn, who in 1956 organized a series of concerts to be held on Sunday afternoons for the University Of Pittsburgh Student Union. Conn hired Marmarosa out of temporary retirement for the above concert.

After the above engagement Marmarosa began to appear in public more regularly again. He is said to have played in the orchestras of Al Noble and trumpeter Whitey Scharbo and performed with a trio of his own called the "Deuces Wild" at Pittsburgh's Midway Lounge at least two times in 1957/58.

The first engagement ran from October 7 to 27 in 1957 (with Spider Rondinelli on drums and an unknown bass player), the second from March 3 to 9, 1958. During the latter week some private recordings were made by Danny Conn (see March 1958).

DANNY CONN QUINTET   STUDIO RECORDINGS

Danny Conn (tp) Buzzy Renn (as) Dodo Marmarosa (p), Jimmy DeJulio (b), Chuck
Spatafore (dm)

November 8, 1957, Pittsburgh, Pa., Wayne Pazcuzzi studio

YOU'RE MY THRILL (s)	Uptown UPCD 27.44
DODO'S BLUES (s)	Uptown UPCD 27.44

Note :

*The above two titles were recorded privately at Wayne Pazcuzzi's studio. Pazcuzzi, a bass player with the
Pittsburgh Symphony Orchestra, ran a studio in a barn at the back of his house and had invited Danny Conn
to do some recordings with a group of his choice.*

*DODO'S BLUES is not identical to the tune with the same title on the ATOMIC recording session from January
11, 1946.*

DODO MARMAROSA TRIO   LIVE RECORDINGS

Dodo Marmarosa (p), Danny Mastri (b), Henry Sciullo (dm)

March 5 or 6, 1958, Pittsburgh, Pa., Midway Lounge

MOOSE THE MOOCHE	Uptown UPCD 27.44
ALWAYS	–
CHEEK TO CHEEK	–
ROBBIN'S NEST	–
TOPSY	–
CHEROKEE	–
SWEET MISS (theme)	–
A FINE ROMANCE	–
BODY AND SOUL (incomplete)	–
BILLIE'S BOUNCE	–
CHEERS (incomplete)	–
THIS CAN'T BE LOVE	–
SWEET MISS (theme)	–

Note :

For the above engagement at the Midway Lounge during March 1958 Marmarosa's trio was billed in the Pittsburgh Post-Gazette as "Marmarosa at Midway with the Deuces Wild". The recordings were made privately with a tape recorder by trumpeter Danny Conn.

In 1958 Marmarosa continued his playing in the Pittsburgh area mainly in trios, accompanied at least once by the Pittsburgh born bass player David Izenzon.

In 1959 the "Deuces Wild" appeared once more at the Midway Lounge in Pittsburgh and, as a photograph published in a CD-booklet by Uptown Records shows, also in Conneaut Lake, Pa., in the summer of 1959. The personnel for the latter engagement was Flo Cassinelli (ts), Dodo Marmarosa (p), Danny Mastri (b), and Spider Rondinelli (dm).

In late 1959 or early 1960 Marmarosa went to Chicago, Ill. There he performed at Sir Gants Bar on the North side of Chicago and played in several clubs, which presented jazz nights once a week, such as Figero's, the Southland Hotel, or Clark's Pink Poodle.
For two months probably in the first half of 1960 he also was with a group of his old boss **Johnny "Scat" Davis** playing in the Chicago area.
During the same time he accompanied the singer Johnny Janis on the recording of a few audition dubs in Chicago.

JOHNNY JANIS   STUDIO RECORDINGS
WITH TRIO/QUARTET ACCOMPANIMENT

Johnny Janis (voc) acc. by Ira Sullivan (tp,ts), Dodo Marmarosa (p), Jerry Friedman (b), Guy Vivaros (dm)

<u>ca. early to mid 1960, Chicago, Ill., unknown studio location</u>

LADY BE GOOD (JJv) (/)	Starwell	STR06
I GOT IT BAD (JJv) (/)		–
THIS CAN'T BE LOVE (omit Sullivan) (JJv) (s)		–
TOO YOUNG (omit Sullivan) (JJv) (/)		–
THE SONG IS YOU (JJv) (/)		–
THE THINGS WE DID LAST SUMMER (omit Sullivan) (JJv) (/)		–
NICE WORK IF YOU CAN GET IT (JJv) (/)		–
I'VE NEVER BEEN IN LOVE BEFORE (JJv) (/)		–
YOU DON'T KNOW WHAT LOVE IS (JJv) (/)		–
I'M BEGINNING TO SEE THE LIGHT (omit Sullivan, Vivaros) (JJv) (s)		–
YOU'LL NEVER KNOW (JJv) (/)		–
LET'S GET AWAY FROM IT ALL (JJv) (s)		–

Note :

The above titles were recorded privately by singer Johnny Janis at a Chicago studio location.

According to Janis' own words he had been caught by Marmarosa's playing at a nightclub in Chicago, had introduced himself to the pianist, and immediately put together a quartet to do the above recordings. Janis then stored away the tapes, only to rediscover them some forty years later with other old recording material. He finally released the recording session on his own Starwell label in 2006 under the title "Jazz Up Your Life".

The Chicago promoter Joe Segal got word of Marmarosa's presence in the town from Johnny Janis and managed to meet the pianist at a concert gig with trumpeter Ira Sullivan on South Stoney Island. Segal immediately employed Marmarosa for a series of off-night sessions and tried to arrange a recording date with producer Jack Tracy of the Argo label for him, but the pianist had left town, before the trio session could be set about.

Marmarosa went west, working on the way in Rock Island, Ill., and Davenport, Iowa, and later in Reno and in San Francisco. Paul Smoker, then living with his parents in Davenport, remembers having been hired (most certainly in the fall of 1960) to play trumpet with Marmarosa in a quartet setting together with bass and drums. The quartet played for at least two weeks in a club called "The Jolly Roger" in Rock Island, just across the Mississippi from Davenport. When Marmarosa went through the glass of the club's entrance door, the gig came to an abrupt end.

Towards the end of 1960 the pianist called Segal from California and promised to return to Chicago soon for the scheduled recording date. Instead he went on what he described himself as "a groovy Mexican vacation" and did another gig in Davenport. At the beginning of May 1961 he finally returned to Chicago, Ill., to do the recordings...

DODO MARMAROSA TRIO   ARGO RECORDING SESSION

Dodo Marmarosa (p), Richard Evans (b), Marshall Thompson (dm)

<u>May 9/10, 1961, Chicago, Ill., Ter Mar studios</u>

10901	UP IN DODO'S ROOM	Argo unissued
10902	JERRY JAM	Argo unissued
10903	APRIL PLAYED THE FIDDLE	Argo LP (S) 4012
10904	SOON	Argo unissued
10905	WHY DO I LOVE YOU	Argo LP (S) 4012
10906	EVERYTHING HAPPENS TO ME	–
10907	ME AND MY SHADOW	–
10908	ON GREEN DOLPHIN STREET	–
10909	WHO CAN I TURN TO?	Argo unissued
10910	TRACY'S BLUES	Argo LP (S) 4012
10911	YOU CALL IT MADNESS	–
10912	MELLOW MOOD	–
10914	I THOUGHT ABOUT YOU	–
10918	A COTTAGE FOR SALE	–

Note :

Argo was the jazz subsidiary of the Chicago based Chess label owned by Leonard and Philip Chess (A & R man: Jack Tracy).

TRACY'S BLUES was dedicated to Jack Tracy, former editor of Chicago based Down Beat magazine, who sponsored and supervised this session together with Joe Segal.

The above LP was called "Dodo's Back", and was released in 1962.

LP reissue:

All issued titles also on Argo ARCD 502.

CD reissues:

All issued titles also on Affinity CD AFF 755, on MCA MVCR-20057, and on Lone Hill Jazz LHJ10119.

During the following years Marmarosa seems to have shuttled between Chicago and Pittsburgh continuously.

He was featured with a group of trumpeter Danny Conn at the Crawford Grill in Pittsburgh in 1961, and bassist Johnny Vance remembers to have jammed with him after hours at Pittsburgh's Point View Hotel several times in the early sixties.

In spring 1962 Marmarosa appeared on a television jazz-program in his hometown, in May he was back in Chicago for another recording session.

DODO MARMAROSA & THE ALL STAR QUINTET

TV SHOW FOR WQED PROGRAM "JAZZ SCENE"

Danny Conn (tp) Carlo Galluzzo (ts), Dodo Marmarosa (p), Jimmy DeJulio (b), Chuck Spatafore (dm)

<u>Spring 1962, Pittsburgh, Pa., WQED studios</u>

HOROSCOPE (VIRGO MOVEMENT) (s)	Uptown UPCD 27.44
OBLIVION (s)	–
DODO'S BLUES (s)	–

Note :

The TV Channel 13 WQED in 1961/62 transmitted a Friday night program called "Jazz Scene", on which local Pittsburgh jazz musicians were presented by host Sterling Yates.

Unfortunately the original programs do no longer exist. The above recordings were taken from his TV set by Danny Conn at the time of transmission.

HOROSCOPE is based on a movement from the classical ballet HOROSCOPE by the English composer Constant Lambert.

DODO'S BLUES is the same composition as on the studio recording from November 8, 1957, but not identical to the tune with the same title on the ATOMIC recording session from January 11, 1946.

GENE AMMONS QUARTET / DODO MARMAROSA TRIO   ARGO
RECORDING SESSION

Gene Ammons (ts), Dodo Marmarosa (p), Sam Jones (b), Marshall Thompson (dm)

<u>May 4, 1962, Chicago, Ill.</u>

GEORGIA (s)	Argo unissued
FOR YOU (s)	–
YOU'RE DRIVING ME CRAZY (s)	–
WHERE OR WHEN (s)	–
THE SONG IS YOU (omit Ammons)	–
JUST FRIENDS (omit Ammons)	–
YARDBIRD SUITE (omit Ammons, take 1)	–
YARDBIRD SUITE (omit Ammons, take 2)	–
I REMEMBER YOU (omit Ammons)	–
BLUZARUMBA (s)	–
THE MOODY BLUES (omit Ammons)	–
FALLING IN LOVE WITH LOVE (take 1) (s)	–
FALLING IN LOVE WITH LOVE (take 2) (s)	–
THE VERY THOUGHT OF YOU (omit Ammons)	–

Note :

As Ammons at the time of recording was contractually bound to the Prestige label, Argo had to sell this session to Prestige. It was released for the first time in 1972 as a double LP-album called "Jug & Dodo".

LP reissues:

All titles on Prestige P 24021 and on Prestige Bellaphon BLST 6532.

CD reissue:

Trio titles (THE SONG IS YOU, JUST FRIENDS, YARDBIRD SUITE (both takes), I REMEMBER YOU, THE MOODY BLUES, and THE VERY THOUGHT OF YOU) also on Lone Hill Jazz LHJ10119.

All titles also on Prestige PCD-24021-2.

In June 1962 promoter Joe Segal presented Marmarosa in a concert at the University of Chicago in Chicago, Ill. Among the other performers were Ira Sullivan (tp), Gene Ammons (ts), and Jodie Christian (p).

Marmarosa stayed for a while to play in Chicago and did one more recording session...

DODO MARMAROSA QUARTET   ARGO RECORDING SESSION

Bill Hardman (tp), Dodo Marmarosa (p), Richard Evans (b), Ben Dixon (dm)

<u>November 2, 1962, Chicago, Ill.</u>

11971	DODO'S TUNE (s)	Argo ARCD 502
11972	AUTOMATION (s)	–
11973	ANALYSIS (s)	–
11974	SOMEDAY (s)	–
11975	ONLY A ROSE (s)	–
11976	TAKE HOME PAY ( )	Argo unissued
11977	GONE WITH THE WIND (s)	Argo ARCD 502

Note :

These titles, except for TAKE HOME PAY, have for the first time been issued in 1988!

CD reissue:

All issued titles also on Affinity CD AFF 755.

During the 1960's Marmarosa obviously continued to play publicly in Pittsburgh and Chicago, although documentation of this period in his career is sparse. He is said, e. g., to have been heard playing at a bar near Lawrence Avenue EL-Stop in Chicago in the fall of 1966, or to have appeared one week with the Salt City Six in Pittsburgh, Pa., in the sixties. Until ca. 1975 he seems to have performed on and off as a solo pianist in restaurants and clubs of the Pittsburgh area like the Cowshed (ca. 1968) or the Colony Restaurant (other sources claim, that he did not appear in public again after 1968). Thereafter his long standing diabetes forced him into permanent retirement.

In the 1980s and 1990s Dodo Marmarosa lived alternately in a Pittsburgh Army Veteran's Hospital or with his sister Doris' family in Glenshaw, near Pittsburgh, Pa.
In July 1991 a note in *Down Beat* magazine reported of Marmarosa's visit to a concert of Randy Brecker and Eliane Elias in Detroit, where he exchanged piano-voicings with Elias after the concert.

In September 1993 an article on Marmarosa by Bob Eleff appeared in the Canadian magazine *Coda*. The author had been lucky in arranging a meeting with the pianist in Pittsburgh prior to the publication of his portrait.

In June 1995 Robert E. Sunenblick, producer of the label Uptown Records, interviewed Marmarosa for a CD-release of previously unissued recordings from the late fifties and early sixties. Marmarosa then was living again with Army veterans outside Pittsburgh and had a tremor in his right hand, which prevented him from playing professionally any longer.
On the occasion of the interview a spoken introduction by Marmarosa was taped to be issued with the recordings. The pianist's recollections were as follows:

DODO MARMAROSA

SPOKEN INTRODUCTION TO UPTOWN CD-RELEASE

June 17, 1995, Pittsburgh, Pa.

Dodo Marmarosa (referring to his March 1958 engagement at the Midway Lounge in Pittsburgh):

> *"Hello, this is Mike Marmarosa. Hope you're enjoying the music we're playing at the Midway Lounge. It was a real long place with a bar and booths and some kind of hamacas. The bar was on the left, and then the booths were on the right, and then we had those hammocks, or whatever it was, over on the..... you know, like the Sheik of Araby.....[laughing:] it's weird around to be, as a horde of sheiks gonna walk in any minute!*
> *It's just an impromptu thing, you know, like just somebody said: we get a group together and..... I forever liked to live those days over again."*

A few reminiscences published in an interview with the pianist by the Pittsburgh journalist Nate Guidry in 1998 were the next to be heard of Dodo Marmarosa.

In the summer of 2002 another Pittsburgh journalist, who planned to write a portrait of trumpeter Danny Conn, asked Marmarosa about the mutual friendship between him and Conn. *"Danny is a great artist, trumpeter and arranger,"* Marmarosa replied. *"He's also a great friend. He comes to visit me a lot and it's always a great pleasure to have him. Sometimes Danny and I and Joe Dallas [a friend and trombone player] get together and we have a session for the girls at the veteran's center."*

A few weeks after this short interview, on September 17, 2002, Marmarosa died of a heart attack at the Army Veteran's Medical Center in Lincoln Lemington near Pittsburgh. Before retiring to his room for the final time, he had, according to his sister Doris, once more played the small organ on one of the floors of the center's building.

NOTE: Supplementing the discographical listing is a final line-up of those titles, which are compositions by Dodo Marmarosa and which are known to have been recorded either by himself or by bands he played in:

AMNESIA	- composed and arranged for Boyd Raeburn; see Standard Recordings, Feb. 1946
ANALYSIS	- see Argo Recording Session, Nov. 2, 1962
AUTOMATION	- composed with Bill Hardman; see Argo Recording Session, Nov. 2, 1962
BATTLE OF THE BALCONY JIVE	- see M-G-M Soundtrack Recordings, Sept. 11, 1944
BOPMATISM	- see Dial Recording Session, Nov. 12, 1947 (also titled COSMO STREET on Atomic Recording Session, Dec. 24, 1947)
COMPADOO	- see Atomic Recording Session, Dec. 24, 1947
DARY DEPARTS	- see Dial Recording Session, Nov. 12, 1947
DODO'S BLUES	- see Atomic Recording session, Jan. 11, 1946 (with different tune see private Studio Recordings, Nov. 8, 1957 and WQED TV Program, Spring 1962)
DODO'S BOUNCE	- see Down Beat Recording Session, July 16, 1947 + Atomic Recording Session, Dec. 24, 1947
DODO'S DANCE	- see Dial Recording Session, Nov. 12, 1947
DODO'S LAMENT	- see Down Beat Recording Session, July 16, 1947
DODO'S TUNE	- see Argo Recording Session, Nov. 2, 1962
ESCAPE	- arr. for and rec. by Ray Linn Nonet, Dec. 14, 1945; see also Atomic Recording Session, Dec. 24, 1947
FLIGHT OF THE VOUT BUG	- composed with Tom Talbert; see Atomic Recording Session, Nov. 4, 1946
MELLOW MOOD	- see Atomic Recording session, Jan. 11, 1946 + Argo Recording Session, May 9/10, 1961
OPUS #5	- see Atomic Recording Session, Dec. 24, 1947
RAINDROPS	- see Atomic Recording Session, Sept. 23, 1946 + Atomic Recording Session, Dec. 24, 1947
TONE PAINTINGS I	- see Atomic Recording Session, Nov. 1, 1947

TONE PAINTINGS II	- see Atomic Recording Session, Nov. 1, 1947
(aka MILES' INFLUENCE)	
TRACY'S BLUES	- see Argo Recording Session, May 9/10, 1961
YOU THRILL ME SO	- see Atomic Recording Session, Dec. 24, 1947

Dodo Marmarosa is credited as co-composer in later Dial 10"
LP issues of the following title (for the original 78rpm issue of
the title Howard McGhee was given credit as composer):

UP IN DODO'S ROOM   - composed with Arvin Garrison;
see Dial Recording Session, Oct. 18, 1946

APPENDIX

A. LISTING OF REISSUES CITED IN THE TEXT
(IN ALPHABETICAL ORDER OF LABELS)

Abbreviations in parentheses denote countries of origin of the labels or releases, as far as they could be discerned:

(A)	Austria	(UK)	United Kingdom/England
(Can)	Canada	(It)	Italy
(D)	Denmark	(J)	Japan
(Eu)	Europe	(Sd)	Sweden
(F)	France	(Sp)	Spain
(G)	Germany	(US)	United States of America

1. LP-RELEASES

Affinity AFS 1012	(UK)	"Skyliner - Charlie Barnet" - Charlie Barnet a. h. Orchestra
Aircheck 35	(Can)	"Gene Krupa And His Orchestra - On The Air 1944-46"
Ajax-140	(US)	"Charlie Barnet In Disco Order Vol. 16"
Ajax-147	(US)	"Charlie Barnet In Disco Order Vol. 17"
Ajaz-201	(US)	"Charlie Barnet In Disco Order Vol. 19"

Alamac LP QSR 2441	(US)	"Slim's Jam - Slim Gaillard 1945-6"
Argo LP (S) 4012	(US)	"Dodo's Back" - Dodo Marmarosa Trio
Argo ARCD 502	(It)	"Dodo Marmarosa - the chicago sessions"
Artie Shaw Club ASC-13	(UK)	"The Artie Shaw Gramercy Five"
Big Band Archives BBA 1209	(US)	"Charlie Barnet and his Orchestra - Swingin' On Nothin' "
Black Lion 28 404-2Z	(G)	"The Sunset All Stars - Jammin' at Sunset Volumes 1 & 2"
Black Lion BLP 60106	(UK)	"Wardell Gray - One For Prez"
Big Band Gems BBG 092		"Spotlite On Shaw 1939-1945"
Bluebird AXM2-5579	(US)	"The Complete Artie Shaw Volume VI 1942-1945"
Bluebird AXM2-5580	(US)	"The Complete Artie Shaw Volume VII 1939-1945"
Blue Note BST 84483/84	(G)	"Lester Young - The Aladdin Sessions"
Camden CAL 908	(US)	"September Song - Artie Shaw And His Orchestra"
Capitol ECJ-50077	(J)	"Capitol Collector's Items"
Capitol T 20579	(UK)	"Jazz of the Forties Vol.1 - Swing Into Bebop"
Cicala BLJ 8017	(It)	"The Bop Masters" unissued and rare performances
Cicala BLJ 8022	(It)	"Bop Sessions" rare & unissued performances
Cicala BLJ 8032	(It)	"Keybop" Tadd Dameron / Dodo Marmarosa
Crown CLP 5008	(US)	"Jazz surprise - the modern jazz stars"
Crown CLP 5009	(US)	"Jazz Masquerade"
Déjavu DVLP 2019	(It)	"Tommy Dorsey - 20 Golden Greats"
Dial 201	(US)	"Charlie Parker - Volume 1"
Dial 202	(US)	"Charlie Parker - Volume 2"
Dial 208	(US, released 1951)	"Piano Moods - Dodo Marmarosa Trio"
Dial 901	(US)	"Charlie Parker - The Bird Plays The Blues"
Dial 905	(US)	"Charlie Parker - Unreleased Masters, Volume 2"
Dragon DRLP 29	(Sd)	"Stan Hasselgard - Jammin' at Jubilee"
EMI 1C 056-85 609	(G)	"World of Jazz: Red Norvo"
Fanfare LP 38-138	(US)	"Charlie Barnet and his orchestra - 1944-45 Broadcasts"

Fanfare LP 44-144	(US)	"Gene Krupa And His Orchestra - 1942-43 broadcasts"
First Heard FHR-8	(UK)	"Boyd Raeburn And His Musicians - 1943-1948"
Folklyric LP 9038	(US)	"Cement Mixer Put-ti Put-ti" - Slim Gaillard
Fontana 683907 JCL	(D)	"Dexter Gordon - Wardell Gray - The Master Swingers!"
Golden Era GE-15006	(US)	"The Clarinet Playing Leaders Volume One" - Shaw/Reynolds
Golden Era GE-15014	(US)	"Boyd Raeburn and his Orchestra - Hep Boyds"
Golden Era GE-15078	(US)	"The Clarinet Playing Leaders Volume Three"
Halo 50273	(US)	"Slim Gaillard with Dizzy Gillespie and Orchestra"
Hep 3	(UK)	"The Boyd Raeburn Orchestra - 'on the air' vol 2"
Hep 22	(UK)	"Boyd Raeburn and his Orchestra - Memphis in June"
I.A.J.R.C. 48	(Can)	"Boyd Raeburn - Rare 1944-46 Broadcast Performances"
Jasmine 2515	(UK)	"Gene Krupa - Air Checks 1938 Through 1942"
Jazz Showcase 5005	(US)	"California Boppin' "
Jazztone J 1001	(US)	"Piano Contrasts - Erroll Garner Trio/Dodo Marmarosa Trio"
Joyce LP-1003	(US)	"Spotlight On Artie Shaw 1945"
Joyce LP-1010	(US)	"Spotlight On Artie Shaw - Volume II - "
Joyce LP-1042	(US)	"One Night Stand with Tommy Dorsey - Volume 2"
Joyce LP-1148	(US)	"One Night Stand with Artie Shaw at the Steel Pier"
Joyce LP-2004	(US)	"The Radio Discs of Tommy Dorsey"
Joyce LP-3001	(US)	"Film Tracks of Charlie Barnet"
Joyce LP-3006	(US)	"Film Tracks of Tommy Dorsey"
Joyce LP-4012	(US)	"Spotlight On Alvino Rey, Boyd Raeburn and Bob Chester"
Joyce LP-5010	(US)	"Boyd Raeburn's Jubilee - 1945"
Joyce LP-5011	(US)	"Boyd Raeburn's Second Jubilee"
Keynote 18PJ-1051-71	(J)	"The Complete Keynote Collection"

Manhattan MAN 501	(It)	"Well, Git It! - Tommy Dorsey"
MCA2-4069	(US)	"The Best Of Charlie Barnet"
MCA 510.181	(F)	"Lionel Hampton No. 7 - Hamp's Small Combos"
MCA Coral 6.22181	(G)	"Lionel Hampton Vol. 7 1947-1949"
Mercury 830.121	(US)	"The complete Keynote Collection"
Movietone MT S 4005	(G)	"Tommy Dorsey's Hullabaloo"
Musicraft MVS-510	(US)	"Mel Tormé And The Mel-Tones with Sonny Burke & His Orchestra - It Happened In Monterey"
Norma Vantage NLP 5011	(J)	"Dodo Marmarosa/Lorraine Geller - West Coast Piano Touch"
Official LP 3050	(D)	"Slim Gaillard - Laughing In Rhythm"
Onyx ORI 212	(US)	"Central Avenue Breakdown; Volume 1"
Onyx ORI 215	(US)	"Central Avenue Breakdown; Volume 2"
Onward To Yesterday	(US)	"Boyd Raeburn And His Orchestra (1944-46)"
Philips 6641 170	(G)	"Remember Tommy - Tommy Dorsey"
Phoenix LP-20	(US)	"Dodo Marmarosa - Piano Man"
Polydor Special 545 107	(UK)	"Slim Gaillard & Friends - Chicken Rhythm"
Prestige P 24021	(US)	"Gene Ammons & Dodo Marmarosa - Jug & Dodo"
Prestige Bellaphon BLST 6532	(G)	"Gene Ammons & Dodo Marmarosa - Jug & Dodo"
Raretone 5020 FC	(It)	"dodo marmarosa - Experiment In Bop"
RCA LPV-544	(US)	"Esquire's All American Hot Jazz- With 22 Esquire Poll Winners"
RCA NL 86757	(Eu)	"Esquire's All-American Hot Jazz Sessions"
RCA NL 45154	(G)	"Tommy Dorsey In Concert"
RCA PM 42403	(F)	"Artie Shaw And His Orchestra Volume 2 (1941-1945)"
Savoy SJL 1177	(US)	"Charlie Parker / Dizzy Gillespie - Bebop's Heartbeat"
Savoy SJL 2215	(US)	"Black California"
Savoy SJL 2242	(US)	"Black California Vol. 2 - Anthology"
Savoy SJL 2247	(US)	"The Modern Jazz Piano Album"
Savoy WL 70510	(Eu)	"The Modern Jazz Piano Album"
Savoy SJL 2250	(US)	"Boyd Raeburn - Jewells"
Solid Sender SOL 514	(G)	"Small Label Gems Of The Forties Vol. 3"

Sounds of Swing LP 101	(US)	"Artie Shaw And His Orchestra - The Big Band Years"
Spotlite 108	(US)	"Dodo Marmarosa" (same as UK release "Spotlite SPJ-128")
Spotlite SPJ-101	(UK)	"Charlie Parker On Dial Volume 1"
Spotlite SPJ-103	(UK)	"Charlie Parker On Dial Volume 3"
Spotlite SPJ-128	(UK)	"Dodo Marmarosa - Dodo's Dance"
Spotlite SPJ-131	(UK)	"Howard McGhee - Trumpet At Tempo"
Spotlite SPJ-134	(UK)	"Wardell Gray - Stan Hasselgard"
Spotlite SPJ-150 D	(UK)	"Charlie Parker - Every Bit Of It"
Sunbeam SB-220	(US)	"Tommy Dorsey And His Orchestra featuring Gene Krupa and Buddy Rich 1944-1946"
Sutton SU 281	(US)	"Mel Tormé and the Romantics - in a romantic mood"
Swing Era LP-1019	(US)	"Charlie Barnet And His Orchestra - Rhapsody In Barnet"
Swing House SWH-8	(UK)	"R & B And Boogie-Woogie"
Swing House SWH-10	(UK)	"Dodo Marmarosa - A 'Live' Dodo"
Swingtime LP ST 1018	(D)	"Slim Gaillard 1945 - Tuitti Fruitti"
Swing Treasury LP ST-109	(US)	"Great Moments In Jazz - Volume 2 - Alto Masters"
Totem LP 1006	(US)	"Al Jolson "On The Air"
Totem LP 1030	(US)	"Al Jolson "On The Air" Volume Four"
Verve 2304 554	(F)	"Slim Gaillard - Opera in Vout"
Verve MGV-8060	(US)	"The Jazz Scene"
Verve 840 032-1	(G)	"Jazz-Club - Piano"
Vogue VJT 3003	(F)	"Gene Norman's Just Jazz Concerts"

2. MC-RELEASES

Nostalgia 0026	(?)	title ? (A set of four cassettes, containing AFRS "Jubilee" programs, incl. "Jubilee" Show No. 278)

3. CD-RELEASES

ABM ABMCD 1065	(UK)	"California Boppers"
Affinity CD AFF 755	(UK)	"Dodo Marmarosa - the chicago sessions"
Audiophonic ABR06082	(US)	"Boyd Raeburn - Out Of This World!"

Bear Family Rec. BCD 16117	(G)	"Ella Mae Morse - Barrelhouse, Boogie, And Blues"
Black Lion BLCD 760106	(G)	"Wardell Gray - One For Prez"
Black Lion BLCD 760171	(G)	"Sunset Swing"
Bluebird CD 07863 66087 2	(G)	"RCA Victor Jazz - The First Half Century: The Forties"
Blue Moon BMCD-1003	(Sp)	"Lester Young - The Complete 1936-1951 Small Group Sessions" Vol.3 1944-1946
Blue Moon BMCD-1008	(Sp)	"Charlie Parker - The Complete Bird 1944-1948"
Blue Moon BMCD-1046	(Sp)	"Jimmy Giuffre - The Complete 1947-1953 Small Group Sessions Vol. 1"
Blue Note CDP 7243 8 32787 2 5	(US)	"The Complete Aladdin Recordings of Lester Young"
Capitol TOCJ-5621-28	(J)	"Capitol Jazz Classics"
Circle CCD-112	(US)	"Charlie Barnet and his Orchestra - 1942"
Classics 24	(F)	"Complementary Tracks" (3 CD Set)
Classics CD 864	(F)	"The Chronogical Slim Gaillard - 1945"
Classics CD 911	(F)	"The Chronogical Slim Gaillard - 1945 Vol. 2"
Classics CD 932	(F)	"The Chronogical Lester Young - 1943-1946"
Classics CD 962	(F)	"The Chronogical Slim Gaillard - 1946"
Classics CD 980	(F)	"The Chronogical Charlie Parker - 1945-1947"
Classics CD 994	(F)	"The Chronogical Lionel Hampton - 1947"
Classics CD 1089	(F)	"The Chronogical Howard McGhee - 1946-1948"
Classics CD 1096	(F)	"The Chronogical Gene Krupa - 1942-1945"
Classics CD 111	(F)	"The Chronogical Lucky Thompson - 1944-1947"
Classics CD 1165	(F)	"The Chronogical Dodo Marmarosa - 1945-1950"
Classics CD 1221	(F)	"The Chronogical Slim Gaillard - 1947-1951"
Classics CD 1242	(F)	"The Chronogical Artie Shaw - 1942-1945"
Classics CD 1277	(F)	"The Chronogical Artie Shaw - 1945"
Classics CD 1297	(F)	"The Chronogical Benny Carter - 1948-1952"
Classics CD 1368	(F)	"The Chronogical Artie Shaw - 1946-1950"
Collector's Choice (unnumbered)	(US)	V-Discs - Tommy Dorsey (3 CD Set)
Cool & Blue CD 115	(Sp)	"Teddy Edwards - Steady With Teddy"
Echo Jazz EJCD 13	(UK)	"Boyd Raeburn"
EPM 152382	(F)	"Be Bop Story Volume 2"

EPM/Xanadu CD FDC 5174	(F)	"Be Bop Revisited Vol. 1"
EPM/Xanadu CD FDC 5175	(F)	"Be Bop Revisited Vol. 2"
Fresh Sound FSCD-156	(Sp)	"Sonny Criss - California Boppin' 1947"
Fresh Sound FSCD-1019	(Sp)	"Dodo Marmarosa - Dodo's Bounce"
Giants of Jazz CD 53097	(It)	"An Unforgettable Session" (April 29, 1947)
Hep CD 1	(UK)	"Boyd Raeburn and His Orchestra - Jubilee performances - 1946"
Hep CD 22	(UK)	"Boyd Raeburn - March Of The Boyds 1945-1948"
Hep CD 39	(UK)	"Tommy Dorsey and His Orchestra - the All Time Hit Parade rehearsals"
Hep CD 40	(UK)	"Tommy Dorsey and His Orchestra - the Carnegie Hall V-Disc session April 1944"
Hep CD 42	(UK)	"Boyd Raeburn and His Orchestra - the transcription performances 1946"
Hep CD 70(3)	(UK)	"Artie Shaw and His Orchestra - 1944-45"
Hep CD 84/85	(UK)	"Artie Shaw - The Complete Spotlight Band1945 Broadcasts"
Hindsight HCD 264	(UK)	"Charlie Barnet - Those Swingin' Years"
I.A.J.R.C. CD-1001	(Can)	"the tenor sax of Lucky Thompson - the beginning years"
Indigo IGO CD 2104	(UK)	"Lucky Thompson - Smooth Sailing"
Jasmine JASMCD 2537	(UK)	"Tommy Dorsey And His Greatest Band"
Jasmine JASCD 337/8	(UK)	"Kay Starr - A Rising Star"
Jass JCD 14	(US)	"Tommy Dorsey And His Orchestra - Well, Git It!"
Jazz Anthology CD 550282	(F)	"Slim Gaillard Trio - Quartet - Orchestra Los Angeles 1945"
Jazz Archives CD 85	(F)	"Charlie Barnet Vol. 2 - Skyliner - 1940-45"
Jazz Classics CD-JZCL-6008	(US)	"Dodo Marmarosa - Up In Dodo's Room"
Jazz Hour JH-1044	(US)	"Gene Krupa & His Orchestra - featuring Roy Eldridge, Charlie Ventura, Sam Donahue"
Jazz&Jazz CD JJ-614	(It)	"Tommy Dorsey & his orchestra - boogie-woogie"
Joyce CD 1016	(US)	"Spotlight on Artie Shaw"
Living Era CD-AJA-5288	(UK)	"Charlie Barnet & His Orchestra - Cherokee"
Living Era CD-AJA-5346	(UK)	"The Velvet Fog - Mel Tormé: Early Hits 1944-1949"
Living Era CD-AJS-2007	(UK)	"Artie Shaw & His Gramercy Five - Summit Ridge Drive"

Lonehill Jazz LHJ10119	(Sp)	"Dodo Marmarosa Trio - Complete Studio Recordings"
Masters of Jazz MJCD 171	(F)	"Wardell Gray - Volume 4, 1947"
MCA CD GRP 16122	(US)	"Charlie Barnet & His Orchestra - Drop Me Off In Harlem"
MCA CD GRP 16392	(US)	"A Piano Anthology"
MCA MVCR-20057	(J)	"Dodo's Back! - The Return Of Dodo Marmarosa"
Mercury CD 830.923-2	(US)	"Roy Eldridge And The Swing Trumpets"
Mosaic MD 12-170	(US)	"Classic Capitol Jazz Sessions"
Musicraft MVSCD-50	(US)	"Artie Shaw and his Orchestra with Strings Volume 1 - For You For Me Forevermore"
Musicraft MVSCD-51	(US)	"Artie Shaw and his Orchestra with Strings Volume 2 - You Do Something To Me"
Musicraft MVSCD-54	(US)	"Mel Tormé and The Mel-Tones - A Foggy Day"
Musicraft MVSCD-60	(US)	"Mel Tormé And The Mel-Tones - There's No One But You"
Ocium OCM 0013	(Sp)	"Willie Smith - A Sound of Distinction"
Ocium OCM 0038	(Sp)	"Lucky Thompson - Lucky Moments"
Prestige PCD-24021-2	(US)	"Gene Ammons & Dodo Marmarosa - Jug & Dodo"
Proper INTRO CD 2055	(UK)	"A Proper Introduction to dodo marmarosa - dodo's dance"
RCA CD ND 82177	(Eu)	"The Bebop Revolution"
RCA CD ND 89914	(F)	"The Indispensable Artie Shaw - Volumes 5/6 (1944-1945)"
Reader's Digest RC7-007-1/3	(US)	"Tommy Dorsey - His Greatest Hits and Finest Performances"
Rhino R 2 75283	(US)	"Tommy And Jimmy Dorsey - Swingin' In Hollywood"
RST JUBCD 1005 2	(A)	"The Best Of AFRS Jubilee Volume 5 - No. 291 & 271"
RST JUBCD 1007 2	(A)	"The Best Of AFRS Jubilee Volume 7 - No. 169 & 81"
RST JUBCD 1011 2	(A)	"The Best Of AFRS Jubilee Volume 11 - No. 163 & 162"
Sandy Hook CD S.H. 2001	(US)	"One Night Stand with Tommy Dorsey"
Savoy SV-0185	(J)	"Boyd Meets Stravinsky - Boyd Raeburn & Orchestra"
Savoy SV-0272	(J)	"The Modern Jazz Piano Album"

Savoy SV-0274	(J)	"Black California Vol. 2"
Savoy ZDS 1177	(US)	"Charlie Parker / Dizzy Gillespie - Bebop's Heartbeat"
Savoy ZDS 4425	(US)	"The Modern Jazz Piano Album"
Sea Breeze SB-2069	(US)	"Tom Talbert - Jazz Orchestra 1946-1949"
Soundcraft CD SC-50117-50118	(US)	"The Victory Parade of Spotlight Bands - 1943-45 Wartime Broadcasts"
Sounds Of Yesteryear DSOY 610	(UK)	"Dodo Marmarosa & The All Stars - A 'Live' Dodo"
Spotlite SPJ-CD 4-101	(UK)	"Charlie Parker on Dial - the complete sessions"
Spotlite SPJ-(CD) 128	(UK)	"Dodo Marmarosa on Dial - the complete sessions"
Spotlite SPJ-(CD) 131	(UK)	"Howard McGhee on Dial - the complete sessions"
Starwell STR06	(US)	"Johnny Janis - Jazz Up Your Life"
Storyville STCD 8313	(D)	"Boyd Raeburn And His Orchestra - 1945-46"
Storyville JazzUnlimited 201 2088	(D)	"Artie Shaw - 1945 Spotlight Bands Broadcasts"
The Audio File DVSB450	(US)	"Victory Parade of Spotlight Bands"
Topaz TPZ 1028	(UK)	"Swing Into Bop"
Toshiba EMI TOCJ-6206	(J)	"Piano Moods/Dodo Marmarosa - the dial collection"
Uptown UPCD 27.44	(US)	"Dodo Marmarosa, Pittsburgh, 1958"
Vantage BA 006	(J)	"Dodo Marmarosa/Lorraine Geller - West Coast Piano Touch"
Verve 840 032-2	(G)	"Jazz-Club - Piano"
Verve 314 521 661-2	(US)	"the jazz scene"
Verve 521 651-2	(UK)	"Slim Gaillard - Laughing In Rhythm: The Best of the Verve Years"
Verve PCD-1401	(J)	"Slim Gaillard - Sabros! Here's Smorgasbord!"[1]
Vintage Jazz Classics VJC-1043	(US)	"Judy Garland On Radio, Vol.1 [1936-44] - All The Things You Are"
Vogue CD 600 126	(F)	"Just Jazz Concert "Vol.1" - Civic Auditorium Pasadena 1947"

---

1. Spanish "Sabroso" is spelled as given here in the title for this Japanese release.

B. BIBLIOGRAPHY

1. DISCOGRAPHIES AND FILMOGRAPHIES

DELAUNAY, Charles
New Hot Discography,
New York, Criterion, 1948

DOYLE, Mike / LOWE, Peter
Slim Gaillard Discography,
in "Discographical Forum" (Malcolm Walker ed.),
London 1985, No. 49, p.4,No. 50, p.3

GARROD, Charles
AFRS One Night Stands 1001 Thru 2000,
Zephyrhills, Fl., Joyce Music Publ., 1996 (working draft)

GARROD, Charles
Charlie Barnet And His Orchestra, 1933-1973,
Zephyrhills, Fl., Joyce Music Publ., 1996 (revised edition)

GARROD, Charles / KORST, Bill
Bob Crosby And His Orchestra Volume Two, 1946-1985,
Zephyrhills, Fl., Joyce Music Publ., 1996 (revised edition)

GARROD, Charles / SCOTT, Walter / GREEN, Frank
Tommy Dorsey And His Orchestra, Volume One,
Zephyrhills, Fl., Joyce Music Publ., 1988 (revised edition)

GARROD, Charles
Ted Fio Rito And His Orchestra plus *Ina Ray Hutton And Her Orchestra*, Zephyrhills, Fl., Joyce Music Publ., 1988

GARROD, Charles
Gene Krupa And His Orchestra, Volume One, 1935-1946, Zephyrhills, Fl., Joyce Music Publ., 1996 (revised edition)

GARROD, Charles / KORST, Bill
Boyd Raeburn And His Orchestra, Zephyrhills, Fl., Joyce Music Publ., 1985 and 1997 (revised edition)

GARROD, Charles / KORST, Bill
Artie Shaw And His Orchestra, Zephyrhills, Fl., Joyce Music Publ., 1986

GARROD, Charles
MacGregor Radio Transcriptions 1 to 920, Zephyrhills, Fl., Joyce Music Publ., 1990

GARROD, Charles
MGM Record Listing 10001 Thru 13506, Zephyrhills, Fl., Joyce Music Publ., 1989

GIBSON, Frank
Dodo Marmarosa Discography, in "Jazz Journal", XVIII/5, 6, 12 and XIX/6, London 1965/1966, p.37 (May 1965), p.25 (June 1965), p.43 (December 1965), p.25 (June 1966)

HIRSCHHORN, Clive
The Hollywood Musical, New York, Crown Publishers Inc., 1983 (revised edition)

HOOGEVEEN, Gerard J.
Michael ‚Dodo‘ Marmarosa's Small Combo Recordings, in "Names & Numbers" (editors Erik M. Bakker, Han Enderman, a.o.), Amsterdam 2003/2004,
　　Part 1: 1944-1946, No. 27 (October 2003), p.3-14,
　　Part 2: 1947-1962, No. 28 (January 2004), p.10-18

HULME, George
Mel Tormé: A Chronicle of His Recordings Books and Films, Jefferson, N. C., McFarland & Company Inc. Publishers, 2000

JEPSEN, Jorgen Grunnet (Ed.)
Jazz Records 1942-80: A Discography, Vol. 1 to 8, Copenhagen 1963-68

KINER, Larry F. / MACKENZIE, Harry
Basic Musical Library, "P" Series, 1-1000,
Westport CT, Greenwood, 1990

LORD, Tom
The Jazz Discography,
Vols. 1 to 34, West Vancouver and
Redwood, N.Y., Cadence, 1992-2004

LOTZ, Rainer E. / NEUERT, Ulrich
*The AFRS "Jubilee" transcription programs; an exploratory
discography*, Vols. 1-2, Frankfurt (Main), Ruecker, 1985

MACKENZIE, Harry / POLOMSKI, Lothar
One Night Stand Series, 1 - 1001,
Westport, CT, Greenwood, 1991

MACKENZIE, Harry
Command Performance USA! A Discography,
Westport, CT, Greenwood, 1996

NASCIMENTO SILVA, Luiz Carlos do
Artie Shaw On Musicraft,
in "IAJRC (International Association of Jazz Record Collectors)
Journal", Indianapolis 1998, Vol. 31, No. 4 (Winter 1998), p. 17-20

RABEN, Erik (Ed.)
Jazz Records 1942-80: A Discography, Copenhagen, Stainless/
Wintermoon, Vol. 1: A-Ba, no year, Vol. 2: Bar-Br, no year,
Vol. 3: Bro-Cl, no year, Vol. 4: Cla-Da, 1993, Vol. 5: Dav-El, 1995

SEARS, Richard S.
V-Discs: A Histography And Discography,
Westport, CT, Greenwood, 1980

SEARS, Richard S.
V-Discs: First Supplement, Westport, CT, Greenwood, 1986

STRATEMANN, Klaus
Buddy Rich and Gene Krupa: a Filmo-discography,
Lübbecke, Germany, 1980

WHEELER, Geoffrey
Jazz by mail; record clubs and record labels 1936 to 1958,
Manassas, Va., 1999

WHEELER, Geoffrey A.
  Gaillard-Gillespie-Parker Bel-Tone Date, in "Names & Numbers"
  (editors Erik M. Bakker, Han Enderman, a.o.), Amsterdam 2007,
  No. 43 (October 2007), p.15-17

YANOW, Scott
  Jazz on Film: The Complete Story of the Musicians & Music Onscreen,
  San Francisco, Cal., 2004

2. BIO-/DISCOGRAPHIES

BERGER, Morroe / BERGER, Edward / PATRICK, James
  Benny Carter: A Life In American Music,
  Metuchen, N.J., Scarecrow, 1982, 2 Vols.

CHILTON, John
  Roy Eldridge, Little Jazz Giant , New York, Continuum, 2002

DAVIS, Miles
  Miles. The Autobiography, New York, Simon and Schuster, 1989

KUEHN, John / ASTRUP, Arne
  Buddy DeFranco: A Biographical Portrait and Discography,
  Metuchen, N.J., Scarecrow, 1993

LEVINSON, Peter J.
  Tommy Dorsey, Livin' In A Great Big Way: A Biography,
  Cambridge, Mass., Da Capo, 2005

MATHER, Dan
  Charlie Barnet: An Illustrated Biography and Discography,
  Jefferson, N.C., McFarland & Company, 2002

RUSSELL, Ross
  Bird Lives!: The High Life and Hard Times of Charlie (Yardbird)
  Parker, Wien, Hannibal, 1985 (German edition)

SIMOSKO, Vladimir
  Artie Shaw: A Musical Biography And Discography,
  Lanham, Maryland, Scarecrow, 2000

TALBOT, Bruce
  Tom Talbert: His Life And Times - Voices from a
  Vanished World of Jazz, Lanham, Maryland, Scarecrow, 2004

TORMÉ, Mel
>   *Traps, The Drum Wonder - The Life Of Buddy Rich,*
>   New York, Oxford University Press, 1992 (paperback edition)

WILLIAMS, Tony
>   *Lucky Thompson Discography and Biography, Part One, 1944-51,*
>   London 1967

ZAMMARCHI, Fabrice / MAS, Sylvie
>   *A Life in the Golden Age of Jazz - A Biography of Buddy DeFranco,*
>   Washington, Parkside Publ., 2002

3. GENERAL

anonymous
>   *Profiling the Players: Gene Krupa and his Orchestra*, in "Down Beat"
>   XX (March 15, 1943), Chicago, Ill., 1943, p.20

ANDERSON, Ernest (Ed.)
>   *Esquire's 1947 Jazz Book*, New York, Smith and Durrell, 1946

BRYANT, Clora / COLLETTE, Buddy / GREEN, William / KELSON, Jack
et al.
>   *Central Avenue Sounds: Jazz in Los Angeles,*
>   Berkeley, University of California Press, 1998

CARR, Roy / CASE, Brian / DELLAR, Fred
>   *The Hip: Hipsters, Jazz And The Beat Generation,*
>   London, Faber and Faber, 1986

COSS, Bill
>   *Cecil Taylor's Struggle For Existence*, in "Down Beat" LXI/7 (July
>   1994), Elmhurst, Ill., 1994, p.52 and 54 (reprint of an interview
>   originally printed on October 26, 1961)

FEATHER, Leonard
>   *Inside Be-Bop*, New York, J. J. Robbins & Sons, 1949

GITLER, Ira
>   *Portrait Of A Legend: Joe Albany*, in "Down Beat", XXX/28
>   (October 24, 1963), Chicago, Ill., p.20

GITLER, Ira
  Swing To Bop: An Oral History Of The Transition In Jazz In The 1940s, New York, Oxford University Press, 1987 (paperback edition)

GRIFFIN, Nard
  To Be Or Not To Bop, New York, Leo B. Workman, 1948

GROVE-HUMPHRIES, Steven / HANSON, Phillip
  Teddy Edwards, in "Jazz Journal International", XXXV/5 (May 1982), London 1982, p.12-13

KORALL, Burt
  Drummin' Men - The Heartbeat of Jazz: The Bebop Years, New York, Oxford University Press, 2002, p.38-47: "Jackie Mills"

LYONS, Len
  The Great Jazz Pianists Speaking of Their Lives and Music, New York, Da Capo, 1989

MILLER, Paul Eduard (Ed.)
  Esquire's 1946 Jazz Book, New York, A. S. Barnes and Co., 1946

SCHULLER, Gunther
  The Swing Era: The Development Of Jazz 1930-1945, New York and Oxford, Oxford University Press, 1989

SHAPIRO, Nat / HENTOFF, Nat
  Hear Me Talkin' To Ya, New York, Rinehart & Company, 1955

TERCINET, Alain
  Be-bop, Paris, P. O. L., 1991

VOIGT, John
  David Izenzon, in "The New Grove Dictionary Of Jazz" (Barry Kernfeld ed.), London, MacMillan, 1995 (reprint), p. 567-68

WILSON, John S.
  This Time Shaw Will Play As Dancers Ask, He Says, in "Down Beat" XXVI (Sept. 23, 1949), Chicago, Ill., 1949, p.3

DOWN BEAT
  issues from 1942 to 1949, Chicago, Ill.

METRONOME
  issues from 1943 to 1949, New York

4. *SPECIAL LITERATURE ON DODO MARMAROSA*

anonymous
   Potpourri (News): "I didn't know he was still alive..."
   in "Down Beat" LVIII/7 (July 1991), Elmhurst, Ill., 1991, p.10

BILLARD, François
   Dodo Marmarosa, in "Dictionnaire Du Jazz" (Ph. Carles/A.
   Clergeat/Jean-Louis Comolli ed.), Paris, Laffont, 1988, p.658-659

BURNS, Tim
   Dodo Marmarosa: An Introduction, in "Jazz Journal", XVII/7 (July
   1964), London 1964, p.28-30

DIETSCHE, Bob
   Dodo Marmarosa, in "Jazz Journal International", XLIV/6
   (June 1991), London 1991, p.10-11

ELEFF, Bob
   The Mystery Of Dodo Marmarosa, in "Coda" No. 251 (Sept./Oct.
   1993), Toronto 1993, p. 20-24

FEATHER, Leonard
   no title, liner notes to Prestige CD-24021-2 "Jug And Dodo",
   Berkeley, CA, 1990

GUIDRY, Nate
   King Of The Keyboard, in "Pittsburgh Post-Gazette",
   Sunday, April 5, 1998, Pittsburgh, PA, 1998, p.G-1

GUIDRY, Nate
   Obituary: Michael "Dodo" Marmarosa / Legendary jazz pianist, in
   "Pittsburgh Post-Gazette", Friday, September 20, 2002,
   Pittsburgh, PA, 2002

HARRISON, Max
   A Note On Dodo Marmarosa, in "Jazz Monthly" No. 7
   (Sept. 1962), London 1962, p.16

HOEFER, George
   The Recorded Flights Of Dodo, in "Down Beat" XXXIII/26
   (December 29, 1966), Chicago, Ill., 1966, p.25-30

HORRICKS, Raymond A.
   Dodo Marmarosa, in "Jazz Journal" IV/10 (Oct. 1951), p.7 and 20

KEEPNEWS, Peter
Dodo Marmarosa, 76, an Early Bebop pianist, in "The New York Times", Friday, September 27, 2002, New York, 2002, p.A27: Obituaries

McCOLLOUGH, Paul
The Vanishing Piano Man, in "Pittsburgh City Paper", September 22-29, 1999, Pittsburgh, PA, 1999, p.18-22

PEASE, Sharon A.
Dodo's Modern Style Is Given Pease Analysis, in "Down Beat" XXIII, December 16, 1946, Chicago, Ill.

PETERSON, Owen
The Consummate Artistry Of Dodo Marmarosa, in "Jazz & Blues", London 1972, No. 1/1972, p.4-8 and No. 2/1972, p.7-10

RÉDA, Jacques
Un oiseau rare: Dodo Marmarosa, in "L'improviste II: Jouer le jeu", Paris, Gallimard, 1985, p. 103-134

RUSSELL, Ross
no title, liner notes to Spotlite SPJ-128 "Dodo Marmarosa - Dodo's Dance", Sawbridgeworth, Herts., 1975

SEGAL, Joe
no title, liner notes to ARGO LP 4012 "Dodo's Back! The Return Of Dodo Marmarosa", Chicago, Ill., 1962

SUNENBLICK, Robert E.
Dodo Marmarosa, Pittsburgh, 1958, liner notes to Uptown UPCD 27.44 "Dodo Marmarosa, Pittsburgh, 1958", Whitehall, Mich., 1997, including an interview by Sunenblick with Dodo Marmarosa from June 19 (17?), 1995

TOLLEY, Trevor
Bebop revisited with Michael "Dodo" Marmarosa, in "Coda" No. 337 (Jan./Feb. 2008), Toronto 2008, p. 20-25

VOCE, Steve
Dodo Marmarosa - Giant among jazz pianists, with a beautiful feel for melodic improvisation, in "The Indepent", Monday, September 23, 2002, London 2002, section: Obituaries

WILLIAMS, Martin
Dial Days - A Conversation with Ross Russell, in "Jazz Changes", New York, Oxford University Press, 1992, p.40-54

TITLE INDEX

Musician Index

Adler, Larry (mouth-organ) 184
Albany, Joe (p) 19, 172
Albright, Max (dm) 202
Allen, Bob (voc) 39, 72, 74-76, 79-83, 85-86,
    88, 90, 92-93, 95-96, 99-100, 102, 104-108,
    111, 113, 115, 117-119, 121
Allen, Dorothy (voc) 133
Allen, Fred (comedian) 54
Allison, Lynn (bs) 59
Allyn, David (voc) 157, 163, 168, 170-171,
    179-182, 184-187, 195
Ammons, Gene (ts) 35, 242, 243
Arslan, Vernon (tp) 202
Ashby, Irving (g) 214
Atkins, Leonard (vl) 72, 80
Auld, George (cond) 67

Babasin, Harry (b, cello) 22, 25-26, 163, 168,
    170, 176, 187, 188, 213, 220, 229
Bailey, Benny (tp) 222
Bain, Bob (g) 38, 84, 93, 95, 102, 109, 113,
    120, 176
Bank, Danny (bs) 38, 63, 65, 69, 231
Barbour, Dave (g) 170, 196, 198
Barnet, Charlie (ld, ss, as, ts) 4-7, 38, 50, 62-
    71, 97-98, 201, 214
Barrios, Gil (p) 232
Bartee, John (arr) 231
Bauduc, Ray (dm) 175
Baxter, Les (voc) 176

Beach, Frank (tp) 176, 190, 192, 196
Beal, Eddie (p) 175
Beller, Alex (vl) 72, 80
Benny, Jack (comedian, vl) 54
Benson, Walter "Red" (tb) 72, 80, 93, 95, 102,
    109, 113, 120
Bergman, Edgar (vl) 192
Berman, Sonny (tp) 191
Bernard, Cy (cello) 192, 196
Bernhart, Milt (tb) 234
Berry, Emmett (tp) 130, 149
Bert, Eddie (tb) 63, 65, 67
Beveridge, Betty (voc) 176
Biondi, Remo "Ray" (g, arr) 54, 59
Blackman, Ben (vl) 80
Blane, Ralph (voc) 192
Block, Sid (b) 5, 38, 72, 80, 86, 93, 95, 102,
    109, 112, 113, 120
Bloom, Kurt (ts) 38, 63, 65, 69, 97
Bluestone, Harry (vl) 189, 191, 196, 198
Bode, Frank (dm) 229
Bothwell, Johnny (as) 59
Bradley, Oscar (dm) 199
Branson, Bruce (cl, ts, bs) 72, 80, 93, 95, 102,
    109, 113, 120, 207
Brecker, Randy (tp) 244
Brice Fanny (comedienne) 105
Briggs, Doris (harp) 38, 80, 93, 95, 102, 109,
    113, 120
Brosen, Charlie (see Branson, Bruce) 202, 207